Rāga Nṛtya Series No. 4

A Companion to Indian Music and Dance

(Spanning a Period of Over Three Thousand Years and Based Mainly on Sanskrit Sources)

Sures Chandra Banerji

SRI SATGURU PUBLICATIONS
A DIVISION OF
INDIAN BOOKS CENTRE
DELHI-INDIA

Published by :

SRI SATGURU PUBLICATIONS
A Division of
INDIAN BOOKS CENTRE
40/5, Shakti Nagar,
Delhi-110007
(INDIA)

First Edition : Delhi. 1990

ISBN - 81-7030-240-4

PRINTED IN INDIA

TO

MY ELDER BROTHER
SRI SAILESH CHANDRA MAJUMDAR,
AS A TOKEN OF REGARD

CONTENTS

APPENDICES

PREFACE

Music and dance are no longer the luxury of the aristocratic people. Nor are these tabooed in the society at large. Interest in these arts is widespread. These have been included in the curricula of academic instituttions up to the Universities. Musicologists do not rest content with merely learning the literature on music and dance. A spirit of research has been instilled into them. Even some foreign enthusiasts are evincing interest in these ancient arts of India.

Indian tradition of music and dance harks back to hoary antiquity, centuries before the dawn of history. Sanskrit texts on these arts are legion. Of them, a very small number has seen the light of day. The vast majority of the texts still lie buried in manuscripts not only in India, but also abroad.

Some works on the history of these Indian arts have been written. Svāmī Prajñānānanda's History stands as a monument to his love of music and profound erudition. It is, however, beyond the ken or means of many a lover of music, particularly of the student community.

The motives of presenting the panorama of Indian music and dance in a succint form, and of stimulating a spirit of research have urged the preparation of the present work.

First of all, we have pointed out the exalted position accorded to music since early times excepting a coterie of writers on Smṛti literature. Then, we have set forth, in a nutshell, the origin and development of these arts ever since the Vedic period. In one chapter, we have given brief accounts of the texts published hitherto. With an eye to the needs of the researchers, a chapter has been devoted to the unpublished works. To give an idea of the magnitude of this literature, we have added a note also on the authors and works known from references only. A separate chapter has been written on the authors of those prominent works which are available in print or in manuscripts. Under each author, we have given as much information about his personal history and date as available materials permit. In one chapter, we have discussed the relation between Indian and foreign music.

The young learner and the general reader find the technical terms and jargon stumbling blocks in their way to the study of the nusicological lore. For facilitating the study of the original texts, we have explained the important technical terms, and noted the references mainly to the *Nāṭyaśāstra* and the *Saṃgitadarpaṇa.*

The following interesting matters, relating to music, have been dealt with in the appendices: influence of nature on music and dance, poetic flashes in literature on musicology. In order to bring out the composite nature of Indian music we have added an appendix on non-Aryan influence on it. Incidentally, we have laid down how music serves as a means of national integration. In one appendix, we have dealt with the influence of Indian music in several countries of the Orient and the Occident. One appendix has been devoted to a discussion on the basic differences between Indian and western music. The important subject of *Mela* is the subjectmatter of a separate appendix. The systems of north Indian and South Indian music have been compared in one appendix. Although this work is mainly based on Sanskrit sources, yet we have given a brief account of the contribution of some medieval performing artistes; because what they did and left for posterity is the warp and woof of Indian music in general and north Indian music is particular.

Finally, we have added an up-to-date bibliography of the important texts, translations and studies in different languages of India and foreign countries.

The author's labours will be amply rewarded if this small work serves the purpose for which it is intended. Suggestions for its improvement will be gratefully received.

In the preparation of this work, the well-known musicologist, Dr. Pradip Ghosh, formerly of Rabindra Bhāratī University, has rendered considerable help. The author's cordial thanks are due to him.

77A, Golf Club Rd.,
Calcutta-33.
New Year's Day,
1397 B.S.

S. C. Banerji

improvement will be gratefully received.

In the preparation of this work, the well-known entomologist Dr. Pradip Ghosh, formerly of Rabindra Bharati University, has rendered considerable help. The author's cordial thanks are due to him.

[illegible]

Calcutta

New Year's Day [illegible]

1977 [illegible]

ABBREVATIONS

Adyar— Cat. of Skt. Mss. in Adyar Library. Pt. I, 1926. Pt. II, 1928.

Alph. List. Beng. Govt.—Alphabetical List of MSS. purchased up to 1891, ptd. at the end of Notices of Skt. Mss. by H.P. Sastri, XI, 1985.

Alwar — Cat. of Skt. MSS. in Library of Mahārājā of Alwar, by Peterson, Bombay, 1982.

Ānandāśrama—Hand-list of Mss. in Ānandās'rama, Poona.

AS - Cat. of ptd. books and MSS. in Jaina Siddhānta Bhavan, Arrah.

Bd. - Report of search for Skt. MSS. in Bombay Presidency during 1887-88, 88-89, 89-90, 90-91, by R.G. Bhandarkar, Bombay, 1897.

Bhau Daji - Cat. of MSS and books belonging to Bhau Daji Memorial; Bombay, 1882.

Bik—Cat. of Skt. MSS. in Library of Mahārājā of Bikaner, by R. K. Mitra.

Bikaner - Cat. of Skt. MSS. in Anup Skt. Lib. by C.K. Raja and M.K. Sarma.

BORI—MSS. in Bhandarkar Oriental Res. Institute, Poona.

BRL—Cat. of Skt. MSS. by A.C. Burnell, London, 1870.

Burnell—Index to Skt. MSS. in Tanjore Palace by A.C. Burnell, London, 1880.

Cuttack—Handlist of MSS. collected for Govt. of Orissa during 1938-40.

I.O.—Cat. of Skt. and Pkt. MSS. in India Office Library, by J. Eggeling.

Jodhpur—Handlist of MSS. in Archaeological Deptt. of Jodhpur State, Jodhpur.

L—Notices of Skt. MSS. by R.L. Mitra.

MD—Des. Cat. of Skt. MSS. in Govt. Oriental MSS. Library, Madras.

MT—Triennial Cat. of MSS.

collected for Govt. Oriental MSS. Library, Madras.

Nepal—Cat. of Palm-leaf and selected paper MSS. in Durbar Lib., Nepal.

Oppert—List of Skt. MSS. in Private Libraries of S. India, by G. Oppert.

Paliyam—Handlist of MSS. in private collection of Paliyam family, Cochin, Kerala State.

Peters—Reports on search for Skt. MSS. by Peterson.

Radh—Pustakānām Sūcīpatram relating to collection of MSS. belonging to Pandit Radhakrishna of Lahore.

R.A. Sastri—Four parts of Diary of Pandit R.A. Sastri's tour in search of Skt. MSS.

Sg—Report on search for Skt. and Tamil MSS. for 1896-97 by Sesagiri Sastri.

Sri Deb—Handlist of MSS. in Srirangam Devasthānam Lib. and Museum, Srirangam.

Stein—Cat. of Skt. MSS in Raghunātha Temple Library of Mahārāja of Jammu and Kashmir, by M.A. Stein.

Sucindram—Handlist of MSS. with P.N. Sarma, Āyurvedās' ramam, Suchindram, Travancore.

TCD—Des. Cat. of Skt. MSS. in Curator's Office Lib., Trivandrum.

TD—Des. Cat. of Skt. MSS. in Tanjore Mahārāj Serfoji's Sarasvatī Mahal Library, Tanjore, by P.P.S. Sastri.

Tirupati—List of rare MSS. in Śrī Veṅkaṭes'vara Oriental Institute, Tirupati.

Tra. Ad. Rep.—List of MSS. collected by Curator for publication of Skt. MSS.; Trivandrum.

Tripunittura—Five handlists of collection of MSS. in Trippunittura, Cochin, Kerala State.

Triv. Cur.—Cat. of MSS. collected by Curator for Pub. of Skt. MSS., Trivandrum, by T.G. Sastri.

Up. Br. Mutt.—Handlist of MSS. in Upanishad Brahma Mutt of Kanci,

Conjeevaram.

WZKM—Wiener Zeitschrift für die Kunde des Morgelandes.

CHRONOLOGY

[Important dates for history of musicology]

B.C.

Indus Valley Civilisation—C. 2500-1500.

Ṛgveda - Commonly accepted date C. 1500-1200 B.C. According to D. Frawley 12,500 (Vide his paper on Astronomical Evidences, etc. in *Glory of India*, Quarterly Jour. on Indology, Vol. V., Nos. 3-4, 1981, Motilal Banarasidass, Delhi).

Sāmaveda—later than *Ṛgveda.*

Brāhmaṇas—C. 1500-1000.

Buddha—Cantonese tradition—b. 566, d. 486.

Aṣṭādhyāyī—See Pāṇini.

Pāṇini—C. 4th. cent.

Mahābhāṣya—See Patañjali.

Patañjali—C. 2nd. cent.

A.D.

Manusaṃhitā—supposed to have assumed present form sometime between 2nd cent. B.C. and 2nd. cent. A.D.

Rāmāyaṇa—present form C. 2nd or 3rd. cent.

Mahābhārata—present form c. 4th. cent.

Gupta rule—C. 320-510.

Nāṭyaśāstra—date highly controversial. Generally believed to have flourished in the fourth cent.

Kālidāsa—earlier than 634 (probably 5th. century).

Śūdraka—variously assigned to different periods from the 2nd. cent. to the 6th. Generally regarded as post-Kālidāsa.

Bhaṭṭi—earlier than middle of 6th. cent.

Pañcatantra—lost original probably earlier than middle of 6th. cent.

Kādambarī—7th. cent.

Māgha—probably earlier than 8th. cent.

Jayadeva—(author of Gītagovinda)—court-poet of king Lakṣmaṇasena of Bengal (C. 1185-1205)

Śārṅgadeva (author of *Saṃgītaratnākara)*—13th. century.

Mughal Rule—1526-1858

Puṇḍarīka Viṭṭhala—17th. cent.

Bhātkhaṇḍe, V. N.—1860-1936

I

INTRODUCTION

SAṂGĪTA—ITS MEANING AND IMPORTANCE IN INDIAN CULTURE

The term *saṃgīta* is derived from root *gai* (to sing), preceded by the prefix *sam* which generally conveys the sense of completeness, perfection, propriety. So, *saṃgīta* means that which is properly or fully sung, i.e. a song. In actual use, however, the term came to denote the threefold art of dance, vocal and instrumental music *(nṛttaṃ gītaṃ vāditraṃ ca trayaṃ saṃgītam ucyate).*

We do not know and, perhaps, shall never know what part *Saṃgīta* played in Indian society of the pre-Vedic age. The Veda is the earliest written record of the Indian life. The Vedic literature sheds lurid light on the *saṃgīta* of these far-off ages. The very accent, which is the most important factor in reciting the Vedic stanzas, is muscial. There is ample evidence of the prevalence of music and dance in the Vedic society.

The Epics and Purāṇas also testify to the recognition, and applause of music and dance as fine arts. Some Tantras attached great importance to vocal and instrumental music, as we shall see later on.

The various prose and poetical works and plays are replete with references to these arts.

The great importance, attached to these arts, can be gauged from the fact that a vast literature, dealing exhaustively with them, came into existence.

The importance of music, as a means of *Sādhana*, worship of or meditation upon God, has been recognised ever since the Vedic age. The *Sāmaveda* is the Veda of the *sāmans* which are nothing but melodious stanzas, meant for recitation as an indispensable element of sacrificial rites. It was the function of the *Udgātṛ* type of priest. It is due to this spiritual significance of *Sāmans* that the Lord says in the *Gītā* (X.22) that He is the *Sāmaveda* among the Vedas *(vedānāṃ sāmavedo'smi)*. The *Skanda-purāṇa* (Viṣṇu-Nārada dialogue) says:

gītaṃ vādyaṃ ca nṛtyaṃ ca nāṭyaṃ viṣṇu kathāṃ mune/

Yah ka[r6]oti sa puṇyātmā trailyokyopari saṃsthitaḥ//

[O sage, one, who sings, plays musical instruments, dances, performs a drama and recites Viṣṇu's narrative, is holy-souled, and resides above the three worlds.] We have the following verse in the *Bṛhannāradīya Purāṇa* (Yama-Bhagīratha-saṃvāda):

devatāyatane yastu bhaktiyuktaḥ pranṛtyati/

gitāni gāyatathana tatphalaṃ śṛṇu bhūpate//

In later times, we find numerous lyrical and sonorous hymns meant for recitation by the devotees. Saṃkarācārya's (born C. 788 A.D.) hymns are the most celebrated among such compositions. The *Gītagovinda* of Jayadeva (12th. cent. A.D.), consisting of various melodies, is a mute monument to the poet's heartfelt devotion to his chosen Lord Kṛṣṇa and His consort Rādhā. The following verse extols song as far superior to *japa* (muttering) or *dhyāna* (meditation) and *Laya* (absorption of mind, deep concentration, exclusive devotion):

japakoṭiguṇaṃ dhyānaṃ dhyānakoṭiguṇo layaḥ/

layakoṭiguṇaṃ gānaṃ gānāt parataraṃ nahi//

The Vaiṣṇavas of Bengal, starting with the great Caitanya (b. 1486 A.D.), used to believe that *Kīrtana*, a species of devotional songs, was a highly effective means of delighting God, and getting His grace. Time was when every nook and corner of Navadvīpa, the birth-place of Caitanya, nay of the whole of Bengal, was flooded with *Harisaṃkīrtana* in which the high and the low took part.

The idea that music and dance please the deitiea was at the root of the institution of *Devadāsīs* (temple-girls). They were virgin girls dedicated to deities whom they were supposed to please by their songs and dance.

The religious and social history of India reveals that many devotees chose vocal music as a medium of their devotion. Mīrā (born C. 1504), Surdās, Kavīr (c. 1440-1518), Rāmprasād (c. 1720-81 A.D.), to mention only a few, belonged to this class of devotees. Rabīndranātha sings—*āmār surguli pāy caraṇ* (my malodies reach your feet).

The spiritualism, associated with music, is vouched by some Purāṇas. For example, according to the *Padmapurāṇa*, the seven *svaras* appeared in bodily forms before sage Gautama when he started singing. It is said that the chief attraction of Vaikuṇṭha is that the *Rāgas* can be directly seen there. According to the *Viṣṇupurāṇa*, *Saṃgīta* alone is the visible form of God. The general attitude of those, who look upon music with a spirit of worship, is that the effort of the man, who being dedicated to music, fails to see *Rāgas* and *Rāgiṇīs* in association with God, is futile.

According to the *Viṣṇudhamottara Purāṇa* (III), the arts of music and dance are inter-dependent. Says the Purāṇa—*ātodyena vinā nṛttaṃ vidyate na kathaṃcana : nṛtta* (dance) does not exist without *ātodya* (instrumental music). Again, it is stated—*na gītena vinā śakyaṃ jñātumātodyamucyate ; ātodya* or instrumental music cannot be learnt without song. In the opinion of the Purāṇa, even *citrasūtra* or the art of painting is difficult to master without *nṛtta* or dance *(vinā tu nṛttaśāstreṇa citrasūtraṃ sudurvidam)*. The supreme importance of vocal music *(gītā)* is declared in the following line :

gītaśāstra-vidhānajñaḥ sarvaṃ vetti yathāvidhī/

One, who is versed in the lore of vocal music, knows everything properly. This Purāṇa equates song with the imperishable Brah man (*brahma cāvyayam*). The great charm of song is thus expressed—*Yathāvidhi kṛtaṃ gānaṃ jaganmohayatyacirāt*; a song, duly sung, enraptures the world in no time. The importance of a musical composition is emphasised in the following verse : *padālī tu padārthānāṃ vācikā na tu darśikā/Svarabandha-viśeṣeṇa rasa-sākṣātkāri tu sā.*

[A collection of words denotes their meaning, but does not reveal the (picture) by being set to tune they lead to the direct perception of *Rasa*[1].]

Music was so popular that it came to be looked upon as an effective medium for pleasing deities even among the Jainas who advocated rigorous asceticism and were sticklers for moral practices. The recital of musical hymns in temples and holy places was a part of their devotional practices. In the Jaina work *Prabandhakośá* (1348 A.D.) of Rājasékhara Sūri, Vastupāla is stated to have made a donation, *inter alia*, of 450 female Jaina singers as also of female dancers.

Sc ıg is based on *Nāda* (sound). The ancient sages believed that *Nāda-brahma* pervades the universe, and is eternal. It reminds one of the theory of the Music of the Spheres, propounded by ancient Greek philosophers.

Thus, we see that the English word music, meaning vocal and instrumental music, does not convey the full connotation of *saṃgīta*; in fact, there is no one English word denoting *saṃgīta*.

---

1. The delectable flavour or sentiment in a literary composition. It has been declared to be like the realisation of the Supreme Being (Brahman)—*brahmāsvāda-sahodara*. The aneients identified the Supreme Being with *Rasa* in the expression *raso vai sah.* Elesewhere in the above Purāṇa (44.101, 106) it is stated that *Gānabrahma* became *Rasa*; Viṣṇu's body became the *Rasa* of *Gānabrahma.*

MUSIC AND DANCE AS A TABOO

We have seen that music originated, and was used in a spiritual atmosphere. The Vedic accents were musical. The songs of the *Sāmaveda*, the earliest specimens of Indian music, used to be sung on the occasion of sacrifices. Gradually, music became professional. There were the bards who used to sing songs for awakening kings in the morning. Among other secular uses of music was to take to this art as a means of livelihood. The travelling singers, the *Kuśīlavas* as they were called, used to sing songs from place to place for the entertainment of the people.

The ancient social leaders were aware of the fact that excessive fondness for music makes a person light-hearted and negligent of duty, and considered it to be a vice. It is for this reason that the scriptures forbid students to indulge in it, and to visit places where musical soirees are held. *Gautama-dharmasūtra*. (ch. XVI) provides that a student should suspend his study when the sound of such musical instruments as *Vāṇa* (= Vīṇā), *bherī* and *mṛdaaṅga* is heard. The distracting effect of music is also recognised in the *Baudhāyana-dharmasūtra* which ordains the cessation of study when vocal music is performed. *Āpastama-dharmasūtra* (I.3.10.19) bans Vedic study as soon as the sound of musical instruments is heard. While prescribing rules about the the do's and don'ts for a student, the *Gautama-dharmasūtra* (II.13,14,18,19,22,23,25) forbids him to play on musical instruments.

The professional dancers and singers were looked down upon, and close association with them was condemned. Manu (VIII.471 includes *taurya-trika* (the threefold arts of vocal and instrumental music and dance) among the vices arising out of passion (*Kāmaja*); Kings are urged to shun these arts. The commentators Medhātithi and Kullūka, however, under Manu VIII.53, make it clear that the occasional enjoyment of music and dance is not categorically prohibited. What is prohibited is addiction *(atip-*

rasakti) which is *Vyasana. Vyasana* means that which causes a person to be indifferent to or negligent of duty (*vi viśeṣeṇa asyate kṣipyate kartavyakarmaṇah anena iti vyasanam).*

An age - old tradition is that poetry is marred by song. *(kāvyaṃ gītena hanyate).* Here also too much indulgence in songs is condemned, not practice or enjoyment in moderation.

It is curious that the very *Sāman* sngs, which had ritual application, were tabooed in certain cases. The Brāhmaṇical law-books ordain that the recitation of the *Ṛgveda* and the *Yajurveda* must be suspended as soon as the sound of a *Sāman* is heard. The *Āpastamba-dharmasūtra* (I.3.10.19) mentions the tone of *Sāmans* among the factors causing the cessation of the study of the above two Vedas ; the other causes are barking of dogs, the cries of wolves and jackals, etc. The reason of the opprobrium, attached to the *Sāmans*, is that *Sāmaveda* owes its origin to pre-brāhmaṇical popular beliefs and magic. The reason that led to the exclusion of the *Atharvaveda* (the Veda of the *Atharvan* or the knowledge of Magic Formulae) from the list of the four Vedic *Saṃhitās*[1], subjected the *Sāmaveda* to anathema. The second part of the *Sāmavidhāna Brāhmaṇa* is a distinct handbook of magic. In it is taught the application of various *Sāmans* for magic purposes.

The low social status of professional dancers and singers in the society can be gauged from the fact that Manu (III.155) includes *Kuśīavas* (i.e. those who take to dancing as a profession, according to Kullūka ; the professional bards, actors, dancers and singers, according to Medhātithi) among those who should not be invited to religious and obseqeuial rites.

Some Purāṇas also attach odium to music and dance. In tne Svargakhaṇḍa of the *Padmapurāṇa.* The *Varāhapurāṇa* brands painters, dancers, singers and actors as unworthy of being invited

---

1. These were called *Trayī* ie the triad of *Ṛk, Yajus* and *Sāmavedas; Manusmṛti*, vii-43, *Arthaśāstra*, I.1.

to *Śrāddha.* In those days, music appears to have been practised by some women for immoral purposes. The above Purāṇa refers to music and dance in connexion with the description of Pretapurī. This might be one of the reasons for condemning these arts.

Despite the deprecatory attitude to music and dance in some Purāṇas, we are told that Śiva is pleased with these arts. We find anecdotes in which those who treated music and dance lightly are stated to have been punished. We are told that as Urvaśī and Purūravas laughed at the time of the former's dance, a severe curse followed. The *Bṛhad-dharmapurāṇa* asks one not to sing before a person who ordered him to sing or dance to test his ability.

In the *Skandapurāṇa* (Kāśīkhaṇḍa), one is prohibited to sing before deities out of temptation for money. The appointment of Devadāsīs to please deities with song and dance dates back at least to the fourth cent. B.C. ; the *Arthaśāstra* mentions (II/2322) this institution.

II

ORIGIN AND DEVELOPMENT OF MUSIC AND DANCE IN INDIA.

INDUṢ VALLEY CIVILISATION

The origin of these arts in India, as in all other countries, is shrouded in obscurity. The ruins of the Indus Valley Civilisation (C. 3000 B.C.) reveal the existence of the flute with seven holes, the *Mṛdaṅga, Vīṇā, Karatāla,* dancing men and women.

VEDIC AGE: SAṂHITĀ PERIOD

Coming down to the age of the *Ṛgveda* (C. 1500 B.C.[1]) which represents another phase of the prehistoric culture, we find that the accents on the words, viz. *Udātta, Anudā tta, Svarita* are musical. The Eighth Book of the *Ṛgveda* is called *Pragātha* (abounding in songs). The Veda refers to dance (X.72.6), musical instruments like *Gargara* (VIII.69.9), *Vāṇa, or Vīṇā* (lute)

The *Sāmaveda* is the Veda of Sāmans or chants, songs. The songs of this Veda are divided into two classes, *Grāmageya* and *Araṇyageya.* With the former is related *Uhagāna* and with the latter *Uhyagāna. Grāmageya-gāna* was, perhaps, the precursor of later songs. It should be noted that seven musical notes were current in the Vedic age.

The *Yajurveda,* both White *(Sukla)* and Black (Kṛṣṇa) refers to musical instruments. For instance, the following instruments are mentioned:

---

1. According to a modern European scholar, this Veda dates back to 12,500 B.C. See D. Frawley, Astronomical Evidence etc. in *Glory of India* (Quarterly Journal of Indology Vol. V, Nos. 3-4, 1981, Motilal Banarsidass, Delhi).

Dundubhi (Śukla 2/17/5, Kṛṣṇa 7/5/9/29),

Bhūmidundubhi (Kṛṣṇa 7/5/9/30). From Bhaṭṭa Bhāskara's commentary, we learn that it was the name of a hole in the ground, covered with leather.

Vanaspati (Vājasaneyī 9/12, Taittirīya 6.1.25, Kāṭhaka 3/4/5). Perhaps it denotes the hollow of a tree, covered with leather.

Tuṇava and Vīṇā (Taittirīya 6/1/41)

Āḍambara (Vājasaneyī 30/10/19).

The *Atharvaveda* mentions some instruments; eg.

Karkara, Āghāṭa (4/37/8/5)

Vakra (4/6/2/4). According to some, it denotes *dhanus* which was the precursor of the violin.

Dance is also referred to in 10/7/4/42.43.

Some of the *Kuntāpa hymns* of this Veda (XX. 127-136) are of the nature of songs eulogising great men.

BRĀHMAṆAS

The Brāhmaṇa literature testifies to various kinds of music and dance. For example,

Tāla related to dance *(Aitareya* 5/22/10)

Bhūmidundubhi, Kāṇḍavīṇā (5/1/5).

Simultaneous performance of dance and song (*Śatapatha* 3/2/46)

Vīṇā (I.bid. 13/1/5/3).

Gāna (Ṣaḍviṃśa 2/5/3/2)

Various notes *(svaras)* suitable to *Sāman songs (Ārṣeya* 1/5).

We find, in this class of literature, some songs called *Gāthā Nārāśaṃsī* (e.g. *Śatapatha* XI, 5, 6, 8; *Āśvalāyana Gṛhya* III.3). These were panegyrics in praise of heroes. There are references (e.g.

Śatapatha 13/1/5/3, 10/4/3/3) to the simultaneous playing of instruments like *Vīṇā, Dundubhi*, etc. Some form of orchestra appears to have been in vogue. The *Pañcaviṃsa Brāhmaṇa* (Caland's ed., p. 86) refers to the instruments *Kāṇḍavīṇā* and *Picchorā* played together. *Picchorā* was, perhaps, a sort of *guitar* played with a plectrum (*Lāṭyāyana* 4/2/5-7; *Drāhyāyaṇa* 11/2/6-8). The *Jaiminīya Brāhmaṇa* mentions the instruments called *Karkari, Alāvu, Vakra, Kapiśirṣiṇī, Aiśiki, Apaghātalikā*. Āpastamba (21/17/6,16) mentions *Apaghātalika, Tambalavīṇā* and *Piccholā*. According to Garbe, *Tambalavīṇā* denotes Tamil guitar. Baudhāyana (16/20 266, 9-10 ; 267.9-10). refers to the instruments called *Āghāṭī, Piccholā* and *Karkarikā*. The *Ghātakarkari, Avaghāta* and *Kāṇḍavīṇā* are mentioned by Śāṃkhāyana (17/3/12). Though called *Vīṇā, Kāṇḍavīṇā* was, according to some, a bamboo-flute. According to the *Karkabhāṣya*, it means a sort of lute made of *Kāṇḍa* or *S'ara (Saccharum arundanaceum)*.

UPANIṢADS

The *Chāndogya Upaniṣad* directs meditation on *Oṃkāra* as *Udgīta* (from *Udgāna* meaning singing loudly). There is mention also of the seven notes *(svaras)* used in *Udgīta*. These are called *Vinardi* (like the below of a bull), *Anirukta* (not fully audible), *Nirukta* (clearly audible), *Mṛdu* (soft, gentle), Ślakṣṇa (pronounced with little effort), *Krauñca* (like the cry of a curlew), *Apadhvānta* (like the sound produced by striking a broken piece of bell-metal). Among the instruments, the *Vīnā* was the most popular, and most widely used (*Chāndogya* 1/7/6). There is reference, in the Yama-Naciketā dialogue of the *Kaṭhopaniṣad* (1/26), to dance and song.

About song and the notes (*svara*), most of the Upaniṣads declare that *svara* arises from the union of *Vāk* (speech) and *Prāṇa* (vital air, breath). This *svara* is the resort of *Sāman* songs and of the songs in later times.

VEDĀṄGAS
ŚIKṢĀ

Of the works on the Śikṣā (phonetics) Vedāṅga, the *Pāṇinīya-*, *Yājñavalkya-*, *Māṇḍukī* - and *Nāradīya - Śikṣās* contain some information on music and dance. Among other things, Pāṇini (C. 4th. cent. B.C.) mentions the dance of *Naṭarāja, Tāla, Tāṇḍava, Lāsya, Nāda*, etc. The work of Yājñavalkya mentions seven *svaras*. The *Māṇḍukī* mentions, *inter alia*, the similarity between musical notes and the cries of animals and birds.

Of all the Śiksā treatises, that of Nārada (C.1st or 3nd. C.A.D.) deals, for the first time, in greater details, with musicology in a systematic manner. It is stated, in this work (1/2/2), that Nārada has defined *Tāna, Rāga, Svara, Grāma* and *Mūrchanā*. As a matter of fact, however, these definitions do not occur in the extant *Nāradīya Śikṣā*. So, it seems that either there was another work associated with Nārada's name or there was an earlier version of the present text. In the text, now available, the name, number and nature of the *svaras* have been discussed in the first section of the first chapter. There is mention of *Uras* (chest), *Kaṇṭha* (throat) and *Śiras* (head) as three places from which *svaras* emerge in varying degrees of intensity. There is discussion of *svaras*, etc. relating to *Laukika-gāna* (as distinguished from *Vaidika-gāna*) in the sections from the second to the fifth. Besides the heptatonic system,[1] the following elements of music have also been dealt with: Three *Grāmas* (scales), 49 *Tānas* (protracted notes,

---

1. The *Yajñavalkya - Śikṣā saṃgraha*, (Kashi ed. 1. p.p. 1-2) states that seven *svaras* of the *Gāndharvaveda* or *Saṃgītaśāstra* are classed as *Udātta, Anudātta, Svarita*, The evolution of the seven later *svaras* from the basic Vedic *śvaras* been demonstrated thus:

From *Udātta* - *Niṣāda* and *Gāndhāra* ;
From *Anudātta* - *Ṛṣabha* and *Dhaivata* ;
From *Svarita* - *Ṣaḍja*, *Madhyama* and *Pañcama*.

keynotes), merits and defects of songs, definition of *Ṣāḍava* and place of articulation, etc. *Sāman* notes, action of hand, *Śruti*, (suitable tone having no resonance,) *Svarita* (circumflex accent), *Śarīra* (parts of the body related to music), *Vāk* (speech), *Manas* (mind). Great stress has been laid on the selection of the genuine teacher of music, instructions meant for the trainee—these constitute the contents of sections six to the end. There is mention of *Tāna, Rāga, Svara, Grāma* and *Mūrchanā* in 1/2/2. Of the 49 *Tānas*, 15 are in *Gāndhāragrāma*,, 20 in the *Madhyama* and 14 in the *Ṣadja-grāma*. A kind of *Rāga* is called *Grāmarāga* in accordance with the characteristics of *Svara* and *Rāga*. The seven notes, starting from *Ṣaḍja*, have been mentioned. One should avoid undue haste in passing from one *svara* to another as also in unifying one with another. This process will be unimpeded and nice, like the balance between sun-rays and the shadow. This will be *druta* (swift) in practice, *madhya* (medium) in application, and *vilambita* (delayed) in teaching. The *svara*, which oversteps its own *sthāna* (place), is *visvara* in the parlance of *Sāman* singers, and *Virakta* in the language of the lute-players.

Songs are of ten qualities (1/3/1) which are as follows:

Rakta- (delightful), *Vikruṣṭa* (very loud),

Pūrṇa (complete), *Ślakṣṇa* (smooth), *Alamkṛta* (embellished),

Sama (even), *Prasanna* (lucid), *Sukumāra* (delicate),

Vyakta (clear) and *Madhura* (sweet).

The following are the defects of songs : Scared, terrified, agitated, indistinct, nasal, voice resembling the caw of a crow, arising from the head, devoid of proper *sthāna*, bad voice, harsh, disintegrated, uneven, devoid of *tāla*.

It is stated (1/3/14) that preceptors like even songs, the learned prefer separation of the words of songs, the females have a predilection for sweet songs and other people desire too loud songs.

Śrutt in a *svara* is, according to the author (1/6/16), imperceptible like the movement of fish in water or like the movement of birds in the sky. The next verse states that *Śruti can be known by effort, as, through effort, one can know of ghee in curd or of fire in the wood. The Śrutis,* called *Dīptā, Āyatā, Karuṇā, Mṛdu* and *Madhyā,* have been named.

The instruments, *Veṇu* (flute) and *Vīṇā,* have been mentioned. *Vīṇā* is twofold(1/6/1f)—*Dāravī* (made of *dāru* or wood?) and *Gā travīṇā* (that which rests on the body?).

The following are prescribed as the daily duties of a trainee in music :

Rising at dawn, meditation on Brahman (Supreme Being), use of tooth-stick, moderate food, eating best food, eating of the three myrobalans (i.e. fruits of *Āmalakī - Phyllanthus emblica), Harī takī (Terminalia chebula* Retz); *Vaheḍā (Terminalia belerica* Roxb.) taken together, along with salt, drinking *dhūmaghṛta* (hot ghee?), observing silence till breakfast, bating the breath while talking.

The faults of a trainee are stated as follows :

Scared attitude, dullness of intellect, laziness, breathing disease, lack of attention. He should emulate the enthusiasm and perseverance of the white-ants in building up an ant-hill. Ceaseless and repeated practice of what has been learnt is necessary. Excessive sleep is harmful for him. Procrastination in eating and walking should be avoided. He should carefully shun crowd, too many friends and the association of women. Gambling, addiction to dramatic performances and sleep at irregular hours are obstacles to the learning of music. The author emphasises regard for the preceptor, clear and proper pronunciation.

Of the S'ikṣā Vedāṇga, the earliest treatises are known as Prā tiśākhya. Some Prātiśākhyas contain elements of music, eg. *Ṛkprā tiśākhya* (13/42.50). The connotation of the word *Gaṇagīti,* occurring in the *Puṣpasūtra,* a *Prātiśākhya* of the *Sāmaveda,* is not clear. It may indicate folk-song current among the masses or *Vṛndagāna* (song sung by a group of singers). From the second *Kaṇḍikā* (particularly verses 8 and 9) of the ninth *Prapāṭhaka* of this treatise, we learn that two, five, six or all the seven *svaras* were used in the *Sāman* songs; all the *svaras* were not used in every song. In later times also, songs, in which only five *svaras* were used, came to be known as *Auḍava*; those, in which six *svaras* were applied, were called *Ṣāḍava*.

KALPA

In the age of the Vedāṅga, called *Kalpa*, all the four kinds of instruments (i.e. *Tata, Ghana, Suṣira* and *Avanaddha*) were in vogue. The main instruments were known as *Vāṇa* or *Vīṇā, Śaṃkha, Vaṃsa, Tuṇava* (a kind of flute), *Dundubhi, Mṛdaṅga, Āghāṭi (Karatāla), Piñchola* or *Picchora* (a type of flute), *Alābu* (perhaps, made of the outer cover of the bottle-gourd), *Kapiśīrṣiṇī* (with the head or face like that of a monkey?), *Panava* (a kind of *Karatāla*), etc. The *Vīṇā* appears to have been of many types; e.g. *Ghaṭarī, Śodha, Kāṇḍa, Godhā'* (a small-sized instrument covered with the skin of the iguana), *Karkarika, Tambala, Taluka.* The *Kātyāyana Śrautasūtra* (13/32) mentions *Śatatantrī*; it is not clear whether 'Śata' denotes exactly one hundred or many.

MUSIC IN THE GREAT EPICS

RĀMĀYAṆA

Some information on music is available in the *Rāmāyaṇa* the present form of which dates back to about the 2nd. or 3rd. cemt. A.D. The Uttarakāṇḍa, which is generally supposed to be a later interpolation, mentions (cantol) *Kāvyagāna* with *Jātirāga, Sthāna, Laya,* etc. The Ayodhyākāṇḍa (canto 65) refers to *Pāṇivādaka, Sūta, Āśīrgāna* and *Gāthāgāna* The following terms show familirily with all the four kinds of instruments, viz. *Tata Ghana, Suṣira* and *Avanaddha* :-

Vipañci or Vīnā (Sundara 10/40/41)

Veṇu or *Vaṃśa* (Kiṣkindhā 30/51).

Śaṃkha (Yuddha 50/6).

Bherī (Yuddha 50/60).

Ghaṇṭā (Yiddha 124/125).

Of the *Avanaddha* instruments, mention has been made also of *Mṛdaṅga, Dundubhi, Muraja, Paṭaha* and *Maḍḍuka. Svastika* and *Tāla* also figure among the *Ghana* instruments.

There is reference, in the Bālakāṇḍa (4), to seven *Suddha Jātigānas*, and, in the *Sundarakāṇḍa* (1/16), to *Kaiśikarāga*. According to some, the words *gāyakāḥ śrutiśīlāśca* testify to the awareness of *Śrutis* in *svaras*. Svāmī Prajñānānanda, however, explains *śrutiśīla* as 'versed in the Vedas'. He thinks that the concept of 22 *Śrutis* was not known in those times.

In the *Rāmāyaṇa, saṃgīta was known as gandharva* (7/23/50). In Vedic sacrifices, the sages used *mārga-saṃgīta*. The Uttarakāṇḍa (7/3/44) reveals the performance of dance with song. Ḍance was of three kinds—*nṛtya* based on *bhāva* (Ayodhyā 20/10), *nṛtta* based on *tāla* and *laya* (Yuddha 5/17) and *Lāsya* (Ayodhyā 69/4). *Lāsya* denotes tender or gentle dance to the accompaniment of vocal and instrumental music. From Yuddhakāṇḍa 40/44-45, it appears that the requisites of dance were light and swift movement of the limbs, loud song and the expression of emotion on the part of the dancer.

A study of the *Rāmāyaṇa* reveals the prevalence of vocal and instrumental music not only in Ayodhyā and Laṅkā, but also in Kiṣkindhā. On the Prasravaṇagiri, Rāma in separation from Sītā, used to hear the *gīta-vāditra - nirghoṣa* of apes, along with sound of *mṛdaṅga (Mṛdaṇgā ḍambaraiḥ saha)*. Just on entering the house of Sugrīva heard sweet *tantrīgīta* which was perfect.

Rāvaṇa is stated to have been accustomed to leaving bed while listening to auspicious instrumental music (*maṅgalavādya*). Among the things, mentioned by Rāvaṇa to allure Sītā, were *gīta*, *nṛtya* and *vādya*.

The sleeping damsels, seen by Hanūmat in the abode of the Rākṣasas, are described as adept in dance and instrumental music; some of them are stated to have hugged their lutes and others holding the *mṛdaṅga* and other instruments. The city of Ayodhyā is stated to have been full of actors and dancers singing and playing instruments. Rāma himself is said to have been versed in Gandharva-śāstra, Rāma's court is described as adorned by connoisseurs in music and dance, Before this court, Lava and Kuśa are stated to have sung songs with *tantrīlaya*. The songs contained *Jāti* which, according to the commentator, means *ṣaḍjāti - svarū pa*.

MAHĀBHĀRATA

At some places (e.g. Anu (18/32) of the *Mahābhārata* (present form C. 4th. cent. A.D. or earlier), the term *gandharva* denotes song. In the Ādiparvan 152/32, the terms *gīta* and *gandharvasvana* occur side by side. It seems, the word *gandharva* was used also to denote instrumental music. The term *saṁgīta* does not appear to have been used in this epic. But, there is mention of the simultaneous performance of dance, song and instrumental music (e.g. Ādi 200/99, 206/4). Arjuna is stated to have learnt these threefold arts from Citrasena (Vana 44/6-10). He, in his turn, taught music to the daughter of the King of Virāṭa. In this connexion, he refers to his proficiency in dance and song (*bhadro'smi-nṛtye kuśalo'smi gīte*). Besides *Kacchapīviṇā* (Śalya 54/18, S'ānti 210/21), *Bherī* (Aśva, 70/18, Ādi 219/4, 113/45, Virāṭa 68/27), *Mṛdaṅga, Śaṃkha, Āḍambara, Puṣkara, Ghaṇṭā, Paṭaha, Dundubhi, Paṇava, Ānaka, Gomukha, Vaṃśī, Jhallisaka*. etc. are mentioned (Śānti 48/5, 53/4, 120/24; Ādi 101/5, 205/33, 214/9; Sauptika 8/32; Araṇya 132/19; Udyoga 78/16, 142/27; Bhīṣma 15/17; Droṇa 75/30, 70/18; Karṇa 41/14; Anu 65/51 etc...). The meaning of *Śatā-*

ṅga-tūrya (*Ādi188/24*) *is not clear. Does it indicate a hundred kinds of instruments? According to some, Śatāṅgatūrya* was a term used to indicate musical instruments in general, because these were played with the help of nails, fingers, sticks, bows, mouth, etc. The words *saptatantūn vitanvānā* (Droṇa 77/18) clearly refer to the practice of spreading seven strings. This appears to indicate the existence of the seven-stringed *Citravīṇā*. The *Nāṭyas'āstra* (Kashi ed., 29/114) mentions such Vīṇās. Some take it to be the precursor of the later instrument called *Setār*; this term is, however, Persian.

Among the instruments, used by kings in the battlefield to enthuse their own soldiers and to scare those of the enemy, *Bherī, Śaṃkha, Panava, Ānaka, Gomukha, Mṛdaṅga, Dundubhi, Krakaca* or *Kṛkaca, Mahānaka, Jharjhara. Pesi, Goviṣāṇa, Puṣkara, Muraja, Ḍiṇḍima*, etc.

Seven *svaras* as mentioned in the epic (Śānti 184/39 40); this is a very ancient reference to the *svaras*. The word *Brahmagīta* occurs in the Śāntiparvan; it occurs also in the *Nāṭyas'āstra* (31/198). Śārṅgadeva mentions (Saṃgītaratnākara. Tālādhyāya 225, 230) song sung by Brahman. In the opinion of the commentator, Kallinātha, *Brahmagīta* means *Sāmagāna*. The term *Brahmagītikā* refers (Anu 25/19) to *Pāṇitāla* and *Śamyātāla*. The *tāla*, that is done with the right hand, is called *Śamyā*.

A kind of auspicious song, called *Gītamaṅgala* and *Maṅgalagīta*, is mentioned in the *Mahābhārata* (Droṇa 5/41 69/11). It has been dealt with in connexion with classical Sanskrit literature. Reference to many experts in song and dance is found in Sabhā, ch. x and Vana, ch XXXII.

Most modern scholars look upon the *Harivaṃśa* as an appendage to the *Mahābhārata* to which it is supposed to have been added at a later period. This work mentions (Bhaviṣya parvan, 20/9) *Gaṇaprabhāṣa* (classical Gandharvaśāstra) as well as *Brahmaprabhāṣita* (Vedic song), *Saṃgīta*, consisting in the threefold arts, occurs at several places (e.g. *Harivaṃśa parvan* 55/19, *Bhaviṣya-parvan* 27/16, *Viṣṇuparvan* 24/75). The term *Chālikya-gāna*[1] is mentioned in several verses (eg. Viṣṇuparvan 89/67, 81-82, 83). *Chālikya* is the name of a kind of song sung with diverse *rāgas* and *tālas*. Such songs used to be sung by men and women together on festive occasions. In them, six *grāmarāgas* were used. These *rāgas* were manifested in the *sthānas* called *Mandra, Madhya* and *Tāra*.

The *Harivaṃśa* refers (Viṣṇuparvan 20/25-26) to a form of dance called *Hallīsaka*. In it, women, surrounding a man or boy, used to perform dance, sing songs and play instruments. According to Nīlakaṇṭha, a late commentator, if the reading is *Jhallīsaka*, it would denote an instrument in which the seven *svaras* can be sounded.

As regards *Āsārita*, occurring in this treatise, Nīlakaṇṭha suggests that, in it, the following processes take place, one after another:

entrance of the female dancer, dramatic performance, *aṅgahāra* in unison with *tāla* and '*devatācihnarūpa*' dance.

The following information is also available in this work:

Devagandharva-geya (Viṣṇuparvan 92/50) - classical *gāndharva* or *mārgagāna* following *Sāmagāna*.

Āgāndhāra-grāmarāga (Ibid. 93/24) - according to Nīlakaṇṭha, a *grāma* consisting of several *svaras*. It seems, in that age, *gāndhāragrāma* was applied to *laukika - gāna*. Its use, perhaps, gradually died out. There is mention of *gāndhārarāga*.

Gaṅgāvataraṇa (13/25; 93/24, 27)—a kind of *nṛttakaraṇa*. (For *Karaṇa*, Vide *Saṃgītaratnākara* VII. 747-48).

93/32 refers to dance with the leg raised, and miscellaneous dance is mentioned in 92/50.

---

1. Dealt with in a separate chapter in connection with technical terms.

From the expression *nāndīṃ vādayāmāsa*, it seems that *Nāndī* was the name of an instrument. According to Nīlakaṇṭha, it was a sort of instrument covered with leather. He refers to the view according to which this word denotes the sound of the twelve drums called *Paṭahas*. *En passant*, it may be noted that *Nāndī-mṛdaṅga* is one of the instruments mentioned in the Jaina *Rā yapaseniya-sutta*. It may be added that *Nāndī* is the term standing for a preliminary of a dramatic performance, conveying benediction or salutation.

Tālalaya (27/93/25)

The following are some of the instruments mentioned at different places of the work, (eg. Viṣṇuparvan 11/27, 29/111, 30/38, 63/18, 117/4, 121/26, 133/10; Harivaṃśaparvan 54/8):

Tumbīvīṇa, Vallakī, Mṛdaṅga, Tūrya, Bherī, Śaṃkha, Veṇu, Vīṇā, Paṇava, Jharjharī, Ḍiṇḍima, Mahatī Vīṇā (large lute?).

Dance is referred to at several places.

PĀLI AND PRĀKRIT LITERATURES

Some Pāli and Prākrit works contain information on music and dance. The following Pali *Jātakas* may be mentioned in this connexion:

Andhabhūta—lute-playing. It testifies to the practice of singing particular songs at the time of playing dice.

Pañcaguru—vocal and instrumental music and dance.

Bandhanamokṣa—dance. The Buddhist *Gaṇḍīstotra-gāthā*, attributed to Aśvaghoṣa (C. 1st cent. A. D.), is a musical work. It seeks to describe in words the religious message carried to the hearts of men by the sounds produced by beating a long strip of wood with a short club.

Music was a favourite art among the Buddhists. Rhys Davids refers to the different types of musical instruments, viz. *Tata*, *Suṣira*, etc. It is on record that the devout Buddhists preached Indian music in China to a considerable extent. The cave-paintings of Ajantā are mute witnesses to the attitude of the society from the second century B.C. to the fifth century A.D. Among them are various delineations of dance, vocal and instrumental music.

The caves of Bāgh in Madhyapradesh, reveal many pictures of Buddhist inspiration dating from the fifth and sixth century A.D.; male and female human figures engaged in dance. The *Saṃyukta Nikāya*, probably of the pre-Christian era, mentions the sweetness of the sound of the lute, besides various other instruments.

The following Prākrit works deserve mention in this connexion:

Gāthāsaptaśatī of Hāla (1st. cent. A.D., according to some; after 3rd. cent., according to others).

Verse iii. 53 hints at the practice of coating the ends of such per cussion instruments as *Muraja* so that they may produce sweet sound. vi. 60 refers to the sound of a lute struck with a bow.

vi. 57 mentions the notes of flutes.

vi. 26 refers to the playing of drums.

iv.42, vii.43 refer to the practice of singing songs in festivals relating to marriage.

iv. 18 refers to the custom of girls playing flutes.

Karakaṇḍacariū of Kanakāmaramuni (11th. cent. A.D.) ii. 9 mentions drums, tabors, lutes and flutes.

Nāyakumāracariu of Pupphayanta (10th. cent. A.D.) v. 7.11, viii. 77—musical instruments called *Ālapanī, Mṛdaṅga, Tantrī, Mardala, Paṭaha, Dundubhi, Ḍhakkā, Bukka, Bherī, Śaṃkha, Jhallarī, Ghaṇṭā, Tūrya. vii.12, ii.18.2,* if 9-dance *Lāsya* and *Tāṇḍava.*

Bhavisayattakahā of Dhanayāla (10th.cent. A.D.) 1.9 -dance.

References to music and dance in the Jaina *Prabandhakośa* have been noted in the introduction in connexion with the importance of music.

MUSIC IN PURĀṆAS [1]

MUSIC IN TANTRAS[2]

CLASSICAL SANSKRIT

PĀṆINI

The following musical terms occur in the *Aṣṭādhyāyī* of Pāṇini:

Apavīṇa (6/2/187)—song sung without *Vīṇā*. It seems, the general practice was to sing to the accompaniment of the lute.

Maḍḍuka (a kind of small drum), *Jharjhara* (4/4/56 - a kind of *Karatāla*).

Tūrya (2/2/3)-Orchestra or a kind of instrument.

Gāthia (6/4/165)—Singer or composer of songs. *Gāthikā* or *Gāyanī* perhaps denotes a female singer.

Sammada (3/3/68) - a festival mainly consisting in dance, vocal and instrumental music.

Dardurika (4/4/34) - perhaps one who used to play earthen drums.

Pāṇigha (3/2/55) and *Tāḍagha* - perhaps, it denotes keeping time by clap. According to some, *Pāṇigha* means the playing of the *Mṛdaṅga*, *Karatāla*, etc. with both the hands. They think that *Tāḍagha* denotes persons who used to play instruments with sticks.

PATAÑJALI

The following terms occur in the *Mahābhāṣya* of Patañjali (C.2nd. cent. B.C.):

---

1. Dealt with in a separate chapter.
2. *Ibid.*

Piṭhara—perhaps, an instrument like a pan or some other vessel.

Nartakikā (6/3/42) - female dancer.

Śailalino Naṭī (4/2/66)-perhaps, a troupe of dancers or actors.

KĀMASŪTRA

Music and dance are included among the four arts mentioned in Vātsyāyana's *Kāmasūtra* (dating from a period between the sixth century B.C. and sixth century A.D.)

PROSE, POETRY, DRAMA

Plenty of materials relating to music and dance occur in prose, poetical and dramatic works in Sanskrit.

VIKRAMORVAŚĪYA

Act iv of the drama contains some elements of musicology. In this connexion, it should be mentioned that the above elements occur in some verses in Apabhraṃśa language. Some scholars think that these verses are later interpolations,[1], Genuine or spurious, whatever they may be, the fact remains that these verses throw some light on India musicology of the medieval period, if not of the ancient.

The musicoogological elements are as follows:

Kinds of songs—*Khaṇḍadhārā, Ākṣiptikā, Carcarī, Bhinnaka, Khaṇḍaka, Mandaghaṭī, Khaṇḍika, Kulikā.* Names of *Rāgas*—*Balantikā, Kakubhā.*

Type of dance—*Khuraka*

---

1. On this problem, see S.K. De, *History of Sanskrit Literature*, 1947, p. 139, f.n. ;

The word *Laya* also occurs in this context. Though primarily meaning rhythm, it is used to convey the sense of harmony in dance, vocal and instrumental music.

MĀLAVIKĀGNIMITRA

• In the *Mālavikāgnimitra, (Viṣkambhaka* preceding Act I.), the word *saṃgītaśālā* occurs. In this drama, the term *saṃgīta* appears to have been used to denote only vocal music; e.g. Prologue, Pāripārśvika's speech preceding verse 21 in the first act.

The word *Upagāna* occurs in the *Mālavikā*, between II.3 and II.4. *Upagāna*, perhaps, stands for ancillary song, not the principal one. In the same context occurs the expression *catuṣpada-vastu gāyati.* This is followed by a song composed in four feet. So, it seems that *'pada'* in *catuṣpada.* means *pāda'.* The use of *pāda* for *pada* is well-known in Sanskrit.

The following musical instruments are named in the *Mālavikāgnimitra* (NSP. ed, 1950):

Mṛdaṅga - Act I, p.p. 19,20:

Muraja - I. 22

Puṣkara - I.21

In the above drama, Kālidāsa reveals his familiarity with not only the art of dance, but also the qualifications of the dancing girl. Such a girl should be possessed of large eyes, a face beautiful like the autumn moon (*Śaradindu-kānti*), the arms bent at the shoulders, heaving and plump breasts, sides as if polished, a very thin hip, heavy buttocks, covered toes.

Kālidāsa generally refers to female dance, and not to the dance of males. There is, however, reference to the dance of Śiva (e.g. *Meghadūta*, I. 40). While describing a dancing girl, he writes as follows: (*Mālavikā*, II. 6):

the bangles at the wrists are static as the body is motionless, the left hand placed on the buttocks, the right hand hanging loose, like a *Śyāmā* creeper, the right foot removing, with the big toe, the flowers strewn on the jewelled pavement of the dancing hall, the eyes steadfastly gazing at the ground, half the body from the foot to the navel straight and stretched.

The description in II. 8 is as follows: though tight-lipped, yet conveying all the intended sense by gestures, rhythmic steps, immersed in *Rasa* (sentiment), acting very delicate and smooth.

In Gaṇadāsa's speech in the beginning of the second act of the *Mālavikāgnimitra*, the expression *Chalikaprayoga* occurs. Monier Williams explains *Chalika* as "a song consisting of four parts, recited with gesticulation, a kind of drama." In the above context, there is reference to *Chalika-prayoga* being heard. So, by *Chalita* Kalidasa appears to mean a kind of song. There is, however, reference to *Chalika Nāṭya* in the *Viṣkambha* preceding the first act. It seems that the term was used, in those times, to indicate both a kind of song and a type of drama.

The word *rāgabandha* in ii.8 of the *Mālavikā* denotes a song with *rāga*.

KUMĀRASAMBHAVA, RAGHUVAMSA, MEGHADŪTA.

Kālidāsa uses the term *Saṃgīta* at several places, e.g. *Kumārasambhava* V. 56, *Meghadūta*, I. 56, *Śakuntalā*, V, line 1, Vidūṣaka's speech. In the *Kumāra*, the word denotes only song. In the *Śakuntalā*, the word *saṃgīta-śālā* occurs. It menas 'a room for *saṃgīta*'. It is not clear whether *saṃgīta* here means song only or instrumental music and dance too.

In the *Meghadūta*, there is mention of both vocal and instrumental music at the time of Paśupati's (i.e. Śva's) *nṛtya* (understood). In Verse 11.25 of this work, the terms *geya* and *mūrchanā* occur. According to Mallinātha, *geya* means gānārhaprabandhādi; i.e., composition, etc. fit for being sung.

The term *mūrchanā* occurs in *Kumāra* VIII. 85 too. This term appears to have been used in the sense in which it is generally used in *Saṃgīta-śāstra*.

In the *Meghadūta* (II.16), there is reference to dance being performed to the accompaniment of *tāla*. The consort of the exiled Yakṣa is described as causing the domestic peacock to dance by *tā la*.

In the *Kumārasambhava* (VIII.85), the terms *gītamaṅgala*, *mūrchanā* and *Kaiśika* occur. According to commentator, Mallinātha, *Kaiśika* is the name of a *Rāga*. Some would prefix *maṅgala* to *Kaiśika*, and hold that, here, the *Rāga Maṅgalakaiśika* is intended by Kālidāsa. As a matter of fact, however, the two words seem to be independent of each other. A distinct *Rāga*, named *Kaiśika*, was, perhaps, used to be sung on auspicious occasions.

In the *Raghuvaṃśa* (I.39), we have the expression *Ṣaḍja-saṃvādinī kekā* (the peacock's cry resembling the *svara* called *Ṣaḍja*). From this it is clear that Kālidāsa knew that the above *svara* had been derived from the peacock's cry.

Elements of folk-songs are also noticeable at some places of Kālidāsa's works. For example, in the *Raghuvaṃśa* iv 20, there is reference to the *Śāligopīs* (female guards of paddy fields) singing of the glory of Raghu. This reminds one of what is called *Sārigān* in Bengal. Songs of this sort are sung by labourers who work in unison as a means of relief and entertainment in the midst of hard labour and also to foster esprit de corps.

Kālidāsa being the greatest Indian poet, we note below all the terms relating to musical instruments contained in his works, for ready reference. For this purpose, we include also the *Ṛtusaṃhāra* and the portion of the *Kumārasambhava* from canto IX to the end, Kālidāsa's authorship of which is doubted by some scholars.

The following abbreviations have been used here:

A - Abhijñānaśakuntala, NSP. ed.

K - Kumārasambhava, ed. Suryakanta, Sahitya Akademi, New Delhi, 1962.

Mal - Mālavikāgnimitra, NSP ed., 1950.

Me - Meghadūta, ed. K.B. Pathak, Poona, 1916.

R - *Raghuvaṃśa*, ed. J. Vidyāsāgara, Calcutta, 1902.

RS - Ṛtusaṃhāra, included in *Kālidāser Granthāvalī*, in Bengali characters, Calcutta, 1322, BSS.

V - *Vikramorvaśiya*, ed. H.D. Velankar, New Delhi, 1961.

Terms arranged in English alphabetical order

Bherī - K XIV.27,44,48

Dundubhi - R X. 76; K XI.37

Ghaṇṭā - R VII.41

Mṛdaṅga - R XIII.40, XVI. 14,64; XIX. 5
Mal. I. pp. 19,20.

Muraja - Me. 58,66.K VI.40. Mal. I. 22

Paṭaha - Me. 36; IX.71; K XIV, 18, 33, 46; XV.11.

Puṣkara - Me. 72; R XVII.11, 14 Mal. I. 21

Śaṃkha - R Vi. 9; KXI. 38; RS. III. 4

Sutantrī - RS. I.3

Tūrya - R III. 19, VI. 9, 56, X.76, XVI. 87 V IV. 12; K VII. 10

Vallakī - R VIII. 41; RS. I. 8.

Veṇu - R XIX. 35

Vīṇā - R VIII. 33, XIX, 35; Me. 91

ŚŪDRAKA (C.6th. cent. A.D.)

MṚCCHAKATIKA

This drama by Śūdraka affords a glimpse of music in vogue in the contemporary society. While speaking of Rebhila's song, a good song is characterised as follows:

It gives rise to '*rakta*' or *anurāga*, i.e., it is attractive. It is also sweet, even throughout, without any lapse anywhere, very clear, possessed of emotion, the charming *Mūrchanā* having a high tone in the middle and soft at the end, having *rāgālāpa*, harmony of *svaras* with instruments like the *Vīṇā*, etc. Among musical instruments, mention has been made of the following: *Vīṇā*, Vaṃśa (Veṇu), Dardura, Panava or *Mṛdaṅga.*

Women also appear to have played the *Mṛdaṅga. Seven svaras* used to be manifested through the seven holes of the flute. The system of *Vṛndagāna* was in vogue.

In the fourth act, various matters, relating to dance, music, etc. have been mentioned while describing the house of Vasantasenā.

BHAṬṬI (C. earlier than middle of 6th.cent. A.D.)

In ii. 16, while describing the beauty of autumn, the poet writes:

vivrtta-hāraṃ rucirāṅgahāraṃ

samudvaha-ccāru-nitamba-ramyam/

āmandra-mantha-dhvani-dattatālaṃ

gopāṅganā-nṛttamanandayattam//

The dance of cowherd-women gave him (Rāmacandra) delight. In it, their sides were moved in a curved manner; the movement of their body or limbs was graceful. Their beautiful buttocks were raised, the dance became charming. In this dance, *tāla* was given in deep sound. The terms *Aṅgahāra*, *Mandra* and *Tāla* (all explained under Technical terms) reveal the author's familiarity with the musical lore or musicology.

MĀGHA (C. 7th. cent. A.D.)

Verse XI.1 of the *Siśupālavadha* is as follows:

*śruti-samadhikamu-ccaiḥ pañ*camaṃ pīḍayantaḥ

satatamṛ-ṣabhahīnaṃ bhinnakīkṛtya ṣaḍjam

praṇijagadur-akāku śrāvaka-kaṇṭhāḥ

pariṇatimi - ti rātrer-māgadhā mādhavāya.

It means as follows: The bards, having left out the *Svaras Ṣaḍja* and *Pañ*eama, intimated, to Kṛṣṇa, the end of the night by loudly singing in this way. That note of them extended afar, and was sweet, and, in it, there was no change. There was no *Ṛṣabha* note in the stringed instrument which accompanied that song.

The following expressions in the above verse are significant:

Srutisamadhika

Abounding in *Śruti.*

This, according to Mallinātha, indicates the *Svara, Ṣaḍja* or *Pañ*cama. According to Hemacandra (*Kāvyānuśāsana*, NSP.ed., ch. 3. 190) *śruti-samadhika* means *śrutyā samadhikaṃ pañcaś-*rutikam, i.e. having more *śrutis* (i.e. 5 instead of 4).

The *Saṃgītaratnākara*, however, holds that the number of Śrutis of a particular *Svara* cannot be increased.

Pīḍayantaḥ

According to Mallinātha, it means *parityajantaḥ* (while giving up). According to Hemacandra, it means *śrutihrāsena alpī kurvantaḥ (i.e. while making scantier by the reduction of Śrutis).*

Satatam

Accompanied by stringed instruments (*tata*) like lute, etc.

Ṛṣabhahīnam

Devoid of the *Svara* called *Ṛṣabha.*

Bhinnakīkṛtya

Different opinions about interpretation are as follows:

1) *Bhinna* means *Vikṛta* (Kallinātha)

2) *Bhinna* means one of the five classes of *Rāgas* as stated in ancient musicology. (Bhātkhaṇḍe).

3) *Bhinna* means the giving up of the prohibited *svaras.* (Mallinātha and Premacandra Tarkavāgīśa, commentator on the *Kāvyādarśa*).

4) *Ṣāḍava* or *Auḍava* (Mataṅga).

Akāku

Avikṛta-dhvani (Mallinātha).

PAÑCATANTRA

(Earlier than 570 A.D.)

Through fables, certain matters, relating to *Saṃgīta,* have been stated. The following are the main topics:

Seven *svaras,* three *Grāmas,* 21 *Mūrchanās,* 49 *Tānas,* three *mātrās,* three *layas,* three *sthānas,* three *Yatis,* nine *Rasas,* 36 *Rāgas,* 40 *Bhāvas,* 185 *Gītāṅgas.*

It may be noted that 36 *Rāgas* are mentioned, but nothing has been said about *Rāgiṇīs.* The fact seems to be that the term *Rāgiṇī* came to be used long after this period.

KĀDAMBARĪ (7th. cent. A.D., earlier half)

(Kale's ed., 1928)

The word *gīta-śruti* occurs at p.26. The word *dantakoṇa* (pp 107, 146), perhaps, denotes a triangular instrument made of ivory.

STAGES OF DEVELOPMENT OF ANCIENT INDIAN MUSIC

The earliest written record of the Indian civilisation and culture is the Veda. The degree of Vedic culture obviously presupposes a preparatory period. It has been aptly said that Vedic civilisation has dawn, but no twilight. As stated in the Introduction, the relics of the Indus Valley Civilisation, which is generally supposed to be pre-Vedic, reveal the existence of a few musical instruments and of the art of dancing.

Coming down to the Vedic age, we find music in a considerably developed form. We have given a rapid survey of the musical elements in the Vedas and the ancillary works.

GĀNDHARVA-SAṂGĪTA

In connexion with ancient Indian music, we come across the words Gandharva and *Gāndharva-saṃgīta.* Originally, Gandharva denoted a celestial musician, a class of demi-gods regarded as the singers and musicians of gods. Then it came to mean a singer in general. In musical lore, there are many traditional Gandharvas, e.g. Nārada, Tumburu, Kohala, Viśākhila, Citrasena, Bharata, Dattila, etc. Some of them are looked upon as creators and propagators of *Gāndharva-saṃgīta.*

Now, what is this kind of *Saṃgita*? It has been defined in the *Nāradīya Śikṣā* (iv.12) and *Nāṭyaśāstra* (Kashi ed., xxviii. 9). According to the *Śikṣā*, as explained by Śobhākara, the word *gāndharva* means what has been derived from *gandharva.* It was the kind of song sung with *svara, tāla* and *pada.* This characteristic of *gandharva* is clearly stated by Bharata who says—*yattu tantrī gataṃ proktaṃ nānātodya-samāśrayam/ gāndharvamiti vijñeyaṃ* svaratālapadāśrayam//

Though this kind of *gāna* was post-Vedic, yet of its prevalence several centuries before Christ, there is literary evidence. For instance, the Ceylonese Buddhist treatise *Mahāvaṃśa* testifies to the vogue of *gāndharva-saṃgīta* before the Nandas (c. 362-322 B.C.) and even earlier during the time of the Śiśunāga king

Bimbisāra (accession C. 546 B.C.), and Ajātaśatru (C. 516-489 B.C.). The account, left by the Greeks, also testifies to the wide cultivation of *gāndharva-saṃgīta* in these times.

The *Rāmāyaṇa*, the *Mahābhārata* and the *Harivaṃśa* reveal the currency of *gāndharva-saṃgīta*. There are indications, in these works, of the use of *Sāmagāna* in connexion with sacrifices like *Rājasūya*, *Aśvamedha*, etc. It should be noted that, in the above works, there is no mention of *Jāti*, *Vikṛta* or *Miśra* and of *Jātirāga*. After the *Nāradīya Śikṣā*, the *Nāṭyaśāstra* is, perhaps, the first treatise to mention *Grāmarāga* (ch. 32, Kashi ed), which arises from *Jāti* or *Jātirāga*.

We have seen that Bharata has defined *gāndharva-saṃgīta* as song based on *svara*, *tāla* and *pada*. Śārṅgadeva, who flourished at a time when *mārgasaṃgīta* reached a high stage of development, defines *gāndharva-saṃgīta* as a kind of song which, coming down traditionally from time immemorial, is applied by Gandharvas:

anādi saṃpradāyaṃ yad gandharvaiḥ saṃprayujyate/
niyataṃ śreyaso hetus-tad gandharvaṃ jagur budhāḥ//
Saṃgītaratnākara IV.2

Anādi-saṃpradāya means traditionally current through the succession of *Gurus* and *Śiṣyas*. Kallinātha says that such songs are *apauruṣeya* i.e., not created by men.

Niyata is explained by Siṃhabhūpāla as *grahā-ṃśa-mūrchanādi-niyama-yukta*.

Gāndharva—Kallinātha takes it to denote *mārgagīta*. Kallinātha clearly brings out the real characteristics of *gāndharva-saṃgīta* in the following lines:

Svaragata-rāgavivekaoyr-jātyādi-antarabhāṣāntaraṃ yaduktaṃ tad gāndharvam. He means to say that not only Jāti or *Jātirāga*, but a conglomerate of *Grāmarāga*, *Bhāṣārāga*, *Vibhāṣārāga* and *Antarabhāṣā* and the songs of artistes Nārada and the like is called *gāndharva-saṃgīta*. That is to say that *gāndharva-saṃgīta* is animated by not only *Jātirāga*, but also by the *Rāgas* known as *Bhāṣā*, *Vibhāṣā* and *Antarabhāṣā*—*Bhāṣā* is the name of a rāga following a *Jātirāga*.

The words in the expression *svara-tāla-padāśrayam* or - *padātmakam* in Bharata's definition of *gāndharva* mean as follows:

(1) *Svara*—it includes *Śruti*. *Grāma*. *Mūrchanā*, *Sādhāraṇa*. 18 *Jātis*, *Jātirāga*, four *Varṇas*, *Alaṃkāra*, *Śamyā*, Tāla, Sannipāta, Parivarta, etc.

(2) *Tāla*—it stands for *Śamyā*, *Pāṇi*, *Sannipāta*, *Parivarta*, *Vastu*, *Mātrā*, *Vidāri*, *Aṅguli*, *Mati*, *Prakaraṇa*, *Gānāvayava*, etc.

(3) *Pada*—includes *Svara* and *Vyañjana*-varṇas, Sandhi, Vibhakti, Ākhyāta, Upasarga, Nipāta, Chandas, Vṛtta, Jāti, etc.

The origin of seven *Śuddhajāti-rāgas*, taking their names from the seven *svaras* (e.g. *Ṣāḍjī*, *Ārṣabhī*., etc.), is quite old. Already in the *Rāmāyaṇa*, we find reference to seven *jātis* in the expression *jātibhiḥ* in the verse *pāṭhye geye ca*, etc. in the Fourth Book.

At the time of Bharata, the permutation and combination of the above *Jātirāgas* led to the creation and currency of eleven additional *Jātirāgas*; thus, the total number of *Jātirāgas* came to 7+11=18. The eleven *Jāti-rāgas*, arising out of a combination of *Śuddha* and *Miśrarāgas*, are as follows:

Name of *Rāga*	Names of combined *Rāgas*
1. *Ṣaḍjamadhyamā*	*Ṣāḍjī* + *Madhyamā*
2. *Ṣaḍjodīcyavā* of *Ṣaḍjodīcyavatī*	*Ṣāḍjī*, + *Gāndhārī* + *Dhaivatī*
3. *Ṣaḍjakaiśikī*	*Ṣāḍjī* + *Gāndhārī*
4. *Gāndhārodīcyavā*	*Ṣāḍjī* + *Gāndhārī* + *Dhaivatī* + *Madhyamā*

5. *Madhyamodīcyavā*	*Gāndhārī, Pañ*camī + Dhaivatī + Madhyamā
6. Raktagāndhārī	Gāndhārī + Pañcamī+Naiṣādī + Madhyamā
7. Āndhrī	Gāndhārī + Ṣāḍjī
8. Nandayantī	Gāndhārī + Pañcamī + Ārṣabhī
9. Gāndhāra-pañcamī	Gāndhārī + Pañcamī
10. Kārmāravī	Naiṣādī + Ārṣabhī + Pañcamī
11. Kaiśikī	Dhaivatī + Ārṣabhī

III

AUTHORS OF PUBLISHED AND UNPUBLISHED WORKS

In this chapter, we shall present a list of the authors of the published and unpublished works on musicology. Under each name will be given as much information as can be gathered.

(In English alphabetical order)

AHOBALA (Also written as Ahobila)

Author of the *Saṃgīta - pārijāta.* Flourished in the 17th. cent. A.D. He refers to the *Rājataraṅgiṇī* (11th-12th cent. A.D.), and defends the views of Rāmāmātya (16th. century), author of the *Svaramela-kalānidhi* (c. 1550 A.D.).

AŚOKAMALLA

Author of the *Nṛtyādhyāya.* Son of King Vīrasiṃha. He quotes Kīrtidhara, Abhinavagupta and a little known work, entitled *Sudhābdhi.*

BĀLARĀMAVARMAN

Nephew of Bālamārtaṇḍa Varman, he was born in 1724 A. D., installed on the throne of Travancore in 1753 A.D., and died in 1798 A.D. He is credited with the authorship of the *Bālarāmabharatam.* The Travancore State Manual (I. 417) records that Bālarāmavarman ruled in 1798-1810 A.D. (See also *Ibid.,* II. 435). But, the above work and an inscription, published in *Travancore Arch. Series, IV.* 106, testify to the fact that Rāmavarman, the predecessor of Bālarāmavarman (*Trav. State Manual* I. 369) was also known as *Bālarāmavarman, and was the author of this work, See also Tra. State MSS.* II. 434.

BHARATA

Believed to be the author of the *Nāṭyaśāstra.* Date not yet determined with certainty. According to some scholars, he probably flourished earlier than the fourth or fifth century A.D. Sometimes referred to as Ādi Bharata. The author of the *Nāṭyaśāstra* appears to have propounded, for the first time, the theory of *Rasa* in connexion with drama. A work on music, entitled *Gītālaṃkāra,* is also attributed to Bharata.

(For life, works and identity, see S.K. De, *History of Sanskrit Poetics,* Calcutta, 1960)

BHĀSKARĀCĀRYA

A descendant of Varadaguru of Śrīvatsagotra, he lived in Sriperumbudur (Chingleput District) probably in the 18th century A.D. His *Sāhityakallolinī* deals with poetics and the art of dance. The work cites the *Rasārnava-sudhākara.*

BHĀTKHAṆḌE, V.N. (1860-1936 A.D.)

Son of Nārāyaṇā and trained in music by Raoji B.B. Begker, he was a renowned musicologist. Born in Bombay city. As a college student, he learnt *Sitar* from G.V. Dāmuljī. He was long associated with the Gāyana Uttejakamandalī, an institution of music established by the Pārsi community of Bombay. He learnt many *Dhrupadas* from Bolbāügkar and Āshāk Ālī of Jaipur. He deeply studied Sanskrit works on musicology. In 1907 A.D., he came to Calcutta, and became very intimate with Rājā Śaurīndra Mohan Ṭhākur. At his initiative, the first All—India Music Conference was held at Baroda. In accordance with his advice, the Music School of Baroda was re-established. With it were associated many renowned musicians including Faiyāz Khān, court-musician of Baroda. With his co-operation, the Music College of Baroda was established in 1918. In 1926, Maurice College was established at Lucknow. He prepared the course of studies there, and started conducting it. He died in 1936. At Maurice College, his renowned disciple Ratanjankār, along with Rājeswar Bali, Umānāth Bali and

Dhurjaṭiprasād, created a group of which the famous Atulprasād was the very soul. Bhātkhaṇḍe grouped the current *Rāga-saṃgīta* into ten main *Ṭhāṭas*. In accordance with different *Svaras*; he divided the *Rāgas* into two classes, viz. *Pūrvāṅga* and *Uttarāṅga*. He specified the application of particular *Svaras* or *Pākaḍ* indicative of the special characteristics of each *Rāga*. The subsidiary *Rāgas* which, according to him, are associated with principal *Rāgas*, are regarded as accessories (*aṅga*) of the latter; e.g. *Kānāḍā Aṅga*, etc. He collected the original melody of many Ḥindustani songs of the types of *Dhrupada*, *Kheyāl*, *Sādrā*. etc., and published their notations.

Of his many published works, the following deserve special mention: *Śrīmallakṣya-saṃgītam*, *Abhinava-rāga-mañjarī*, *Hindustāni Saṃgītapaddhati* and *Kramika-pustaka-mālikā*.

The following articles of Bhātkhaṇḍe speak volumes for his learning:

(1) Modern Hidusthani Rāga System and the simplest method of studying the same (read at Lucknow Conference, 1925.

(2) Music systems of 15th, 16th and 17th. centuries (pub. in first four parts of the quarterly Journal *Saṃgītā* published from Maurice College, Lucknow).

(3) A short historical survey of music of Upper India, 1917.

For details about the author, see S.N. Ratanjankār, *Paṇdit Bhātkhaṇḍe*, 1967.

BHĀVABHAṬṬA

His ancestors used to live in Ābhīra Maṇḍala in Mālava region. His father, Saṃgītarāya Janārdana Bhaṭṭa, was grandson of the musician, Tāna Bhaṭṭa, and composed the following works in the court of king Anūpasiṃha of Bikaner (1674-1709 A.D.):

Anūpasaṃgītaratnākara, Anūpasaṃgītavilāsa, Anūpasaṃgītāṅkuśa, Saṃgītavinoda, Muralīprakāśa, Naṣṭoddiṣṭaprabodhaka, Dhrauvapadaṭīkā.

BHŪLOKAMALLA

Epithet of Someśvara (q.v.).

(Mummidi) CIKKADEVARĀYA III

Ruler of Mysore (1672-1704 A.D.), he wrote the *Bharata-sāra-saṃgraha* which is an incomplete work in 2,500 verses, and sets forth the views of Bharata, Mataṅga and Vidyāraṇya. [See *Cikkadevarāya-vaṃśāvalī*, Ed. Mysore. and *Cikkadevarāja-vaṃśapraśasti.* TC. IV. No. 3919]

DĀMODARA

Also called Catura Dāmodara and son of Lakṣmīdhara (according to I.O. Cat. of MSS., II. 318), he was one of the connoisseurs of music at the court of

Emperor Jāhāṅgir or Shāh Jāhān in the 17th. cent. Author of the *Saṃgīta-darpaṇa.* Supposed, by some, to have been a descendant of Catura Kallinātha (q.v.).

Haribhaṭṭa or Harivallabha appears to have been another name of the author. (See Krishnamachariar, *Hist. of Class. Skt. Lit.*).

DATTILĀCĀRYA

Author of the *Dattilam.* The name is mentioned, in the *Nāṭyaśāstra,* as that of a son of Bharata. Some think that a larger work by him is lost. Dattila is mentioned by Abhinavagupta in his *Abhinava-bhāratī,* ch. IV, among ancient authorities. He is cited also by Mataṅga in the *Bṛhaddeśī.* Dattila's precise date is unknown. According to some, he was a contemporary of Bharata. Among his predecessors, he mentions Kohala and Nārada.

DEVANĀCĀRYA

Author of the *Saṃgītamuktāvalī.* Probably the same as Devaṇabhaṭṭa, author of the celebrated Smṛti digest, entitled

Smṛticandrikā, and described as son of Keśavāditya Bhaṭṭa. Also known as Devānanda, Devendra, Devagaṇa, he was a South Indian. According to P.V. Kane, he flourished probably in the second half of the 12th. century A.D. or the first half of the 13th. According to M. Krishnamachariar, he wrote in the Court of King Prauḍha Devarāja of Vijaynagar (1406-22A.D.). He mentions, *inter alia*, the writers named Rudrasiṃha and Someśvara. (King) Gajapati Vīraśrī Nārāyaṇadeva, Son of Padmanābha, he ruled at Parlakimedi (Orissa) about 1700 A.D. Belonging to the race of Uttuṅgagaṅga, he learnt music under Puruṣottama Kaviratna (q.v.). His work is entitled *Saṃgīta-nārāyaṇa*.

GAURANĀRYA

Author of the *Lakṣaṇadīpikā*, he was son of Ayama (Ayalu?) prabhu, brother of Potana, Minister of Siṅgaya Mādhava, King of Rācakonda of Recarla dynasty, who ruled about 1427 A.D. (18th. cent. - See Krishnamachariar, *Hist. of Class Skt. Lit.*, p. 787).

(GOPAPUTRA) GOPENDRA TIPPA BHŪPĀLA

Author of the *Tāladīpikā*, he belonged to Saluva dynasty of Vijaynagar, and flourished in the 15th century A.D.

GHANAŚYĀMA

Author of a commentary on *Hastamuktāvalī*, a treatise on dance.

See Intro. to *Nāgarasarvasva*, ed. Tanusukharama Sarma, Bombay.

GOPĪNĀTHA KAVIBHŪṢAṆA

Son of Vāsudeva Pātra of Karaṇa family, priest and physician of King Gajapati Jagannātha Nārāyaṇa of Khimindi of Gaṅga race (reign C. 1766-180 A.D.). His elaborate work on poetics is entitled *Kavicintāmaṇi* in 24 chapters the last of which includes music. He wrote also a musical poem, *Rāmacandravihāra*.

GOVINDA DĪKṢITA

Real author of the *Saṃgītasudhā* which is known as a work by king Raghunātha of Tanjore. As a matter of fact, Govinda dedicated this work to Raghunātha Nāyaka (accession 1614 A.D.) under whom he was a Minister, Govinda's son, Veṅkaṭamakhin, author of the *Caturdaṇḍiprakāśikā* states that Govinda wrote, *inter alia.* a treatise named *Saṃgītasudhā-nidhi.*

GOVINDA

Author of the *Rāga-tāla-pārijāta-prakāśa* in which mention is made of Śārṅgadeva (q.v.). He must have lived later than the 13th. cent. A.D. Among other writers, he mentions Samīraṇa, Nandin, Guha, Mataṅgaja, Nārada.

Another person of the same name wrote the *Saṃgīta-śāstra-saṃkṣepa.* He is taken to represent the music of later times, and is considered to have superseded Veṅkaṭamakhin's (q.v.) views. In two chapter-colophons, the work is purported to be a part of the *Skandapurāṇa,* and composed by Ṣaṇmukha. He supports Tyāgarāja (1758-1846 A.D.) of Tiruvarur. Supposed by some to have been a friend of Tyāgarāja (b. 1758 A.D.).

The following information is contained in footnote l,p, 875, of *Hist. of Class. Skt. Lit.* of Krishnamachariar, 1974, "Rāmakrishnakavi says that Govinda was an Āndhra, that he wrote a work called *Rāgatālacintāmaṇi* that he followed *Rāmāmātya* and his 20 *melas* and that the Adyar MS. contains a few sheets in the beginning of this work which had got mixed up with an anonymous work called *Saṃgraha-cūḍāmaṇi,* described as a part of the *Skandapurāṇa.*"

The detractors of Govinda declare that he was probably a friend of Tyāgarāja, and that he deliberately composed the work in the guise of an extract from Purāṇa to depopularise Veṅkatamakhin.

Govinda refers to the *Vīṇā* (lute) of Acyutarāya who ruled at Tanjore in 1572-1614 A.D.

His son, Pratāpamalla, was a poet. His another son, Jagatprakāśamalla, compiled an anthology, *Padmasamuccaya.* At the initiative of his daughter's son, Ananta, Ghanaśyāma wrote a commentary on the *Hastamuktāvali*, a work on dance. [Vide Intro. to *Nāgarasarvasva*, ed. T. Sarma, Bombay.]

HAMMĪRA

Probably King of Mewar and fifth ancestor of King Kumbhakarṇa (1431 or 1433-1469 or 1468 A.D.) who commented on the *Gītagovinda* of Jayadeva. Hammīra died in 1394 A.D. In his *Saṃgīta-śṛṅgāra-hāra*, he mentions an earlier writer (king) Jaitrasiṃha.

HARIBHAṬṬA

To an author of this name are attributed the three works on music, entitled *Saṃgītadrpaṇa*, *Saṃgīta-sāroddhāra* and *Saṃgīta-kalānidhi.*

In the introductory verses of the Tanjore MS. (XVI. 7266) Haribhaṭṭa appears to be another name for Catura Dāmodara.

HARIPĀLA

Also called Haripāladeva or Hari, he was son of Kumiri (?) and grandson of Somanātha. He was probably king Haripāla of Yādava dynasty of Devagiri (1312-1318 A.D.) who was slain by Mubārak in 1318 A.D. He does not seem to be identical with king Haripāla of the Cālukya Dynasty of Anhilvāḍ (1145-1155 A.D.). Our Haripāla calls himself *Vicāracaturmukha* and *Vīṇātantra-viśārada.*

Author of the *Saṃgīta-sudhākara*, in which he is mentioned as an author on music along with Śārṅgadeva among the *Ādhunikas* (moderns).

In the anonymous *Abhinaya-Śāstram* (DC XXII, 8720-21), there is a reference to *Hari-bhūbhuja* which, perhaps, refers to our Haripāla.

HṚDAYANĀRĀYAṆA

King of Garrh or Gaḍhadurga (Jabbalpore), who ruled about 1667 A.D. In the colophon to the *Hṛdayaprakāśa*, he describes himself as Mahārājādhirāja-Mahārāja-Gaḍhā-durgādhipa-mahārāja-śrī Hṛdayanārāyaṇa-deva. He wrote two works on music, entitled *Hṛdayaprakāśa* and *Hṛdaya-kautuka*. He utilised Locana Kavi's *Rāgataraṅgiṇī* for elaboration.

JAGADEKAMALLA PRATĀPACAKRAVARTIN

A Cālukya king of Kalyāṇ (1138-1150 A.D.). Mentioned respectfully by Śārṅgadeva. A follower of Abhinavagupta, he composed the *Saṃgīta-cūḍāmaṇi*.

JAGADDHARA

Son of Ratnadhara, he flourished sometime about the 15th. cent. A.D. His work on music is the *Saṃgīta-sarvasva*. He also commented on the *Sarasvatīkaṇṭhābharana*.

JAGAJJYOTIRMALLA

Son of Tribhuvanamalla, he was the ruler of Bhaktapura (Bhatagamva), a tributary (1617-1633) of the king of Nepal. A great musician as he was, he noticed that there was no reliable and authoritative work on music in the north.

So, he brought Abhilāṣa's *Saṃgītacandra* into Nepal, and had a commentary, *Saṃgītabhāskara*, written on it by a scholar named *Vaṅgamaṇi* of Mithilā. He himself composed the *Saṃgīta-sārasaṃgraha* in Nepal Era 799. His other work on musicology is the *Svarodayadīpikā*. He wrote works also on other subjects.

At the instance of his daughter's son, Ananta, one Ghanaśyāma wrote a commentary on the *Hastamuktāvalī*, a work on dance.

JĀYASENĀPATI

Author of the *Nṛttaratnāvalī*. He flourished in the thirteenth cent. A.D. He was the commander of elephant-forces under Kākatiya Gaṇapati, king of Warangal (1200-1265 A.D.). For Jāyasenāpati's Inscriptions dated Śaka 1135, 1157, see *Epigraphia Indica.* III, 84; V.143, VI. 39. For Gaṇapati's inscription, see *Indian Antiquary,* XXI.20. Some unpublished ones from Nizam's dominions are with M.R. Kavi, Madras.

(Catura) KALLINĀTHA

A noted commentator on Śārṅgadeva's *Saṃgīta-ratnākara.* Son of Lakṣmīdhara and Nārāyaṇī of Śāṇḍilyagotra and grandson of Tullāleśvaradeva, he adorned the Court of Immadi Devarāya, alias Mallikārjuna, son of Prauḍha Devarāja or Devarāya II of Vijaynagar (1446-85 A.D.).

His commentary, called *Kalānidhi,* is defective at places. So, he has been bitterly criticised by Raghunātha. He quotes, as an authority, Gopālanāyaka who is believed to have been a friend of Āmir Khusru, and respected by Alauddin Khilji (reign 1296-1316 A.D.) Vide Isvariprasād, *Medieval India,* 542. He was familiar with the earlier works, *Aumāpatam* and *Saṃgītameru.*

KIKARĀJA

Author of a work, entitled *Saṃgīta-sāroddhāra* which is to be distinguished from a work of the same title by Haribhaṭṭa.

Kikarāja was known as Śāradānandana. See B. O.R.I. MS. 1886-92, No. 832.

KOHALA

Mentioned among the direct disciples of Bharata to whom he is ranked next in the quality of writings. It is stated, in the *Nāṭyaśāstra* (XXVIII.18), that Kohala will compose a treatise on *Prastāratantra.* His work is lost except for a fragmentary *Tālādhyāya.* The *Abhinayśāstra,* attributed to Kohala, may be a part of his lost work or an abridgement of it. The *Dattila--kohalīya* appears to be a narration, by Kohala, to Mataṅga. Kohala's work appears also to have been narrated to Śārdūla, as is attested by Kallinātha in his commentary on the *Saṃgītaratnākara* and by Raghunātha in his *Saṃgītasudhā.*

Kohala is often quoted by later writers, particularly by Abhinavagupta (10th-11th.cent.) and Kallinātha (15th. cent.).

The citations from Kohala indicate that, though mainly following in the footsteps of Bharata, he improved upon the *Nāṭyaśāstra* in details of classifications, e.g. in the case of *Cārī* (see Glossary).

KṚṢṆĀNANDA VYĀSADEVA RĀGASĀGARA

He was the chief singer in the court of Udaypur, authored an encyclopaedic work called *Rāgakalpadruma.* He is known to have been born in the last decade of the 18th. century.

KṢEMAKARṆA

Another name of Kṣemendra (q.v.).

KṢEMENDRA

Also known as Kṣemakarṇa, he was the author of a *Rāgamālā* (1570 A.D.). written at the instance of Jalava Bhūpati. Not to be confused with the Kashmirian polymath, Kṣemendra (11th. cent. A.D.).

KUMBHA, KUMBHAKARṆA OR KUMBHA RĀṆĀ

Belonging to the race of Guhilas (Brahmin kings) of Medapata (Mewār), he was son of Mokala and husband of the famous saint Mīrā Bāi, and father of Rājamalla. Besides being a great conqueror, he was a poet, musicologist and litterateur. His *Rasikapriyā* commentary on the *Gītagovinda* speaks eloquently of his aesthetic taste and literary skill. Author of the *Saṃgītarāja.* He ruled at Citrakūṭa (Chittor) in 1431-1469 A.D. (or, according to some, 1433-1468 A.D.).

From a quotation (*Śikhariṇī Chandas, tallakṣaṇaṃ saṃgītarāje*, etc.), in his commentary on the *Gītagovinda,* he appears to have written a chapter on metres in the *Saṃgītarāja.*

From the concluding verses of the cantos in his *Rasikapriyā,* it appears that be wrote the works called *Saṃgīta-krama-dīpikā, Ekaliṅgāśraya* and *Kumbhasvāmi-mandāra.*

He wrote also a commentary on the *the Saṃgītaratnākara.*

For details of his life and activities, sea Todd, *Annals of Rajasthan.*

LAKṢMAṆA BHĀSKARA

Author of the work, entitled *Mataṅgabharata.* He was earlier than the Nāik King of Tanjore, and may have lived about the 14th. cent. A.D.

LAKṢMĪDHARA

Author of the *Bharata-śāstra-grantha.* He flourished in the Court of King Tirumalarāya of Vijayṇagar (1570-73 A.D.), and lived at Cerukuru in Guntur District. In his commentary on the *Gītagovinda* (Tanj. XVI. 7333), he mentions the following works:

Rāgadīpikā, Raṅgalakṣaṇa-vilāsa, Vāmadevīya and king Pratāpa's *Saṃgīta-cūḍāmaṇi.* In his above work, he cites his work *Ṛtukrīḍāviveka.*

LAKṢMĪNĀRĀYAṆA (Bhandāru)

Author of the *Saṃgītasūryodaya,* he was son Bhandāru Viṭṭhaleśvara and Rukmiṇī of Bharadvājagotra. He was the State Musician (*Vāggeyakāra—vācaṃ ca geyaṃ ca karoti yasmād vāggeyakāraḥ kathitas-tato'sau*) of Emperor Kṛṣṇadevarāya of Vijaynagar (1509-29 A.D.). The prologue of his work gives an account of the Emperor of Vidyāpura, and is of considerable historical value.

LOCANA KAVI (Or, PAṆḌITA)

To him are attributed the *Rāgataraṅgiṇī* and the *Rāgasaṃgītasaṃgraha (Raṅgasaṃgītasaṃgraha,* according to Krishnamachariar). The colophon to the former states that it was composed in Śaka 1082(=1160 A.D.). The question of Locana's date, however, is puzzling. In the work, there is mention of Vidyāpati, and his songs are quoted. Vidyāpati, who adorned the courts of some kings of Mithilā, including the famous

Śivasiṃha (close of 14th. cent.), is believed to have lived from 1350 to 1440 A.D. This date militates against the above date. Again, the work mentions Muslim *Rāgas* like *Iman, Phirodast* etc. These *Rāgas* are known to have originated with the great musicologist, Āmir Khusrau (1253-1325). In the circumstances, one of the following alternatives is possible. Either the date, stated in the colophon, is wrong. Or, the reference to Vidyāpati and the quotation of his songs and also the mention of Muslim *Rāgas* are later interpolations. Such interpolations are not unknown in works on Sanskrit literature. These were quite facile at a time when works were written by hand. It is generally found that the greater the popularity of a work, the greater is the scope and facility of incorporating extraneous matters into it. It is, however, difficult to choose between the above two alternatives. The lower terminus of his date is fixed by the use of the *Rāgataraṅgiṇī* by Hṛdayanārāyaṇa, author of the *Hṛdayaprakāśa* and *Hṛdayakautuka*. who ruled about 1667 A.D.

According to Kṣitimohan Sen, Locana was a protégé of the Sena kings of Bengal; he, however, does not state the source of his information.

MADANAPĀLA

Appears to have been a king to whom works on Smṛti, astronomy and medical science are attributed. Of the Smṛti works, the most well-known is the *Madanapārijāra*. Supposed to have flourished about the middle of the 14th. cent. A.D.

MAHĀVAIDYANĀTHA ŚIVA

One of the most noted musicologists of South India. He wrote the *Melarāga-mālikā*.

MATAṄGA

Author of the *Bṛhaddeśī*, a work on music. According to some, *Laghudeśī* was the title of his other work which is lost.He mentions Bharata, Yāṣṭika, Dattila, etc., and quotes passages from Kohala (q.v.). He is referred to by such eminent writers as

Abhinavagupta (10th-11th cent.) and Śārṅgadeva (13th century). There is a tradition that Mataṅga's sons were Dattila and Kohala. Mataṅga differs from Bharata on certain matters, particularly in the introduction of 12 *Svaras* in *Mūrchanā*. Among Prabandhas, Mataṅga is stated to have introduced the form *Harivilāsa*, and, in dance, a species is called *Jakkinī*.

Mataṇga is believed, by some, to have flourished at a time not very long after Bharata. It is noteworthy that Mataṅga is a legendary name occurring in the *Raghuvaṃśa*, *Rāmāyaṇa* (Araṇyakāṇḍa) and the *Mahābhārata*. Mataṅga, as a writer on music and dance, is mentioned in the Tamil epic *Cilappatikaram* which is generally believed to date back to a period not later than the fourth cent. B.C.

Mataṅga quotes passages from Kohala and Śārdūla.

Mataṅga is mentioned by later writers as the originator of a new school.

Svāmī Prajñānānanda places the author of the *Bṛhaddeśī* in the Gupta Age.

NĀGĀRJUNA

To an author of this name is attributed the work on music, entitled *Arjuna-bharatam*. More persons than one appear to have borne this name. Of them, the most famous is the Buddhist philosopher who probably flourished in the latter part of the 2nd cent. A.D. For several Nāgārjunas, See S.C. Banerji, *A Companion To Sanskrit Literature*.

NANDIKEŚVARA

Author of the *Abhinayadarpaṇa* and the *Bharatārṇava*. Probably flourished a little before the fifth century A.D. He has been cited by Mataṅga in his *Bṛhaddeśī*, and followed by Nārada in his *Saṃgītamakaranda*. He appears to have created some *tālas*, and has the distinction of having been the first writer of the post-Bharata period to deal with *tālas* exhaustively.

NĀNYADEVA

Also known as Nānyapati or Nānyabhūpāla, he is credited with the authorship of the commentary, called *Bharatabhāṣya* or *Bharata-vārtika*, otherwise known as *Sarasvatī-hṛdayālaṃkā ra*. He is known as the founder of the Karṇāṭaka dynasty of Mithilā, who ruled from 1097-1147 A.D. He is styled *Mithileś-vara* in one verse, and the colophons describe him as *Mahāsā-mantādhipati*. He mentions the *Granthamahārṇava* as another work written by him.

About the contents and characteristics of the above work, we reproduce below an excerpt quoted by Krishnamachariar (*Hist. of Class. Skt. Lit.*, para 1002);

"Every step in the advancement of music was closely traced to the rites of the Vedic Epoch, and every instrument was brought face to face with that used in the sacrificial rites by sacred Ṛṣis. He gives full information on every subject except on flute, where he is eclipsed by a voracious royal scholar, Kumbhakarṇa. Some chapters treat of *sapta-gītis, deśī-gītis* and the ancient *tāla* system which are now obsolete. The first of these topics was elaborately dealt with by Bharata, while the *deśī-gītis*, the source of later *prabandhas* took a prominent place in the grand work of Mataṅga. Dattila and Abhinava seem to have bestowed greater attention upon the *sapta-gītis*, knowledge of which was indispensable to the right understanding of the Vedic rites in *Aśvamedha* and *Rājasūya*. Those seven sacred chants were first sung by Dakṣabrahma to propitiate gods. *Ekatantrī, Pinākī* and *Kinnarī vīṇās* were introduced to produce all the graces of the seven songs when sung by the *ṛṣis*. Nānyadeva gives details for about 140 *rāgas*. He is always careful to quote his authorities, and thus on *rāgas* his chief masters are Kāśyapa and Mataṅga. Śārṅgadeva covered a wider range of 260 *rāgas*, many of which were abandoned long before his day. Nandin also discused about the same number. But Śā-rṅgadeva was not much indebted to Nandin for his materials which were directly taken from Nānyadeva for *rāgas* and from Abhinava for all critical matters, though he never mentions his creditors anywhere. A close comparison of Śārṅga's work with the production of Abhinava will reveal the astonishing insight with which he studied the psychology of the great philosopher Abhivava."

See M.R. Kavi in *IHQ*, III ; R.C. Majumdar in *IHQ*, VII, 679; K.P. Jayaswal, *JBORS*, IX.310, X.87.

NĀRADA

To him are ascribed the works on music, entitled *Saṃgīta-makaranda*, *Nāradīya Śikṣā*, *Pañ*cama-sāra-saṃhitā and *Rāganirūpaṇa*.

Judging by the fact that centuries elapsed between the origin of the *Nāradīya Śikṣā* and the *Saṃgīta-makaranda* as well as by the archaic character of the language of the former, it is obvious that the authors of these two works could not be identical. Some think that the name Nārada is legendary. The author or authors concerned, perhaps, associated their works with the name of the divine sage, said to have been an adept in music, particularly in playing the lute, in order to impart a halo of sanctity and antiquity to their works. But, the fact that the author of the *Saṃgītamakaranda* pays homage to sage Nārada seems to point to the fact that he was different from the legendary sage.

The author mentions, *inter alia*, Mataṅga, Tumburu, Mātṛgupta, Rāvaṇa, Vikrama (Candragupta II?), etc. The reference to Mātṛgupta tends to prove that the author could not possibly be earlier than the seventh century A.D. ; according to some, a poet Mātṛgupta flourished about 550-600 A.D.

It should be noted that a Mātṛgupta is stated by Kalhaṇa as a predecessor of Pravarasena. (C. 5th. cent. A.D.), king of Kashmir. He may or may not have been identical with Mātṛguptācārya, commentator on the *Nāṭyaśāstra*.

According to a tradition, Kālidāsa is identified with one Mātṛgupta.

The *Nāradīya Śikṣā* reveals some similarity with the *Nāradopaniṣat* (pub. Bombay). According to some, the *Śikṣā* is the borrower as it develops the principles laid down in the Upaniṣat. Pradip Ghosh seeks to establish that the *Saṃgītamakaranda* dates back to the 16th-17th. century A.D. (Vide Preface to his ed. of the *Saṃgītamakaranda*).

The chronological relationship of this Nārada and Śārṅgadeva has been dealt with in connexion with our observations on the *Saṃgīta-makaranda*.

NARAHARI CAKRAVARTĪ

A very prolific composer of Vaiṣṇava lyric poems. In his poems, he gives his name as Naraharidāsa or Ghanaśyāmadāsa. He appears to have been a junior contemporary of the celebrated compiler of the Vaiṣṇava work, entitled *Padāmṛta-samudra*, whose date is 1699-1777 A.D.

NĀRĀYAṆA MIŚRA KAVIRATNA

Son of Puruṣottama Kaviratna (q.v.), he wrote the *Saṃgītasaraṇi* besides the *Prabandhas* entitled *Balabhadravijaya. Śaṃkaravihāra, Uṣābhilāṣa, Kṛṣṇavilāsa, Guṇḍicāvijaya, Navanāgalalita.*

The author classifies Prabandhas as *Suddha* and *Sūtra*. The former contains songs set to different *Rāgas*, e.g. *Gītagovinda*; the latter has throughout only one *Rāga*. He composed the *Rāmābhyudaya Sūtraprabandha*. His father wrote a work of the same title which is *Śuddhaprabandha*.

NĀRĀYAṆA DEVA

King Gajapati Vīraśrī Nārāyaṇadeva, son of Padmanābha, ruled at Parlakimedi (Orissa) in about 1700 A.D. He belongs to the race of Uttuṅgagaṅga. He learnt music from Kaviratna Puruṣottama. Author of the Saṃgītanārāyaṇa. Besides other works, he quotes his own *Alamkāracandrikā*.

PĀNINI

The celebrated author of the *Aṣṭādhyāyī*. This grammar contains rules for both Vedic language and the classical Sanskrit. The part of the grammar, dealing with Vedic, deals, *inter alia*, with Vedic accents which, to some extent, were the precursors of the heptatonic system in Indian musicology. Besides the above work, the *Pāṇinīya-śikṣā* is attributed to him. Nothing definite is known about his age; he is, however, generally assigned to the fourth century B.C.

PĀRSVADEVA

Author of the *Saṃgīta-samaya-sāra*. Probably flourished in the 13th. cent. A.D., and was a contemporary of Śārṅgadeva. Son of Ādideva and Gaurī, he calls himself *Śrutijñ* āna-cakravartin. Abhinava-bharatācārya, Saṃgītakāra. He refers to kings Bhoja, Someśvara and Paramardin, and is quoted by Śiṅgabhū pāla.

PRATĀPASIṂHA

Mahārāja of Jaipur (1779-180 A.D.). He compiled an encyclopaedia, entitled *Saṃgītasāgara* with the help of other musicians and musciologists.

PUṆḌARĪKA VIṬṬHALA

Belonging to village Satānurva in Khāndesh, he was a Karṇāta Brahmin of Jāmadagnya-gotra. Under the patronage of king Burhānkhān of Pharata dynasty (which ruled at Ānandavallī in Khāndesh in 1370-1600 A.D.) he started bringing North Indian music into order. He wrote the following works:-

Viṭṭhalīya[1], *Rāgamālā*, *Nartana-nirṇaya*, *Rāgamañjarī*, *Sadrāga-candrodaya*. After the annexation of Khāndesh by Ākbar about 1599 A.D., he went to his court at Delhi. There he

1. In place of this work, mentioned by Krishnamachariar, M. Bose mentions (*Jour, of Asiatic Soc.*, XXIX, No. 1. p. 92) *Sīghrabodhinī-nāmamālā*.

wrote the *Rāganārāyaṇa* at the instance of Chief Mādhavasiṃha[1]

His lucubrations reveal his profound and comprehensive scholarship in northern and southern systems of music. He was probably identical with Viṭṭhala, author of the *Saṃgīta-vṛtta-ratnākara.*

PURUṢOTTAMA KAVIRATNA

He lived at Parlakimedi, Ganjam (Orissa) in c. 1790 A.D. He probably wrote the *Rāgamālikā* or *Kalāṃkura-nibandha.* Besides, he composed the *Rāmodaya, Rāmābhyudaya and Bālarāmāyaṇa.*

RAGHUNĀTHA

King of Tanjore. With him is associated the work entitled *Saṃgītasudhā.* A great musician and musicologist, he discovered a new type of *Vīṇā* called after him. Of his several other works, one is *Bharatasudhā* which deals with dance. Also see our observations on Govinda *Dīkṣita* and *Saṃgītasudhā.*

RĀMĀMĀTYA

Author of the *Svara-mela-kalānidhi.* Son of Timmāmātya, a descendant of Todarmal, a high functionary under Ākbar (1556-1605), he flourished in the court of Aliya Rāmarāja (d. 1565 A.D.) of Vijayanagar, and was the daughterr's son of Catura Kallinātha (q.v.), a renowned commentator of the *Saṃgīta-ratnākara.* It is known that, at the time of Rāmāmātya, there were many changes in *Rāgas.*

RĀMASVĀMĪ DĪKṢITA (1735-1817 A.D.)

Son of Veṅkaṭeśvara and disciple of Veṅkaṭa Vaidyanātha Dīkṣita, he belonged to Govindapuram near Madhyārjuna

---

1. According to Bahura, Paṇḍarīka was the court-poet of Madho Sing, brother of Mān Singh, ruler of Jaipur, A copy of the *Rāgamañjarī* contains a note confirming this information. In the colophon of the *Rāgamañjarī*, the author states that it was written for Madho Sing. (See M. Bose, *Jour, of Asiatic Soc.*, XXIX, No. 1, p.92).

(Tiruvadamarudur). Under the tutelage of Vīrabhadrāya, the master-musician of the time, he became famous at Tanjore, and wrote the *Tālamālikā*.

RUDRA

Also called Rudraṭācārya, he was author of a treatise on music, engraved on a rock at Kudimiyāmalai in Pudukkota State. His identity with Rudraṭa, the poetician (C. 9th. cent. A.D.) is not probable. Mataṅga mentions a Rudraṭa as a writer on music and Śārṅgadeva and Kallinātha also do the same. He declared that the older *Vīṇā Śuddhamela* (Raghunātha's vīṇā) was not fit for illustrating *Śrutis*. He has subjected some views of Śārṅgadeva and Rāmāmātya to carping criticism which, however, is considered by Ahobila as unjust.

His *Caturdaṇḍi-prakāśikā* is a well-known treatise on musicology. The inscription concerned is *Epigraphia Indica* 231, Pudukkota State Inscriptions No. 9. It is not proved that the author was the priest of King Mahendra-vikrama (7th cent. A.D.), author of *Mattavilāsa*.

ṢANMUKHA

Also called Guha, an old writer on music. Author of *Saṃgraha-cūḍāmaṇi* which is, perhaps, a part of this original work now lost. As the work mentions Śārṅgadeva, this author must have flourished after him.

ŚĀRṄGADEVA

From his *Saṃgīta-ratnākara.* we learn that his ancestors belonged to Kashmir. Son of Soḍhala and grandson of Bhāskara, he was a protégé of the Yādava King Śiṇghana who ruled at Devagiri from 1210 to 1247 A.D., He appears to have been a resident of village Yajñapura, and describes himself as the Chief Accountant of the above king.

He refers to himself as *Niḥśaṅka* (devoid of fear). He invented a *Vīṇā* (lute) under this name. While referring to the views of earlier writers, Śārṅgadeva's work is not a mere epitome; the author proceeds on an original definition and discussion.

SIṂHABHŪPĀLA

See under *Saṃgītasudhākara.*

SOMADEVARĀJA

Author of the *Saṃgītaratnāvalī.*

SOMANĀRYA

Author of the *Svara-rāga-sudhārasa.* He quotes one Rāvaṇa among the original writers. A follower of Nārada's school, he often differs from Bharata. He was probably the eminent Telugu poet Nācana Somana, author of *Uttara Harivaṃśa,* who was the donee under a grant dated 1344 A.D. of king Bukka I of Vijaynagar.

SOMANĀTHA (SOMA OR MUDGALAPUTRA)

Flourished in the 17th. cent. A.D., and wrote the *Rāgavibodha.* He was probably an Āndhra of Godāvarī district. According to some, he was a Telugu Brahmin of the East Coast, probably Rājamandry. Appears to have been a performing artiste as well as a scholar and poet.

SOMESVARA

At least three kings of this name belonged to the Cālukya dynasty of Kalyāṇī. This king appears to have been Someśvara III, styled Bhūlokamalla, the son and successor of the seventh king Vikramāditya VI. He ruled from C. 1127-38 A.D. He cultivated music and dance vigorously; so much so that models of south Indian music assumed the appellation of Karṇāṭa, the land ruled over by him. Thenceforward South Indian music started developing into two distinct schools in the Karṇāṭa and Andhra countries. They were often blended, almost unconsciously, by vernacular representation. For instance, Veṅkaṭanātha, in his *Haṃsasandeśa* (13th. cent.) observes:

ikṣucchāye ..... śālisaṃrakṣikāṇām
Karṇāṭāndhra-vyatikara bhidākarbure gītibhede, muhyantīnāṃ-madana-kaluṣam maugdhyamāsvādayethāḥ//

It is not known whether or not he was the same Someśvara as mentioned by Śārṅgadeva and Śāradātanaya along with Bhoja.

The *Abhilaṣitārtha-cintāmaṇi* or *Mānasollāsa* is attributed to Someśvara.

The *Saṃgītaratnāvalī* (Vide list of authors on music in *Saṅgīamakaranda*, GOS, p. 56), attrbuted, in Catalogues, to Somarājadeva, is, perhaps, by a *Pratihārī* of the Cālukya king Ajayapāla of Gujarat (1174-77 A.D.) See Intro. to *Bhāvaprakāśa*, GOS, pp 72-5.

Our Someśvara is to be distingushed from his namesake (c. middle of 13th. cent.) who is credited with the authorship of the poetical work entitled *Kīrtikaumudī*, *Surathotsava*, the drama called *Ullāgharāghava*, the hymn *Rāmaśataka* and the anthology *Karṇāmṛtaprapā*.

For a biographical account of our Somesvara, see S.C. Banerji. and A.K. Gupta, *Vikramāṅka-devacarita*, Eng. trs.; also see B.J. Sandesara, *Pro. of A.I.O. Conf.*, 1951.

ŚRĪNIVĀSA

Author of the *Rāgatattva-vibodha*. Supposed to have flourished in the latter half of the 17th cent.

ŚUBHAṂKARA

Son of Śrīdhara and Subhadrā, he is author of the *Saṃgīta-dāmodara*. Supposed to have flourished in Bengal in the 15th. cent. A.D. The above work is cited in the *Saṃgīta-nārāyaṇa* (chap. III) of the 17th. cent. A.D. He wrote a commentary on the *Nāradīya Śikṣā*.

SUDHĀKALASA

Author of the *Saṃgītopaniṣat*, he was a Jain and a pupil of Rājaśekharasūri (C. 9th-10th. cent. A.D.)

TULAJARĀJA (TUKKOJI) OR TULAJAJI

King of Tanjore (1729-1735 A.D.), he composed the *Saṃgīta-sārāmṛta*. It is a prore work dealing with all the topics found in the *Saṃgītaratnākara* of Śārṅgadeva. In MS. No. XVI/7288 of Śāstrī's *Tanjore Catalogue*, the author's genealogy is given. His *Nāṭyavedāgama* deals with dance.

UMĀPATI

Probably Umāpatiśivārya of Cidambaram, the renowned writer on Śaivite worship, who, according to Krishnamachariar *(Hist. of Class. Skt. Lit.*, para 990), must have flourished earlier than the 12th. cent. A.D.

VEDA

Probably son of Ananta who was son of Catura Dāmodara (q.v.), he is author of a work, entitled *Saṃgīta-makaranda* (to be distinguished from a treatise of the same title, attributed to Nārada). Veda was a court-poet of Shāhaji, father of Śivāji, who was known as Makarandabhūpa. Veda was also a tutor of the king's son Śambhu, elder brother of Śivāji, early in the 17th cent. A.D. His other work is entitled *Saṃgīta-puṣpāñjali*.

VEṄKAṬA VAIDYANĀTHA DĪKṢITA

A resident of Tiruvadamarudur, he was grandson of the paternal uncle of Veṅkaṭamakhin whose musical talent was inherited by him. Himself an adept in playing the *Vīṇā*, he wrote an exposition of Veṅkaṭamakhin's *Caturdaṇḍiprakāśikā*. He lived in 1735-1817, and wrote the work *Tālamālikā*. Rāmasvāmī Dīkṣita became *Vaiṇika-śikhāmaṇi* under the tutelage of Vaidyanātha.

VEṄKAṬEŚA OR VEṄKAṬA MAKHIN

Son of Govindamakhin (or-dīkṣita) and brother of Yajñanārāyaṇa, he was in the court of King Vijayarāghava who ruled at Tanjore till 1672 A.D. He was a pupil of king Raghunātha and tutor of Nīlakaṇṭha. He was the author of the *Sāhitya-sāmrājya-kāvya*, *Vārtikābharaṇa* (Mīmāṃsa) and *Citrabandha-rāmāyaṇa* besides his celebrated work on musicology and *Lakṣaṇagītas* (printed in *Saṃgīta-sampradāya-pradarśinī*). Generally following Bharata, he introduced a system of notation in the expression of Srutis, discovered a type of lute (*Vīṇā*), *a mela in Siṃharava-rāga* and called *Madhyamela*. He declared that the older *Vīṇā Śuddhamela* (Raghunātha's *Vīṇā*) was not fit for illustrating *Śrutis*. He has subjected some views of Śārṅgadeva and Rāmāmātya to carping criticism which, however, is considered by Ahobala as unjust.

His *Caturdaṇḍi-prakāśikā* is a well-known treatise on musicology.

1. See Krishnamachariar, *Hist. of Class. Skt. Lit.*, para 1006.

VIDYĀRAṆYA

Name assumed by Mādhava after he became an ascetic and the Head of Sringeri Maṭha. Virtually the founder of Vijaynagar formally founded in 1336 A.D. by his disciple, king Harihara I, with the help of his brother Bukka I (reign 1354, A.D. till death in 1377).

Son of Māyaṇa and Śrīmatī, and elder brother of the famous Vedic exegetist, Sāyaṇa with whom he is identified by some. May or may not be identical with Mādhava, author of the *Sarvadarśana-saṃgraha*. Appears to have been a versatile scholar and a prolific writer. Works on Smṛti, grammar, etc. are attributed to him. His work on music is entitled *Saṃgīta-sāra*. He died C. 1387 A.D. His contribution lies in the fact that he introduced sixteen *Melaṣ* or *Janakarāgas* and fifty *Janyarāgas*. For an account of Vidyāraṇya by S. Veṅkaṭādri, see *Andhrapatrikā*, Annual No. 1921-22, 158-9. Also see Taylor, *Oriental Historical Manuscripts*, Madras 92; *I.A.* XLV. 1., and *Sources of Vijaynagar History*, 47-51; L. Sarup in' *B.C. Law Vol.*, II, Poona, 1946.

AUTHORS KNOWN FROM REFERENCES ONLY.

ĀÑJANEYA

Mentioned in several works of musicology as an authoritative musicologist. Vide *Journal of Music Academy*, Madras, VI. III, pp 18, 94, 95.

KĀŚĪNĀTHA

A Bengali and author of a musicological work in which he follows Hanūmat and Bharata. A contemporary of Sāmaṇṇasūri who mentions him in his *Gīta-sāhitya-saṃgraha-dīpikā*. Vide Raghavan, *Jour. of Music Academy*, Madras, XXI, i-iv, p. 210.

KAŚYAPA

An ancient authority on musicology. Mentioned in various works; eg. *Nāradīya Śikṣā*. *Saṃgīta-makaranda* of Nārada, *Bṛhaddeśī* of Makaranda, *Abhinavabhāratī* of Abhinavagupta, *Saṃgīta-ratnākara* of Śārṅgadeva, *Viśvapradīpa* of Bhuvanānanda. Vide V. Raghavan in *Jour. of Music Academy*, Madras, III; *Saṃgīta-Nāṭaka Akademi Bulletin*, New Delhi, No.5, 1956; V. Raghavan in *Arts and Letters, Jour. of Royal India, Pakistan, Ceylon Society, London, XXVIII, i. 1953; Jour. of Music Acadamy*, Madras, XXV. 1954; *Bulletin of Saṃgīta Nāṭaka Akademi*, New Delhi, No. 4, 1956.

KĀTYĀYANA

Author of an authoritative work on musicology. Mentioned in the *Saṃgīta-darpaṇa* of Catura Dāmodara.

KṚṢṆA DATTA

Mentioned in Nārāyaṇadeva's *Saṃgītanārāyaṇa*.

IV

PUBLISHED WORKS

For the present purpose, we have selected the prominent published works on musicology. Under each work we have given a rapid survey of its contents highlighting its noteworthy features and contribution to musicology or dance-lore as the case may be. As an exhaustive bibliography has been added at the end, we have not given the details of the edition, place and year of publication under each title.

It should be noted that there is generally a lack of critical editions of the published works. For this purpose, the collaboration of musicologists and Sanskritists is necessary.

(In English alphabetical order)

ABHILAṢITĀRTHA-CINTĀMAṆI

(Also called *Mānasollāsa)*

Attributed to Cālukya king, Someśvara. The work was composed in Śaka era 1051(=1129 A.D.) It contains 2,500 verses on vocal and instrumental music, especially *Prabandhas.*

[Ed.GOS, Baroda, 1961. Critical ed. of the Music and Dance sections by V.Raghavan. See S.S.Misra, *Mānasollāsa of Someśvara—a* cultural study, Benares.]

ABHINAYA-ḌARPAṆA

By Nandikeśvara. It deals with histrionic art, mainly with gestures and postures in drama and dance.

[Ed., with Eng. trs and notes, by Ghosh, 1975(3rd ed.) See *Mirror of Gestures* with Eng. trs., intro. and illustrations by A.K.Coomaraswamy and G.K. Duggirala, Cambridge, Mass., 1917.]

ABHINAVA-RĀGAMAÑJARĪ

Written by Bhātkhande under the pen-name Viṣṇuśarmā. It may be characterised as a follow-up and supplement of the author's *Śrīmallakṣya-saṃgīta*.

In this work, of which the earlier part is in Sanskrit and the latter in Hindī, the author gives accounts of 120 *Rāgas* in a simple style.

[Published in Bombay,1921.]

ANŪPASAMGĪTA-VILĀSA

By Bhāvabhaṭṭa, it is named after his patron, Anūpasiṃha of Bikaner, Rajasthan.

The author shows close familiarity with south Indian music; this is, perhaps, due to the fact that his ancestors, living in the south, migrated to the north. He has grouped *Rāgas* under 20 Ṭhāṭas; his *Śuddhaṭhāṭa* is the South Indian *Kanakāṅgī*. He has tried to arrange north Indian *Rāgas* according to the south Indian mode. The 20 basic *Rāgiṇīs*, according to him, are: *Ṭoḍi, Gauḍa, Varāṭī, Kedāra, Śuddhanāṭa, Mālavakauśika, Śrī, Hambīra, Āhīrī, Kalyāṇī, Deśākhyā, Deśakāra, Sāraṅga, Karṇāṭa, Kāmoda, Hijjāja, Nādarāmakriyā, Hindola Mukhārī, Soma.*

Mostly a compilation, the work cites the *Saṃgītapārijāta* at several places, besides the *Rāgamañjari, Rāgakutūhala* and *Rāgakautuka*. This work is referred to in the author's *Samgītāṅkuśa.*

[Only three chaps. printed by Āryabhusan Press, Poona, 1921. See *Jour. of Music Academy*, Madras, IV, p.p.69-70.]

AUMĀPATAM

By Umāpati. An ancient but incomplete work on music, *Tāla*, dance and muscical instruments. It is in 38 chapters, and in the form of a narration of Śiva to Pārvatī. It begins with the origin of sounds *(nāda)*, and their development into musical harmony. It has wide difference from the treatises of Bharata, Mataṅga and Kohala. For example, the author gives 126 minor divisions of *Svaraṣ* whereas Bharata gives 22 and Mataṅga 66.

In his *Saṃgītasudhā*, Raghunātha, King of Tanjore (accession 1614 A.D.) informs us that it is a modern epitome of *Nandīśvara-saṃhitā*. The entire fifth chapter is quoted by Kallinātha (15th. cent, earlier half). in his commentary on the *Saṃgītaratnā kara.*

[Published in Madras,1957]

BHARATABHĀṢYA

Also called *Bharatavārtika* or *Sarasvatīhṛdayā-laṃkāra, it is by Nānyadeva or Nānyapati or Nānyabhūpāla. It is not a direct commentary on the Nāṭyaśāstra.* Planned in four parts (aṃśas), it promises to devote one part to each of the four kinds of *Abhinaya*. The extanṭ portioṇ deals only with *Vācika Abhinaya*, and relates mainly to chapters 28 to 33 of the *Nāṭyaśāstra*, dealing with music. Besides Bharata, the old authorities, quoted in it, are Nārada, Śātātapa, Dattila, Kāśyapa, Mataṅga, *Bṛhaddeśī*, Nandimata, Yāṣṭīka, Kīrtidhara, Viśākhila. It seems that Śārṅgadeva is the only author who cities Nānyadeva (as Rājā Nānya,*Saṃgītaratnākara, I.18).*

The work, existing in a unique MS., No 111 of 1869-70, in BORI-Cat. of MSS.., xii, p.p. 377-83, is understood to have been edited by C.P.Desai of Tārāpur, Thana, Bombay, for Khairāgarh Music University, M.P.

BHARATĀRṆAVA

By Nandikeśvara. The first post-Bharata writer to discuss *tālas* exhaustively. It testifies to the origin of quite a number of *tālas*, in the period following the *Nāṭya-śāstra*. It mentions nearly 112 *tālas* of different names.

The work exists in the following MSS: DC. XXII.8735; TC III.2435; II.1360. The *Tālādhyāya* is with M.R. Kavi, Madras.

The MS. in Tanjore Library, containing chaps. 5-14, is on *Abhinaya*, and is entitled *Guheśabharataprakāśa*. The colophon reads: *iti nandikeśvara-viracite-bharatārṇave nāṭyārṇave sumatibodhake sapta-lāsya-prakaraṇaṃ nāma caturdaśo' dhyāyaḥ*.

Thus, it appears to be a part of a larger chapter, called Nāṭyārṇava.

While the N.S. mentions only two *Aṅgas*, viz., *Laghu* and *Guru*, this work mentions additional *Aṅgas* called *Druta*, *Pluta*, *Haṃsapada* and *Virāma*. There is mention also of the different names of each of the *Aṅgas*. A noteworthy feature of this treatise is the basic principle of dividing the classes of *tālas*.

While the *NS.* mentions only two classes of *tālas*. viz. *Tryasra* and *Caturasra*, this work mentions a few more; viz. *Khaṇḍa*, *Sama*, *Asama*, *Miśra*, *Pūrṇa*, etc.. Coming to *Varṇatāla*, *we find that this work distinguishes such tālas* as *Caturasra-varṇa*, *Miśravarṇa*, *Tryasravarṇa*, *Khaṇḍavarṇa*, etc. *Kaṅkāla-tālas have been divided as Pūrṇa*, *Khaṇḍa*, *Sama* and *Asama*. Another distinguishing feature of the *tāla*-system in it is the division of *tālas*; e.g.1/2, 1/4, 3/4, etc. The work is important in view of the fact that it appears to have influenced subsequent writers in matters relating to *tāla*.

[Ed.K.B.Sastri, Tanjore, 1957.]

BHARATAVĀRTIKA

Same as Bharatabhāṣya (q.v.).

BṚHADDEŚĪ

Attributed to Mataṅga, it originated between the 5th and the 7th cent. A.D. according to some, a little later than 9th. cent., according to others. The title indicates that it discusses *Śuddha Deśī Saṃgīta*. But, it deals also with *Śruti* and *Svara*. The author holds that songs, sung by common folk like cowherds as well as by kings of their own accord in their own lands, are called *Deśī*. He deals particularly with the *rāgas* and *tālas* of the *Deśī* type;

this perhaps, explains the significance of the title of the work. Following the *Nāṭyaśāstra* it states 18 kinds of *Jāti*, distinguished as *Śuddha* and *Vikṛta*. The extant work seems to be truncated, because the concluding verse of the existing work indicates that a discussion on *Vākya* will follow, but that is not found. In this discussion on the concept of *Nāda*,the author reveals considerable influence of grammar and Tantra. In this work, the division of songs as *Nibaddha* and *Anibaddha* has been admitted. Though recognising 22 *Śrutis* the author holds that the basic *Śruti* is one, and the others are its illusory manifestations (*prabtibhāsa*). He recognises two *Grāmas* (q.v.), called *Ṣaḍja* and *Madhyama*. In connexion with the discussion on the difference between *Mūrchanā* and *Tāna*, it is stated that the ascent of the *Svaras* (q.v.) is called *Mūrchanā*, while their descent is also called *Tāna*. But, from the reference to Mataṅga's views in the work, called *Rāgaviboda*, it appears that the ascent and descent of the *Svaras* are called *Mūrchanā*, while ascent is called *Tāna*.

Mataṅga mentions Bharata, and follows him in certain matters, as pointed out above. But, he differs from Bharata at several places, particularly in the introduction of 12 *Svaras* in *Mūrchanā*. Among *Prabandhas*, *Mataṅga* is stated, in the *Yāṣṭikamatam* (Ms. No.12 of 745, Orinental MS. Library, Madras) to have introduced the form *Harivilāsa*. Mataṅga appears to have introduced a dance called *Jhakkinī* (See M.Krishnamachariar, *Hist. of Cl. Skt. Lit.*, 1974, p, 824).

That difference in certain matters existed in his time is clear from Mataṅga's work. For instance, while mentioning *Kauśika*, he states that, according to some, *Ṛṣabha* will be *Apanyāsa*, according to others, like *Aṃśa*. *Gīta* is of seven kinds; according to Yāṣṭika, it is of five varieties, viz. *Śuddhā*, *Vesarā*, *Bhinnā*, *Gauḍā*, *Sādhāritā*.

Mataṅga divides *Bhāṣā* into four kinds, *Mūla*, *Saṃkīrṇa*, *Deśaja and Chāyāmātrāśraya* (from *Uḍu* meaning star); it indicates the number five, as *ākāśa* is the fifth gross element (*Kṣiti-*

ap-tejaḥ-marud-vyoma). The author has dealt with *Ṭakkarāga, Boṭṭarāga, Mālavapañcama, Mālavakauśika, Revagupta*, etc.

Mataṅga quotes passages from Kohala and Śārdūla. Among others, he mentions Kāśyapa, Dattila, Nandikeśvara, Nārada, Bharata, etc.

CATURDAṆḌI-PRAKĀŚIKĀ

BY Veṅkaṭeśa or Veṅkaṭa Makhin, it is in six chapters, and is designed mainly as a treatise on music, with special reference to the instrument called *Vīṇā* (lute). *Caturdaṇḍī* means four parts of a *Rāga*; viz *Sthāyī, Ārohī, Avarohī and Saṃcārī*. The main topics of discussion are: *Vīṇā, Śruti, Svara, Mela, Rāga, Ālāpa, Sthāya, Gīta, Prabandha.*

In the Svaraprakaraṇa, the author has discussed *Tālāṅga*. There are names of many mixed *Rāgas* in the fifth section. The work is a classic on Carnatic music as practised in the 17th.cent. A.D.V.N.Bhātkhaṇḍe, the noted exponent of Hindustāni music, frequently referes to it. Being an innovator of the *Melakartā* system, Veṅkaṭamakhin is a potent force in northern Indian music too.

In his time,*Mārgasaṃgīta* was in a moribund state. He composed his work to revive it.

It is interesting to note that the work refers also to the culture of songs among Muslims.

As regards *Deśī Rāgas*, the author states that *deśasamudbhave rāgas* arise in various ways. As these are produced from the mixture of various *Svaras* and *Rāgas*, and as they are infinite, he does not deal with them.

After criticism of some earlier writers, the author introduces many new ideas, and suggests novel methods. He criticises earlier writers, particularly Rāmāmātya. He is believed to have introduced, for the first time, the 72 *Melakartās* now in vogue in South India. This introduction, as observed by M. Krishnamachariar, is, like older classification, "mnemonic rather than logical". To what extent credit is due to Veṅkaṭamakhin for this introduction cannot be determined. The following observations of M.R. Kavi deserve careful consideration:

The system of *Melakartās* is elaborated in *Saṃgraha-cūḍāmaṇi* purported to have been composed by Ṣaṇmukha in *Skandapurāṇa*. The existence was doubted by Subharāma Dīkṣita of Ettiya-puram, in his *Saṃgīta* work. "Happily an old manuscript is available with me and Venkatamakhin's origniality can be disproved." Gopālanāyaka has been mentioned as an authority on *Caturdaṇḍī*.

Veṅkaṭamakhin's views have been bolstered up in the *Melādhikāra-lakṣaṇa* of C.18th. cent. A.D.

[Ptd. by Vidvat-sabhā, Madras,1934. An elaborate exposition has been published by V.V.Wazalwar, Santiniketan, West Bengal, 1970.]

For a critical review of its contents, see T.L.V. Iyer, *Jour. of Music Academy*, Madras, Vol I.

CATVĀRIṂŚAC-CHATARĀGA-NIRŪPANA

Another name of *Rāganirūpaṇa* (q.v.).

DATTILAM

Attributed to Dattilācārya, and consisting of nine sections, it, following the *Nāṭyaśāstra*, discusses *Gāndharva-saṃgīta*. While recognising the heptatonic system of *svaras*, *Ṣaḍja*, etc, the author admits only two *Grāmas* (q.v.) called *Ṣaḍja*, and *Madhyama*. In the names and number of *Mūrchanā, etc., the author follows in the footsteps of the author of the Nāṭyáśāstra*. Dattila recognises 84 *tānas*. According to him, the number of *Jātirāgas*, divided as *Śuddha* and *Vikṛta*, is 18. He discusses also *Saṃkarya jāti* or those produced by a mixture of *Suddha* and *Vikṛta*. There is a discussion on *tāla* also.

The other topics, briefly touched upon, are: *Śruti, Vṛtti, Sthāna, Sādhāraṇa, Varṇa, Alaṃkāra,* seven kinds of *Mārgarīti,* 22 kinds of *Dhvani. According to Dattila, as also to Mataṅga and Śāṛṅgadeva, the thirteenth and the ninth Śruti* are *Saṃvādī.* It should be noted that Dattila mentions also the southern mode of music in verses 198 and 239. Dattila recognises the *Laukika* songs of the *Sāmaveda,* current in different regions. Thus, it is obvious that both *Mārga* and *Deśī* were in vogue in his time.

Dattila's work, according to his own admission, is an epitome of the view of earlier writers (*pūrvā-cārya-matasyaitad diṅmātraṃ samudāhṛtam*)..

[Ed. K.S. Sastri, Trivandrum, 1930; with Hindī comm., Hathras, U.P. Text with Bengali trs. by P.K.Ghosh, Calcutta, 1984. A Study of Dattilam, Eng. trs. by M.Loth.]

GĪTAGOVINDA

Though the *Gītagovinda* is not a work on musicology, yet it cannot be passed over in an account like this.

This lyrical composition of Jayadeva, depicting the love-sports of Kṛṣṇa and Rādhā in Vṛndāvana, is a unique contribution to not only Sanskrit literature by creating a new literary genre, but also to the history of music. The staple of the work is the songs set to different *rāgas* and *tālas*. Thus, it testifies to the prevalance of certain *rāgas* and *tālas* at least in Bengal at the time of Jayadeva. The *rāgas*, mentioned by him, are:

Bhairavī, Deśākhya, Gauḍamālava, Gauḍī, Gurjarī, Karṇāṭa, Mālava, Naṭa, Rāmakari (or-kali), Varāḍī, Vasanta, Vibhāsa.

The following *tālas* have been mentioned: *Eka, Parimaṭha, Rūpaka, Yati.*

[Of many eds,, the one by V.M.Kulkarni, with Mānāṅka's comm., 1963, is noteworthy.]

HṚDAYAPRAKĀŚA and HṚDAYAKAUTUKA

Works on music, by Hṛdayanārāyaṇadeva. The first one is a short tract of 87 verses. It defines some basic concepts of musicology, viz.*Mela, Svaras* called *Vādī, Vivādī, Anuvādī, Aṃśa, Nyāsa, Alaṃkāra, Sthāna, Tāna, Auḍava, Ṣāḍava. Mūrchanā.* The work enumerates *Śuddhasvaras, Vikṛtasvaras and Gamaka.* The greater part of the work is devoted to *Mela* which is twofold—*Śuddha* and *Vikṛta.* The *Janaka Melas* and the *Janya Rāgas,* according to the scheme of the author, are as follows:

Janaka Mela	Janya Rāga
1. Śuddhasvaramela Bhairavī	Saindhava, Bhairavī, Nilāmbarī
2. Ekasvara-vikṛta Mela Karṇāṭa	Karṇāṭa, Kakubhā, Jijāvantī, Saurāṣṭrī, Sugharāyī, Kāmoda, Aḍānā, Vāgīśvarī.
3. Do Mukhārī	Mukhārī
4. Dvisvara-vikṛta Mela Toḍī	Toḍī
5. Do Kedāra	Kedāra, Śyāma-naṭa, Khambāvatī, Hammīra, Śaṃkarābharaṇa, Jayatkedāra, Vihāgara, Āhīranāṭa, Māru, Bhīmapalāśikā, Chāyānāṭa, Kedāranāṭa, Mālakauśika, Bhūpāli.
6. Trisvaravikṛta Mela Iman,	Puriyā-Kalyāṇ, Iman Jayatkalyāṇ, Śuddhakalyāṇ.
7. Do Megha	Megha, Suddhnāṭa, Vilāval, Naṭa, Devagiri, 'Gaurasāraṅga, Alahiyā, Devābharaṇa, Deśākhya, Gauḍamallāra, Suhava, Madhyamādi, Mallāra.
8. Do Hṛdayaramā	Hṛdayaramā
9. Catuḥsvara-vikṛta	Gaurī, Mūlatānī, Dhanāsarī,

Mela Gaurī	Srī, Sadrāga, Caitīgaurī, Vasanta, Jayaśrī, Rāma-keli, Paraja, Pañcama, Gāndhāra, Āśāvarī, Deśī Toḍī, Mālava, Bhairava, Bahulī, Gurjarī, Gauḍa,Guṇakari, Dęśakāla, Mālaśrī Vibhāsa, Trivaṇa.
10. Catuḥsvara-vikṛta Sāraṅg	Sāraṅg, Paṭamañjarī, Sāmanta, Baḍahaṃsa
11. Do Pūrvā	Pūrvā
12. Do Dhanāśri	Dhanāśrī

[Ed.and trs. into Bengali by Pradip Ghosh, Calcutta.]

HṚDAYAKAUTUKA

By Hṛdayanārāyaṇa, The *Rāgas* and *Rāgiṇs*, dealt with in it, do not agree with those current at present. For instance, now-a-days *Śuddha-Madhyama* is used in *Rāga* in which the author requires *Tīvra Madhyama.*

[Ed. D.K. Joshi, Poona.]

KALĀNIDHI

Tittle of Kallinātha's commentary on the *Saṃgītaratnākara.* It combines the merits of lucidity and brevity. It is defective at places, and is criticised by Raghunātha.

[Published, with text, by Adyar Library, Madras, 1986.]

(ŚRĪMAT) LAKṢYSAMGĪṬA

Composed by Bhātkhaṇḍe under the nom-de-plume Catura Paṇḍita. In it, the author discusses, in the old style, both ancient and modern music. At first, the author seeks to show the mode by placing *Śuddha svaras* on the *Vīṇā* according to ancient authors. Then he shows the *svaras* on the *Vīṇā* with a table, according to some treatises like the *Saṃgītaratnākara* and contemporary

Hindustānī mode. He has also acquainted us with *Śuddha* and *Vikṛta savaras* according to the contemporary South Indian Style.

In the second chapter, he gives an account of *Rāga* system as *Janaka* (original) and *Janya (derivative) in accordance with the mode obtaining in the South. He has not given the husband-wife relation of Rāgas* and *Rāgiṇīs.* Instead, he has stated several *Melas.* The credit of the author lies in his expression of the views of authoritative formulators of Śāstras in simple language and racy style. A noteworthy characteristic of the work is that it mentions and illustrates such *Muslim melodies* as *Īman, Miān Mallār, Vilāskhānī Toḍī, Husen Toḍī*., etc. The author's main object is to present the views of earlier masters. Occasionally he adds his own notes.

In the appendix, the author has shown the grouping of *Rāgas* as-found in ancient treatises.

[Published in Bombay, 1910.]

MĀNASOLLĀSA

Same as *Abhilaṣitārthacintāmaṇi* (q.v.).

MELARĀGAMĀLIKĀ

By Mahāvaidyanātha Śiva. Based on the *Saṃgraha-cūḍāmaṇi* of Govindācārya.

[Published. from Adyar Library, Madras, 1937]

NĀRADĪYA ŚIKṢĀ

Belonging to the Śikṣā Vedāṅga, it is in two parts, and deals with the music of *Sāman (Sāmaveda)* generally, and as recited at sacrifices. It serves as a link between the Vedic and post-Vedic music, and is the earliest extant record of musical divisions and terminology. The Vedāṅga (accessory of the Veda), of which this work is a part, dates back to pre-Christian times. Śubhaṅkara (q.v.) wrote a commentary on it. Bharata appears to follow the views of Nārada on Sāmasvara, and quotes (XXXXIV.119) a verse from the *Nāradīya Śiksā.* Abhinavagupta refers to it at several places in his *Abhinavabhāratī* commentary on the *Nāṭyaśāstra;* e.g. XXVIII. 18,25. The entire work of Nārada is reproduced in the *Nāradīya Purāṇa.*

As a noteworthy feature of the Śikṣā treatise, we may point out the recognition of *Gāndhāragrāma* which, being beyond the reach of human voice, was ignored by Bharata and his followers. Though Bharata and Nārada agree in definitions and particulars of *Śrutis*, yet they differ in terminology.

In later times, Nārada's views were not accepted in toto. While Bharata differs from him to some extent, Mataṅga shows wider divergence.

Some scholars regard the above treatise as a post-Bharata one. For example, Popley says, 'It shows....... development on the *Nāṭyaśāstra* in its *rāga* system, in a number of matters, agrees with the Kudimiyamalai inscription where that disagrees with the next important treatise, the *Saṃgītaratnākara.* (*The Music of India*, 14). M. Krishnamachariar observes (*Class. Skt. Lit.*, 1974, p.830, f.n.). The imaginary development in the *rāgas* is due to difference in views between Nārada and Bharata. The Kudimiyamalai inscription has not yet been rightly interpreted.

The *Nāradīya Śikṣā* states that the seven *Svaras* in order were derived from the following birds and beasts respectively:

Mayūra (peacock), *Gāvaḥ* (cows), *Ajāvika* (goat and sheep), *Krauñca* (curlew), *Kokila* (cuckoo), *Aśva* (horse), *Kuñjara* (elephant).

This treatise connects the seven *Svaras* of *Sāmagāna* with the seven *Svaras* of classical music in the following way:

Sāman	Classical
Svara 1	Madhyama (MA)
2	Gāndhāra (GA)

3	Ṛṣabha (RI)
4	Ṣaḍja (Sa)
5	Dhaivata (Dha)
6	Niṣāda (NI)
7	Pañcama(PA)

[Ed. S. Samasrami, Bombay, with comms, *Vivaraṇa* and *Vivaraṇaprakāśa*, Mysore, 1949; S.C. Banerjee, with Introduction, Eng. trs., Glossary and a survey of the origin and development of ancient and medieval Indian musicology. Also ed. P.Jha, with his own Sanskrit comm., Tarakeswar, Hughli, V.S.2037. Published with Śobhākara's comm. at Varanasi, 1893 and at Tanjore. Bengali trs. by R. Mitra, Calcutta.]

NĀṬYAŚĀSTRA

Attributed to Bharata, it is the earliest extant work on dramaturgy, musicology and dance. According to some, Bharata is a legendary sage with whose name the work was associated by its author to impart a halo of sancitity to it. It consists of 36 chapters, according to some, 37 according to others. According to Abhinavagupta, it contains 6,000 stanzas divided into 36 chapters. Several commentaries on the work appear to have existed. Of these, only the one by Abhinavagupta exists in an incomplete form. According to some scholars, chapters 28-33, dealing with *Saṃgīta*, were composed by Kohala (q.v). The contents of the chapters of the *Nāṭyaśāstra* are briefly as follows:

Nāṭyotpatti, Prekṣāgṛha-lakṣaṇa, Raṅgadevapūjana, Tāṇḍavalakaṣaṇa, Pūrvaraṅgavidhāna, Rasavikalpa, Bhāvavyañjaka, Upāṅgavidhāna, Hastābhinaya, Śārīrābhinaya, Cārīvidhāna, Maṇḍalavidhāna, Gatipracāra, Pravṛttidharmivyañjaka, Chandovibhāga, Chandoviciti, Vāgabhinaya, Bhāṣāvidhāna, Kākusvaravyañjaka, Daśarūpavidhāna, Sandhyaṅgavikalpa, Vṛttivikalpa, Āhāryābhinaya, Sāmānyābhinaya, Bāhyopacāra, Citrābhinaya, Siddhivyañjaka, Ātodyavidhi, Ātodyavidhāna, Suṣirātodyavidhāna, Tālavyañjaka, Dhruvāvidhāna, Prakṛtivicāra, Bhūmikāvikalpa, Nāṭyāvatāra.

[Ed. M.Ghosh, Calcutta, I,1967; II, 1961.

R.Nagar, with comm. *Abhinavabhāratī* of Abhinavagupta, Delhi, 1981.

M.R.Kavi, GOS.Vol. 1956 (2nd.ed.);Vol II, 1934; Vol, III, 1954, J.K.D.H.Dasgupta, KSS, 1929. Kāvyamālā ed., 1894. Trs. into Eng. by M.Ghosh, Calcutta, 1951.

Trs. into Bengali by S.C.Bandyopadhyaya,. I, Calcutta, 1980; II, Calcutta,1982; III, Calcutta, 1982.]

There is a *Nāṭyaśāstra-saṃgraha* by U.Govindācārya, ed. A.K.M. Row Sahib, G.Nāgarāja, Vol. I,1953.

NṚTYĀDHYĀYA

By Aśokamalla. Mainly following in the footsteps of Śārṅgadeva, the author deals, in its present incomplete form, with *Aṅga, Upāṅga, Pratyaṅga, Cārī, Maṇḍala, Sthāna, Karaṇa, Aṅgahāra* and *Kalāsa.* Starting with hand-poses, it ends with Kalāsa which seems to have been discussed for the first time in this work. Another noteworthy feature of the treatise is the description of *Muḍuacārī* which is believed to be another form of the term *Madhupacārī* which is an *Ākāśikī Cārī* mentioned by Kohala as testified to by Kallinātha's commentary on the *Saṃgītaratnākara.* This appears to be the only treatise to describe *Vartanās* and *Cālakas* fully. These are described by Kohala as quoted by Kallinātha in his commentary on the *Saṃgītaratnākara.* The text of the *Ratnākara,* however, does not contain their description. It should be mentioned that while the *Vartanās* and *Cālakas,* referred to by Kalinātha as having been dealt with by Kohala, occur in the *Nṛtyādhyāya,* the latter.describes some *Vartanās* and *Cālakas* not mentioned by Kohala. In addition to *Kalāsas, Muḍupacarīs, Vartanās* and *Cālakas* the *Nṛtyādhyāya* also deals with new forms of *Deśī Lāsyāṅgas, Sthānas* and *Utplutikaraṇas.*

The very title indicates that it is a part of a bigger treatise which is unknown.

[Ed. P. Shah, GOS, Baroda, 1963.].

NṚTYA-RATNAKOŚA

First part of the *Saṃgītarāja* (q.v.). It is divided into four *Uttaras*. The fourth *Uttara* deals with the stages *pūrvarañja*, four kinds of acting, *Āṅgika, Vācika Sāttvika* and *Āhārya*. In dealing with *Āṅgika Abhinaya*, it follows the *NS* and the *SR*. *Cālakas* (q.v.) and *Vartanās* (q.v.) are described oc the Kallnātha. The second *Uttara* describes *Care, Sthānake* and *Recaka*. [Ed. R. C. Parikh and P.Shaḥ, Vol. I, 1957.]

NṚTTARATNĀVALĪ

A noteworthy work on dance. Attributed to Jāyasenāpati, it contains eight chapters. Written in 1253-54 A.D., it deals with *Mārga* and *Deśī* kinds of music.

In the former, the author follows Bharata, and, in the latter, chiefly Someśvara. The author incorporates the latest improvements in the art of dancing.

[Ed. V. Raghavan, Madras, 1965].

PAÑCAMASĀRA-SAṂHITĀ

Attributed to Nārada, it exists in an incomplete form, and in more versions than one. The version, printed in the *Nāradīya Śikṣā*, ed. S.C. Banerji, contains a good number of verses. There is mention of the second, third and fourth chapters; the first chapter is missing. The text commences with the divine origin of *saṃgīta*, and its subsequent introduction on the earth. Then it mentions the places where the best *naṭas* (actors) live. After this it lays down the qualifications of a *Nāyaka* (hero). Incidentally it is stated that *Vādya* follows *Gīta* and that the attitude of a *Nāyaka* follows all these. *Nṛtya* is defined as a combination of *Dhātu* and *Mātrā*: *Dhātu* is stated to be *nādātmaka*, and *mātrā* indicates a number of *akṣaras*.

Then it mentions the merits and demerits of a singer, defines *abhinaya*, characteristics of *Sāttvikabhāva*, *Tāṇḍava*, *Lāsya*, the classifications of musical instruments.

The second chapter states six *Rāgas*, viz., *Mālava*, *Mallāra*, *Śrī*, *Vasanta*, *Hindola* and *Karṇāṭa*, and their thirty-six consorts (6 each) called *Rāgiṇīs*. Incidentally, the author states the time of the day as well as seasons appropriate for the different melodies. Then follow *dhyānarūpas* of *Rāgas*.

Finally, the *Rāgiṇis* have been dealt with. These are, in brief, the contents of the third chapter which has been given the name of *Rāganirṇaya*. Then follows what is caḷled *Tālā dhyāya*.

The work, of unknown authorship and date, appears to be a sort of music manual compiled for beginners.

In a verse of chapter two, it is stated that the *naṭas* (actors) of Rāḍha are the best. *Rāḍha* was the name of that part of West Bengal which lies to the west of the Ganges including Tamluk, Medinipur and the districts of Hughli and Burdwan. A portion of the district of Murṣidabad was included in its northern boundary. So, the author seems to have been a Bengali residing in Rāḍha.

Printed in the *Fundamentals of Ancient Indian Music and Dance* (Appendix) by S.C. Banerji, L.D. Institute, Ahmedabad, and also in the *Nāradīya Śikṣā*, ed. S. C. Banerji, Calcutta, 1983.

PĀṆINĪYA ŚIKṢĀ

A work of the Śikṣā Vedāṅga. It lays down the sources of the *svaras*. *Niṣāda* and *Gāndhāra* of the gamut are *Udātta* (acutely accented), *Ṛṣabha* and *Dhaivata Anudātta* (unaccented), *Ṣaḍja*, *Madhyama* and *Pañcama* are *Svarita* (circumflexed). In accordance with the measure of time, required in pronunciation or articulation, vowels may be *hrasva* (short), *dīrgha* (long) or *pluta* (prolated).

See A. Weber, *Indische Studien*, 4, 435 f.f.

B. Liebich, Zur Einfuh-rung in die indische einheimische Sprach. Wissenschaft, 11, p. 20. It is stated that, though late in form, it is old in contents.

RĀGAVIBODHA

Composed by Somanātha, who was probably an Āndhra of Godāvarī district, in 1609 A.D., in verse, it commences with the differentiation of *Mārga* and *Deśī*. It deals with the theory of musical sounds, and describes the different types of *Vīṇās* and the modes of using them. The discussion on *Svaras* occupies chapters one, three and four: the fourth chapter is devoted to the types of Vīṇā and the rules relating thereto. The author classifies the *Rāgas* into Primary (*Janaka*) and Derivative (*Janya*). He states a number of melodies developed from the *Rāgas*. The work contains fine poetry in *Āryā* metre. The author speaks of *Rāgas* and *Śrutis* especially with a view to their use on the Vīṇā. He declared twenty-three heptattonic *Melarāgas* and seventy-seven *Janya-rāgas*. His discussion is from the standpoint of South Indian mode. The author has criticised Śārṅgadeva's views on *Śruti*, and shows agreement with Rāmāmātya in the matter of *Svaras*. Taking Hanūmat etc. as authoritative, he has denied the rigidity of *Grāma*, *Śruti*, *Svara*, etc.

The work affords a fine picture of the condition of Indian music towards the close of the 16th century.

According to him, of the twelve *Vikṛta svaras* of Śārṅgadeva, only seven are real *svaras*. Somanātha has recognised seventeen *svaras*, and their Śrutis have been mentioned in consonance with the earlier masters like Bharata.

Four types of *Vīṇā* appear to have been in vogue in his time.

In his *Musical Modes of the Hindus*, William Jones (1746-

1794) highly praises the merit of the work.

Somanātha appears to have been influenced by north Indian Muslim music to some extent. He not only mentions but also depicts the picture of Turuṣka Toḍī in its *Dhyāna.*

The author states that he has composed this work as a means of enlightening the simple-minded people (*bā liśabodhopāya*); it has been left to the wise to form their judgment with their own logic.

[Ed. S. Sastri, Madras, 1945 (with author's own comm., called *Viveka*; by R. Simpson with a table of notations, Leipzig, 1904. With Eng. trs. by M.S.R. Iyer. Partly trs. into Eng. in *Indian Musical Journal*, Mysore, 1912-13. An ed. was pub. in Bombay. There is a gloss on it, called *Rāgavibodha-viveka.*, in Bhandarkar's Deccan College MSS., XIX. I. 430. See Popley, *The Music of India, 18, K.B. Dewal. Theory of Indian Music as expounded by Somanātha*, Poona. *The musical compositions of Somanātha (Sadrāga-candrodaya* was published by Munich University of Germany in 1904. It contains all the notations as found in the manuscript.]

RĀGAKALPADRUMA

A unique encyclopaedic compilation of musicology, in three parts, of Kṛṣṇānanda. In it, the author has collected songs of different Indian languages and of saveral artistes of earlier times. It comprises eight chapters, one on each of the following topics;

Svara, Rāga, time suitable for *Rāgas* and *Rāgiṇis,* their *Dhyānas, Tāla, Nṛtya, Vādya,* collection of songs, etc. In the chapter on *Rāga,* there are divisons of *Rāgas,* their wives, lady-loves, daughters-in-law, etc. There is mention of many *Rāgas* and *Rāgiṇīs* occurring in the ancient musical lore. Several *Rāgas,* obsolete now-a-days, have been left out. It mentions 28 kinds of *Tālas.* It, however, does not include some of the Tālas used in the different styles of *Vaiṣṇava-kīrtana* of Bengal (e.g.

Manoharsāin, Garānhāṭi, etc.). It omits also some *Tālas* applied by the sects known as Sāin, Bāül, Darveś. All the *Tālas*, current in regions like Mālābār, are mentioned in the work. It excludes some *Deśī Tālas* too. In the third part of the work, 27 *Tālas* have been described. In Svarādhyāya, the author deals with *Śruti, Mūrchanā, Alaṃkāra, Svarālāpa, Svara-prastāra* and *Tānaprastāra*, etc.

In the chapter on *Rāga*, we are informed that, according to Nārada, male *Rāgas* are six, viz, *Bhairava, Mālavakośa, Hindola, Dīpaka, Śrī* and *Megha*. According to another view, the male *Rāgas* are *Vasanta, Bṛhallāṭa, Mallāra, Mālava, Pradīpa* and *Kauśika*. Each of them has a wife, unmarried sweethearts, sons, etc. This shows that, with the proliferation of melodies, such divisions multiplied.

Besides *Śuddharāgas*, the author mentions a century and a half of mixed *Rāgas*, e.g. *Multāni-bhīmpalaśrī, Puriyādhanāśrī, Gauḍa-sāraṅga, Gurjarī-ṭoḍī, Śyām-kalyāṇ, Iman - vihāg, Bhairavī-pāhāḍī, Sindhu - multānī Vihārī-khāmbāj*, etc. From the work it is clear that the same melody, according to one, is different according to another.

The author cites the authority of Hanūmat, Bharata, Sārṅgadeva, Kallinātha, *Siṃhabhūpāla*, etc. Among the works cited by him, are the *Saṃgītadarpaṇa, Svaramelakalānidhi, Rāgavibodha, Caturdaṇḍi - prakāśikā, Saṃgītasārāmṛta, Rāgataraṅgiṇī* of Locana, *Hṛdayaprakāśa, Saṃgīta-pārijāta, Rāgacandrodaya, Rāgamālā, Rāgamañjarī*, etc.

A study of the work reveals that a single *Rāga* has assumed different forms. For example, *Ekaṭoḍī, Darbāri Ṭoḍī, Deśī Ṭoḍī*, and so on, *Naṭa Mallāra, Suraṭa Mallāra, Miān Mallāra*, etc. *Miān* stands for Tānsen or his school (*gharāṇā* in common parlance).

The language of the work does not strictly conform to the norm of grammar.

[First part printed in 1842 and last part in 1849]

RĀGAMAÑJARĪ

Attributed to Puṇḍarīka Viṭṭhala. The author is of the view that, in the event of conflict between musical lore or tradition and practice, the latter is to be upheld. For instance, when a person sings in *Ṣaḍja Grāma* instead of *Madhyama* and *Gāndhāra*, as *required* by the Śāstra, *Ṣaḍja grāma* itself must be regarded as chief, no other *grāma* will have predominance (*mukhyatamaḥ ṣaḍja - grāma eva, na cāparau*).

Citing the authority of Hanūmat, he maintains that, though rigid rule is found in Śāstra about *Graha, Aṃśa, Nyāsa*, etc.; there is no restrictive provision in the case of *Deśī Rāgas.*

The author describes himself, in the colophon, as *Karṇāṭa jātiya.* He, however, has attempted a synthesis between the southern and northern systems. His acceptance of the northern mode is demonstrated by his mention of the wives and sons of *Rāgas.*

Towards the end of the work, he has given Persian *Rāgas* as well as application of Persian element in Sanskrit *Rāgas.* A few lines are quoted as specimens.

anyépi pārasikeyā rāgāḥ pharada-nāmakāḥ/

sampūrṇāḥ sarvagamakāḥ kākalyantitāḥ sadā//

deśakāre vākharejaḥ āśāvaryāṃ hijejakaḥ//

RĀGANIRŪPAṆA

Atributed to Nārada, it is a metrical description of 140 Rāgas. It is quoted in the *Saṃgītanārāyaṇa* of Nārāyaṇadeva (c.f. *nārada - saṃhitāyāṃ catvāriṃsacchata-rāganirūpana* etc.)

[Ed. D.K. Joshi, Poona]

RĀGATARANGIṆĪ

Attributed to Locana Kavi (or Paṇḍita). He has dealt elaborately with *Svaras.* The seven *Śuddha Svaras*, according to him, are in the proper place among the 22 *Śrutis.* His *Vikṛta. svaras* are the *tīvra* or *komala* forms of Suddha svaras. According to him, *Prācya Rāgas* are twelve in number the names and characteristics of which have been given by him. These are the parent (*Janaka*) *Rāgas* from which derivative (*janya*) *Rāgas* were produced. The *Janaka Rāgas* and the number of *Janya Rāgas*, according to him, are as follows:-

Janakas	No. of Janya Rāgas
Bhairavī	2
Gaurī	27
Karṇāṭa	20
Kedāra	13
Iman	4
Sāraṅga	5
Megha	10
Dhanāśrī	2
Ṭoḍī	1
Pūrvā	1
Mukhāri	1
Dīpaka	1

The author has stated that, for fear of bulk, he has not mentioned the *Āroha* and *Avaroha* of various *Rāgas.* The author has elaborately dealt with the mixed *Rāgas* (*sakala-deśasādhāraṇa - guṇi-gaṇa - prasiddha - rāgasaṃkaraḥ*) current in different regions. He has laid down different views about the time suitable for different *Rāgas.* As regards *Tālas,* the author has mentioned the ancient ones, *Cañ*catpuṭa, Cācapuṭa, etc.

For the songs of Vidyāpati and Muslim *Rāgas,* mentioned in the *Rāgataraṅgiṇī*, see our observations on the author.

[Published at Poona, 1918]

RĀGATATTVA - VIBODHA

By Śrīnivāsa, The object of the work is to enlighten the ignoramus in simple language. So, it does not contain much of jargon. According to the author, *Śrutis* in relation to *Svaras* are only 12; the remaining *Śrutis* are redundant. In the concluding verse, he says *anantā api rāgāḥ syurgamakodgrāhabhedataḥ* i.e. the number of *Rāgas* is infinte depending on the difference of *Gamaka* (see Glossary) and *Udgrāha* (see *Ibid*).

[Ed. D.K. Joshi, Poona]

SAṂGĪTA - DĀMODARA

Written by Śubhaṃkara, it consists of seven chapters, and deals with a variety of topics relating to dance, drama and music. The author tries to explain music and dramaturgy as originating from Kṛṣṇa (Dāmodara). The title of the work, however, seems to have been given after the name of King Dā modara to whom the work is dedicated.

It is very popular among the Vaiṣṇavas of Bengal. The work is largely a compilation of materials from the ancient works on music and dramaturgy, and shows little originatity of the author.

As it is cited in the *Saṃgīta - nārāyaṇa*, it must have originated before the 17th, cent. A.D.

[Ed. G. Sastri & G. Mukherjee, Calcutta, 1980. A critical ed. by V. Raghavan was to be published].

SAṂGĪTA - DARPAṆA

Written by Dāmodara or Catura Dāmodara, son of Lakṣmīdhara, about 1625 A.D. in the reign of Jāhāngir, it is on the northern school of Indian music. It deals also with dance. It borrows freely from the *Svarādhyāya* of the *Saṃgītaratnākara*. The pictorial descriptions of the different *Rāgas*, given in it, are mostly based on Somanāth's *Rāga-vibodha*.

The author follows Hanūmat in discussing the varieties of *Rāgas* and *Rāgiṇīs*. He distinguishes between *Mārga* and *Deśi*

Rāgas. The characteristics of the latter, according to him, are that they do not conform to any hard and fast rule regarding *Śruti, Svara, Grāma, Jāti,* etc. and that they contain modes of various countries (*nānādeśagata-cchāyā*).

The number of *Tānas,* according to him, is 3,17,930. According to Popley, this work lays down modes which are still current in north India.

This work, written in simple language and lucid style, explains the four parts of a song very clearly as follows:-

Āsthāyī : It is that part in which a song rests (*yatropa-viśyate rā gaḥ*)

Ābhoga : the concluding portion.

Antarā : the part in between the above two.

Saṃcārī : that arises out of the mixture of all the above.

[Ed. with comm. of Ratansi- Līlādhara and Gujarati trs. by L. Thakkara, chaps. 1 and 2 only, Bombay, 1910]. There is another work of the same title by Haribhaṭṭa.

See Des. Cat. of Skt. MSS. in Oriental MSS Library, Madras, XXII. No. 18017. Tanjore Cafalogue, XVI. 7266.

In introductory verses of the latter, Haribhaṭṭa is stated to be another name for Catura Dāmodara.

SAṂGĪTA - MAKARANDA

There are twò works of this title, one by Veda and the other attributed to Nārada. The former exists in a manuscript (*Tanjore Catalogue,* XVI. 7268) dated 1650 A.D.

Herę, we are concerned with the one by Nārada. Consisting of two parts, *Saṃgīta* and *Nṛtta,* each divided into four chapters, it is attributed to Nārada and may, perhaps, be assigned to the 11th. cent. A.D. It mentions Mahāmāheśvara, i.e. Abhinavagupta. Śārṅgadeva seems to have borrowed a few verses from it. Its definition of *Gāndhāra* is almost wholly repeated by Śārṅgadeva. It mentions two divisions of *Rāgas,* viz. Principals (6) and their wives, and classifies musical sounds into five kinds according to the source of percussion; viz. *Nakhaja, Vāyuja, Carmaja, Lohaja* and *Śarīraja*. The author mentions *Rāgas* to be sung at different times. According to him, the *Rāgas* are 32, but, those prevailing in different regions are infinite. He holds that full *Rāgas* number 500 *Śāḍava - Rāgas* 200 and *Auḍava* 100. Among other special features of the work are (1) Determination of the places of origin of the *Svaras*, their sage, *Gotra Varṇa*, etc.

(2) Naming the 22 *śrutis* in a manner different from that of Bharata, Śārṅgadeva, Ahobala and Dāmodara.

(3) Discussion on *Mūrchanā*, etc. of *Gāndhāra-grāma*. According to him, *Mūrchanā* means the ascent and descent of the seven *svaras* in order.

(4) Classification of *Rāgas* as male, female and eunuch. The total number of *Rāgas* is ninety-three.

(5) Use of the word *daśaprāṇa* in connexion with *tāla*, and elaborate discussion.

(6) Introduction of a special mode, called *Daśaprabandha*, of using *tāla*.

The author has discussed the sources of the five *Mārgatālas* viz. *Caccatpuṭa, Cācapuṭa, Ṣaṭpitāputraka, Saṃpakveṣṭaka* and *Udghaṭṭaka*. In section two of the chapter on dance, the author mentions (verses 1,2) the names of deities, sages and others as the formulators of the different ancient facts about *tāla*. The author lays down the characteristics of the theatre, the assembly of spectators, the president of the assembly, etc.

In the same section (verses 3-16) he names 101 *tālas* which are not divided as *Mārga* and *Deśi* as in the *Saṃgītaratnākara*. The author does not mention some of the *tālas*; enumerated in the *Bharatārṇava*, but mentions five new *tālas*; viz. *Rāgavardhana, Utsava, Samatāla, Antarakrīḍā and Catustāla.* From the list of *tālas* in the *Bharatārṇava* he omits the following: *Śrīnandana, Karṣuka, Pana - tāla Bhadravāna, Druta-śekhara, Jhombaḍa, Kataṇa, Anyamaṇṭha,* etc.

Verses 17-74 of the above section are devoted to the determination of the *mātrās* of the *tālas.* In this matter, the author by and large follows the *Bharatārṇava.*

In the third section of the above chapter, the author discusses ten *Tāla-prabandhas,* a concept attributed to Nandikeśvara. Verses 33 to 47 discuss *Aṅga-tālas. This is followed by a discussion on the origin of tāla* incidentally indicating the ten *Tālaprāṇas.*

The author discusses various units of time, e.g. *Kṣaṇa, Lava, Kāṣṭhā, Nimeṣa, Kalā, Druta, Anadruta, Laghu, Guru, Pluta,* etc.

He refers to the *Mārgas* like *Dakṣiṇa, Vārtika, Citra, Vicitra, Citratara, Aticitratara,* etc.

iii. 61 of the *Nṛtta*-chapter mentions, for the first time, two main *Kriyās* viz. *Mārga* and *Deśī.* The author gives 33 as the number of *Naṭī-bhāvas* prevailing in the different countries taken together.

The author mentions five *aṅgas* (accessories) of *tāla; viz. Anadruta, Druta, Laghu, Guru* and *Pluta.*

On the authority of earlier writers, he states three kinds of *Graha* (q.v.) ; viz. *Sama, Atīta, Anāgata.*

As regards *Jāti,* he follows Bharata in mentioning the kinds of it called *Tryasra, Caturasra, Miśra* and a *Khaṇḍa Jāti.* He mentions eighteen *Jātis.* Some discussions on *Laya, Yati* and *Prastāra* are also found.

He names nineteen *alaṃkāras.*

As regards musical instruments, he mentions different kinds of *Mṛdaṅga, Vīṇā,* etc. Nineteen varieties of *Vīṇā* have been described.

The influence of this work on some later treatises is obvious. The major portion of the discussion on *Tāla,* contained in

Jagadekamalla's *Saṃgīta-cūḍāmaṇi* is similar to that in the *Saṃgīta-makaranda* and *Bharatārṇava*. Pārśvadeva's *Saṃgīta-samayasāra* contains *Tāloddeśa-sloka* which is almost the same as in the *S. Makaranda*.

The chronological relationship of this work with the *Saṃgītaratnākara* is intriguing. The verse of the *Saṃgītamakaranda* (section four of chapter I), describing the characteristics of a singer, is the same as that of *Saṃgītaratnākra* on the same topic. It is not possible to determine the borrower. The possibility of interpolation, however, cannot be ruled out; the popularity of the *Saṃgītaratnākara* may have prompted a later scribe to add the verse concerned in the other work. The *Makaranda* does not appear to follow the *Ratnākara* for several reasons. For example, unlike Śārṅgadeva, Nārada does not divide *Tālas* into *Mārga* and *Deśī*. The latter deals succintly with dance, whereas the former discusses it in one long chapter. The *Saṃgītamakaranda* is written in simple language and in old style but the other work is rich in language and diction, and deals with the topics scientifically with meticulous attention to details. Had the author of the *Makaranda* followed Śārṅgadeva, he would have, perhaps, mentioned Rudraṭa, king Nānya, Someśa, Lollaṭa, Udbhaṭa, Abhinavagupta, etc. mentioned by the latter.

Nārada does not cite Śārṅgadeva. The arrangement of the contents of the two works is totally different. All this tends to point to the *Makaranda* as the earlier work. This conjecture is supported by the fact that Śārṅgadeva cites Nārada.

[Ed. M.R. Telang, Geos, 1920]

There is a large treatise of the same title, by Veda. It mentions the later forms of modern dancing, as influenced by European and modern art. It deals with *Rasadṛṣṭi, Gati, Cārī, Hasta, Nṛtya* and *Rasa*.

SAṂGĪTAPĀRIJĀTA

Written in the 17th. century A.D., it is an important treatise on the northern system of Indian music, by Ahobala. The topics, dealt with in it, are *Uddeśa, Svara, Grāma, Mūrchanā, Prastāra, Naṣṭoddiṣṭa, Varṇa, Alaṃkāra, Gamaka, Śuddha* and *Vikṛta Svaras, Svarasthāna, Rāga,* time suitable for *Rāgas.* It mentions 29 *Śrutis* and 122 *Rāgas. Ahobala,* for the first time, describes the 12 *Svaras* (vowels) in terms of the length of the string of the *Vīṇā.* The author holds that all *Śrutis,* when used in *Rāgas,* became *svaras.* The work mentions ancient writers, and is based particularly on Hanūmān's work. The author refers to *Rāgataraṅgiṇī, Rāgavibodha* and the *Rājataraṅgiṇī* (11th-12th. cent.). He supports the views of Rāmāmātya.

Ahobala has used, for *Rāgas,* seven *Śuddha-svaras* and five *Vikṛta-svaras;* he has applied *Komala Ni, Tīvra GA, Tīvratara MA, Komala Dha* and *Tīvra* NI.

Besides a number of pure *Rāgas,* he deals with a few mixed *Rāgas,* e.g. *Vasantabhairava, Toḍī, Varāṭī,* etc.

The modest object of the work is to enlighten those who are devoid of the sense of *Svaras (Svarajñāna-vihīnebhyo mārgo'yaṃ bodhito mayā).*

SAṂGĪTARĀJA (also known as *Saṃgīta-mīmāṃsā*)

Attributed to Kumbha or Kumbhakarṇa, it deals with music, vocal and instrumental. It is divided into five chapters (*Ratnakoṣas*), called respectively *Pāṭhya, Gīta, Vādya, Nṛtya* and *Rasa.* Each chapter consists of four sections, called *Ullāsas,* each of which is sub-divided into four *Parīkṣaṇas.* It consists of 16,000 stanzas, each comprising 32 letters.

[Ed. P. Sharma, Vol. I, Benares, 1963].

SAṂGĪTA - RATNĀKARA

A huge and highly authoritative work by Śārṅgadava, dealing with music, both vocal and instrumental and dance. Its seven chapters are named as follows:-

I. Svaragatādhyāya.

II. Rāgādhyāya.

III. Prakīrṇakādhyāya.

IV. Prabandhādhyāya.

V. Tālādhyāya.

VI. Vādyādhyāya.

VII. Nartanādhyāya.

The work, *Chandoviciti*, mentioned in the *Prabandhādhyāya* above, is regarded, by the commentator, Siṃhabhūpāla, as a work by Śārṅgadeva himself.

Besides Siṃhabhūpāla, the other commentators are Kallinātha, Keśava, Haṃsabhūpāla and Kumbhakarṇa. The titles of the commentaries of Siṃhabhūpāla, Kallinātha and Keśava are respectively *Saṃgītasudhākara*, *Kalānidhi* and *Kaustubha*. Of all the commentaries, the one by Kallināth is the most popular. There is also an anonymous commentary, named *Candrikā*. There is a Hindī commentary by Gaṅgārāma (*Tanjore Palace Library Cataloge of MSS*, XVI, 7279).

In comparison with the earlier works, this treatise has discussed many more things. For example, it has arranged the *tālas* under two sections, viz. *Mārga* and *Deśī*. In it, we find elaborate treatment of some modes like *Kalāpāta*, *Aṅgulavidhi*, *Tāladhāraṇa*, etc.

Like the present system of counting *Mātrās* on the tips of fingers, in vogue in South Indian music, there was a system in the early times also, as is attested by the *Saṃgītaratnākara*, chap 7, Verses 32-34. Here we find that, in order to show the *mātrās* of the *tālas* of even number, belonging to the class of *Caccatpuṭa*, the following fingers were used.

Little, ring, middle and index.

In the case of *tālas* with odd numbers of *mātrās*, the middle finger is not required.

Śārṅgadeva was, perhaps, the first writer to use *ardha-mātrā* (i.e. *Druta aṅga*) and three *mātrās* (i.e. *Pluta aṅga*) in respect of

Deśī tāla (Vide V. 238 of the S.R.) From V. 255 of this treatise, we learn that *Deśī tālas*, in which there is the use of *ardha-mātrā* and *khaṇḍa-mātrā* like *Virāma*, etc., are also called *Khaṇḍa Tālas.*

The different *tāla-aṅgas*, with the corresponding symbols introduced by Śārṅgadeva, are as follows:-

Aṅga	Symbol
Druta	0
Laghu	1
Guru	S
Pluta	S'

Śārṅgadeva mentions 120 *Deśītālas* which are of the highest number, Most of these *tālas* are, no doubt, found in earlier works, but the present work revelas a distinct mode of arranging them.

It introduces at least 25 new names of which some e.g. Śārṅgadeva, Niḥśaṅkalīla,. Niḥśaṅka are obviously Śārṅgadeva's innovation.

The chronological relation of this work with the *Saṃgītamakaranda* has been discussed in connexion with our observations on that work.

[Ed. S.S. Sāstri, Madras, Vol I (Adhyāya 1), 1943; Vol II (Adhyāyas - 2-4), 1959; Vol III (Adhyāyas 5-6), 1951 by C.K. Rājā, Adyar Library Series No. 51, 1945 (Madras), ch. VII by K.K. Rājā and R. Burnier, *Brahmavidyā* (Adyar library Bulletin), Vol XX111. pts. 3-4, 1959 (Madras), Chap. I trs. into Eng. by R.K. Shringy, Vārānasi, 1978. Trs. into Hiṇdī (chaps. I-IV) by S.C. Banerji, Calcutta, 1380 B.S. Bengali trs. by Sures Chandra Bandhyopādhyāy, Calcutta, 1379 BS].

SAṂGĪTASAMAYASĀRA

In this work, Pārśvadeva discusses music in a simple manner. In nine chapters, called *Adhikaraṇas*, it deals with *Nāda* and *Dhvani, Sthāyins, Rāgas, Vādya, Abhinaya, Tāla, Prastāra*, and ends with *Adhvayoga.* The author mentions king Pratāpa, a Digambara Śaṃkara, Tumburu, Mataṅga, Kaśyapa, Dattila, Kohala and Hanūmat as writers on music. Also mentioned are Bhoja, Someśvara.

Of the persons, named by the author, some are of unknown date. Mataṅga flourished in the Gupta period, according to some, in the ninth century, according to others. But, Bhoja and Someśvara are of known dates. Bhoja flourished in the first half of the 11th cent. Someśvara appears to be the Cālukya king of this name who was the author of the *Mānasollāsa* (also called *Abhilaṣitārtha - cintāmaṇi,* composed in 1129 A.D., which contains a huge number (2.500) of verses on vocal and instrumental music, and is regarded as an authoritative treatise. 1129 A.D. is, therefore, the upper terminus of the date of Pārśvadeva.

Difficulty, however, arises from the occurrence of the terms *Turuṣkatoḍī* and *Turuṣkagauḍa* if we accept them as belonging to the genuine portion of the work, and not interpolated into the text by a later land. If Pārśvadeva used these terms, he must be considered to have flourished after Āmir Khusrau (1253-1325 A.D.), a conclusion which militates against the above conjecture about his time.

The name Pārśvadeva is typically Jain. The title of the work reminds one of the *Samayasāra* of the Jain Kundakundācārya.

The fact that Pārśvadeva is silent about the *Saṃgītaratnākara* tends to indicate that he preceded Śārṅgadeva.

It is, perhaps, due to his Jaina persuasion that he uses many Prākrit terms, instead of Sanskrit, to indicate *Rāgas, Tālas* and other forms of jargon. For instance, the following are some of the peculiar names of *Sthāyas; Gossagāḍha, Peṭṭopeṭṭi Phellophelli, Uṭṭuṇḍula,* etc.

The term *Jhombara, described in Prabandha* Adhyāya, seems, from verbal similarity, to be the precursor of *Jhumur.*, a kind of folk-song prevailing in Bengal. Among *hastapāṭas* (for *pāṭa*, see Glossary) are mentioned *Bollāraṇī*, *Callāraṇī*. A kind of movement of the body in dance is called *Jhaṣka*.

The *Rāgas*, mentioned by him are *Śuddha Vaṅgāla*, *Gauḍa*, *Drāviḍa-varāṭī*, *Karṇāṭa-gauḍa*, *Turuṣkagauḍa*, etc.

He has distinguished between *Mārga* and *Deśī* dances. One, who can teach both kinds of dance, is *Uttama*; one, who can teach *Mārga* only, is *Madhyama*. Some of the *Rāgas* figure in the *Kīrtana* songs of Bengal. Several combined *Rāgas* are also mentioned.

As regards Tāla, he mentions *Caccatpuṭa*, *Cācapuṭa*, etc. followed by *Jhampā*, *Pratibhaṭṭa etc.* Emphasising the importance of *Tāla*, the author says that *Tāla* is the very basis of *Saṃgīta*.

According to Pārśvadeva, among singers he is connoisseur who, having listened to a good song, becomes horripilated, and sheds tears of joy.

[Ed. TSS, 1925; GOS, Baroda, Actually it omits chapter I and the first 40 verses of the second. Vide. *Des. Cat. of Skt. MSS. in Oriental MSS. Library*, Mysore, 2091, called *Saṃgīta-sāra-saṃgraha*.]

SAṂGĪTASĀRĀMṚTA

By Tulajarāja (also called Tulajājī, Tukkojī, It is an extensive prose work on all the topics discussed by Śārṅgadeva. In the beginning, he pays homage to Śiva conceived as the embodiment of *Nāda*. (A portion of this work was published by Sukthankar under the title *Saṃgītasārāmṛtoddhāra*).

SAṂGĪTA - SĀRA - SAṂGRAHA

Written by the Bengali Ghanaśyāmadāsa or Narahari Cakravartī. Date of composition, stated at the end, is Śaka 1729 (=1807 A.D.). It is not clear whether it is the date of the original work or of its copy in which it is written.

Composed in six chapters, its contents are as follows:

I - Gīta-nirṇaya (determination of songs)

II - Vādya-nirṇaya (determination of musical instruments)

III - Nṛtya-nāṭya-prakaraṇa (section on dance and drama)

IV - Āṅgikābhinaya (acting by physical gestures)

V - Bhāṣādi-nirūpaṇa (determination of language, etc).

VI - Chandaḥ-prakāśa-prakaraṇa (section on metres)

[Ed., with an introductions, by Swami Prajnanananda, Calcutta, 1956].

There are three more works of the same title:

(1) Written or compiled by King Jagajjyotirmalla of Nepal (1617-33 A.D., Nepal Era 799).

(2) Telugu work by Tiruveṅkaṭa Kavi.

(3) Compiled by S.M. Tagore, published in Calcutta, 1884.

SAṂGĪTOPANIṢAD-SĀRODDHĀRA

By Sudhākalasa. From the work itself (VI. 152) we learn that a *Saṃgītopa-niṣad* was composed in *Saṃvat* 1380 (=1324 A.D.) and its epitome, that is, the present work, in *Saṃvat* 1406(=1350 A.D.). The colophon to the second chapter describes the author as the disciple of the Jain Rājaśekhara Sūri. This Rājaśekhara, obviously different from his famous namesake (9th, 10th. cent. author, *inter alia*, of the *Kāvyamīmāṃasā* appears to have been author of the Jaina work, called *Prabandhakośa*.

The work reveals some originality in his elaborate treatment of *tālas* in the second chapter. For the first time, it mentions (2.11.2) a new *tālāṅga* called *Vipluta*, consisting of five *Mātrās*. In this work, 73 *tālas* have been arranged into different groups in accordance with the number of *mātrās* ranging from 1 to 10. A noteworthy feature of this work is that the *pāṭa* (popularly called *ṭhekā* in Bengal) of each *tāla* has been mentioned. This treatise mentions the following five *tālas* which are not found elsewhere: *Vardhāpana, Pratāpavardhana, Pūrṇacandra,*

Pṛthvikuṇḍala and *Tālaratnākara*. These appear to be innovations by the author.

[Ed. U.P. Shah, Baroda, 1961.]

SAṂGĪTASUDHĀKARA

Well-known commentary on the *Saṃgītaratnākara*. It is by *Siṃhabhūpāla*, also called Śiṅgabhūpāla, Śiṅgadharaṇīśa, Śiṅgarāja or Śiṅgamahīpati. According to Śeśagiri Śāstri, he was king Śiṇgamanāyaka of Veṅkaṭagiri, who ruled about 1330 A.D. according to some, in the fifteenth century according to others.

His *Rasārṇavasudhākara* is a celebrated work on poetics. He appears to have composed also a work called *Nāṭakaparibhāṣā*.

Krishnamachariar, however, is of the opinion (*Hist. of Class. Skt. Lit.*, para 1004, f.n.1) that the author of the *Rasārṇavasudhākara* is different.

The passage, quoted by Mallinātha (end of 14th. cent. or earlier half of the 15th.) in his commentary on the *Kumārasambhava* (i.25), agrees with i.181 of the *Rasārnavasudhākara*.

[Ed.K. Vedāntavāgīśa and S.P. Ghosh, Calcutta 1879, Published in the Adyar Library ed. of the *Saṃgītaratnākara*, 1986].

SARASVATĪ - HṚDAYĀLAṂKĀRA

Same as *Bharatabhāṣya* (q.v.).

ŚRĪMALLAKṢYASAṂGĪTA

See under *Lakṣyasaṃgīta*.

SVARAMELAKALĀNIDHI

Composed by Rāmāmātya in five chapters in C. 1550 A.D., it is a highly authoritative treatise in South India. It deals exhaustively with *Karṇāṭaka - saṃgīta*, and its division into 72 *Melakartās*.

It is noteworthy that, like Śārṅgadeva, he holds that, in the event of conflict between the current and Śāstric modes, the latter should be interpreted according to the former. Pointing out a flaw in the *svara*-definitions of Śārṅgadeva, he has shown seven *Śuddha svaras* and *Vikṛta svaras.* He has shown contradiction in Śārṅgadeva's account of *Vikṛta svara.*

He declares 20 *Janakamelas,* and 64 *Janyarāgas.*

[Ed. K. Vidyāvīgīśa, Calcutta, 1931; J. Vidyāsāgar, Calcutta, 1884; with Hindī trs, Hathras, U.P.]

MISCELLANEOUS PUBLISHED WORKS

Title	Author	Place and year of publication	Remarks
Abhinava-rāgamañjarī	Viṣṇuśarmā (Bhātkhaṇḍe)	Poona	
Anūpasaṃ-gītāṅkuśa	Bhāvabhaṭṭa	Āryabhūṣana Press, Poona, 1921.	
Anūpasaṃgīta-ratnākara	Bhāvabhaṭṭa	Āryabhūṣana Press, Poona.	In two chapters, it is a recast of the *Saṃgītaratnākara*. Mentioned by the author in his *Anūpasaṃgītāṅkuśa*. See Stein, Extr. p. 267 and *Jour. of Music Academy*, Madras, IV, p.p. 69-70.
Catvāriṃśad-rāganirūpaṇa		Bombay	
Gāyakapārijāta	Śiṅgarācārya	Madras	
Lakṣyasaṃgītā	Bhātkhaṇḍe	Poona	
Mālādhārā	Minappa Veṅkaṭāppā	Mysore	
Rāgacandrikā		Bombay	
Rāgamālā	Puṇḍarīka Viṭṭhala	Bombay	Being serially published in

			the Bengali journal *Sāṃgītika*, Calcutta, from Issue No. 2, April, 1989, with Bengali trs. and notes by Pradip Ghosh.
Sadrāga-candrodaya	Puṇḍarīka Viṭṭhala	Bombay	See Popley, *Music of India.*
Saṃgīta-rājaraṅga			Trivandrum.
Saṃgītasārā-mṛta	Tulajarāja or Tulajājī or Tukkoji, King of Tanjore, 1729-35	Tanj.xvi. 7288	Author's genealogy is given. A part of it was published by Sukthankar under the title *Saṃgīta-sārā-mrto-ddhāra.* The entire work is in prose, and deals with all the topics discussed by Śārṅgadeva.
Saṃgīta-sarvā-rtha-saṃgraha	Kṛṣṇarāo	Madras.	

V

UNPUBLISHED WORKS

The unpublished works on musicology far outnumber the published ones. For a full history of Indian lore on music and dance, and a detailed appraisal of the contents of the works, it is necessary to publish the important manuscripts on these arts. For the facility of those, who are interested in resusciating the unpublished works and bringing them to the light of day, we have made a list of the selected unpublished works along with references to the noteworthy collections in India and foreign countries. Complete manuscripts have generally been preferred to the incomplete ones. In case, however, where no complete manuscript is known, the incomplete one has been mentioned. In selecting the depositories of manuscripts, we have preferred the well-known ones to little or less known collections. Against the titles, we have set forth such information about them as can be gleaned from the manuscripts concerned and from other sources. The study of the manuscripts has a twofold importance. First, some of them furnish internal evidence about their dates of composition. Moreover, by mentioning earlier authors or works, they help determination of the relative chronology.

(Titles arranged in Devanāgarī alphabetical order)

Title	Author	Reference	Remarks
Anūpa-bhāvamañjarī	Bhāvabhaṭṭa	Bikaner 3418	Author was a protégé of King Anūpasiṃha of Bikaner.
Anūpa-rasasāgara	(Anuṣṭubh Cakravartin) Son of Saṃgītarāja Janārdana Bhaṭṭa	Bikaner 3343-45	12 chapters

Anūpasaṃgī-taratnākara	Bhāvabhaṭṭa		In two chapters, it is a recast of Śā-rṅgadeva's *Saṃgīta-ratnā-kara* mentioned in the author's *Anūpa-saṃgītā-ṅkuśa.*
Anūpa-saṃgī-tavartamāna	Bhāvabhaṭṭa	Bikaner 3364-65 iii.pp 107-8	See *NIA*, IV
Anūpa-saṃgī-tavilāsa		Bikaner 1091 (*Nṛtya* with commentary) 3366 (*Svara*), 3367 (*Rāga*), 3368 (*Prakīrṇa*), 3369 (*Prabandha*) 3370 (*Vādya*) 3371 (*Tāla*), 3372 (*Nṛtya*) Stein Extr. p. 267. Only three chapters printed by Āryabhūṣaṇa Press, 1921 A.D. *Journal of Music Academy*, Madras, p.p. 69-70.	Mostly compilation from different works. Mentioned in the author's *Saṃgītāṅkuśa.*

		3373 (*Svara*) 3374 (*Prakīrṇa about Nṛtya*) 3376 (*Svara*) 3377 (*Rāga*) 3378 (*Prakīrṇaka*) 3379 (*Prabandha*) 3380 (*Vādya*) 3381 (*Tāla*) 3382 (*Nrtya*) 3383 (*Rāga*) 3384 (Nṛtya).	
Do	Bhāvabhaṭṭa, son of Saṃgītarāja Janārdana Bhaṭṭa and grandson of Tāna Bhaṭṭa		*The Rāgamañjarī*. Rāga-kutūhala and Rāga-kautuka are quoted.
Anūpa-saṃgītasāgara	Bhāvabhaṭṭa		12 Chapters. Is it different from the aforesaid *Anūpa-rāga-sāgara*?
Anūpa-saṃgītoddeśa	Raghunātha Gosvāmin (son of Bhāvabhaṭṭa)	Bikaner 3398-99	
Arjunādimatasāram	Veṅkaṭācārya	Oriental MSS. Library, Madras	Author, son of Ānandācārya of Naidhruva Kāśyapagotra.

			Resident of Samalkot in East Godāvarī Dist. C. 1880 A.D.
Kalā-ṅkuranibandha			Also called *Rāgamātṛkā* (q.v.)
Kavicintāmaṇi	Gopīnātha Kavibhūṣaṇa	T.C. IV.4225	A work on poetics in 24 chapters the last of which contains discussion on music.
Kīrtanacintāmaṇi or Gītacintāmaṇi.	Raghunātha-Bhaṭṭa Gosvāmī		Deals with the definition etc. of *Kīrtana*. Composed like a dialogue between sages Vālmīki and Bharadvāja.
Kutupādhyāya Kohalamata	Bhāvabhaṭṭa	Bikaner 3401 TCD 1221 (Contains some exposition in Malayalam) Travancore University Catalogue, 1724 T 822	In the form of a dialogue between Kohala and Mataṅga.
Kohala-rahasya		MT 787 (13 Chaps.)	Deals with *Rāgas* suitable for certain special

			topics. Written in the form of a dialogue between Kohala and Mataṅga.
Gītalakṣaṇa		Bikaner 3404	
Gītālaṃkāra	Bharata	Bd. 977 BORI 977 of 1887-91 BORI DXII. 310. Same as *Vādi-mallaga-jāṅkuśa* mentioned in *Saṃgīta-śiromaṇi* as one of its sources. Nepal I, p. 241 RASB. XVI. 68	See V.Raghavan, Later Saṃgīta Literature, *Saṃgīta-Nāṭaka Akademi* Bulletin, 18, April, 1961, pp 10-11
Chalaprakriyā		Adyar I, p.49a Adyar D.I. 798, 799. Alwar 298 Borl, 105/2 of 1886-92 IM 2555A Stein 15 See Burnell, Saṃhitopaniṣad-brāhmaṇa, pp. XV, XVI R. Simon WZKM. XXVII. 325 Adyar D.I. 800-810 Alph.	Index of Saman songs.

Chalākṣara		Lit. Beng. Govt., p.410 42294-9 L 1420, 1559 Sri Dev 351 (C), 374(b), Whish 167	
Jaina-saṃgīta		Adyar	
Tālakalāvilāsa		Sg. II.64	Mentioned in Lakṣmīdhara's *Śrutirañjanī* commentary on the *Gītagovinda.*
Do (Svaramela-kalānidhi),		Adyar II.p. 45 a (incomplete)	
Tālacandrikā	Virūpākṣa	Sucindram 200 Tra. A.D.. Rep. 1104, 128 (Incomplete) TCD 1223	Author was son of Rāmacandrādhvarin and disciple of Vīrarāghava.
Tāladīpikā Gopendra Tippa Bhūpāla	Burnell 60b MT 770	Composed in three chapters, it deals with *Mārga* and *Deśī tālas.* (Mārga tāla-prastārādi-nirūpaṇa) TD 10828-29 (Both incomplete) I.O.	

	8830-31 (Both incomplete with Telugu commentary TC, I. 1015 Tanj. XVI. 7307 S.K. De, SP. II, 84, 109	
Tālaprakaraṇa	Madras University 747 MD 12991 (with Telugu interpretation)	
Tālaprakāśa	Bhau Daji 120	
Tālaprabandha		A Śiva-hymn by Gopendra-Tippabhūpāla designed as containing illustrations of all the *Tālas*. The author, perhaps, composed another work about 108 *Karaṇas* in dance. See V. Raghavan, Later Saṃgīta Literature, *Jour. of Music Academy*, Madras, IV,

			1938, pp 51-52 *Saṃgīta-Nāṭaka Academy Bulletin*, No. 17(1960), p.10 See *Contribution of Kerala to Sanskrit Literature*, p.p. 189, 194
Tālaprastāra	Rāma-pāṇivāda	Burnell 60b MT 5207 (Incomplete) Oppert I. 2850 Paliyam 730(b), 922 TD 10832-36 Trippūṇittura V.26 Uzhuttara Vā-riyar 24 MT2779.	
Tālavādyavidhāna (Taken from *Uḍḍiśa-mantrodaya*)	Travancore University. 8959 (incomplete) with comm. in Malayalam, Triv. Cur. VII 140		
Tālaviṣaya		MD. 12995 (with interpretation in Telugu)	

Tālamañjarī		Adyar (with Telugu commentary) Bikaner 3406	
Tālalakṣaṇa		BORI 7060f 1892-95 Burnell 61a (2MSS) 10 7904 (with Telugu exposition) Peters. V, p. 286, (No. 706a). TD 10837 (with Telugu commentary), 10841 (complete Aṣṭottaraśata-tāla-lakṣaṇa), 10842, 10843-45	
Tāla-sarvasva-sāra-saṃgraha		Cuttack 137	
Tālādhyāya	Kohala	MD. 12996 (with Telugu commentary, incomplete) 12997 (*ibid*) TA 2166, 2167)4	
Tūryatūrya-gīta-Upaniṣad-vivaraṇa	Brahmayogin	Up. Br. Mutt 82 (U)	The author, an ascetic, wrote works on nondualistic Vedānta and *Rāma-bhakti*,

and was a musicologist. Living in Kānchī, he founded the Upaniṣad Brahma Maṭha there.. At first known as Rāma-candrendra, he was named Śivarāma. After writing exposition of 108 Upaniṣads, he came to be known as Upaniṣad Brahma-Yogin. The date of completion of his *Paramādvaita-siddhānta-paribhāṣā* (MT 6521) is writen as 1790 A.D. Besides miscellaneous songs, he wrote some *Gītaprabandhas* in glorification of Śiva etc. See *Journal of Music*

			Academy, Madras, XXVII, p. 123; XXVIII, pp 151, 152
Tūrya-bīja (-atīta) - gīta-vivaraṇa	Upaniṣad Brahmayogin	Do 81	
Tūryavirāṭa (atīta) - gīta-vivaraṇa	Do	Do, 79	
Tūrya-Sūtra (atīta)-gīta-vivaraṇa	Do	Do, 80	
Dakṣiṇī-rāgamālā		BORI.MS.No. 384, 1895-8	Describes six *Rāgas* only.
Dattilakohalīya		Burnell 606 Tirupati 267	See *Journal of Śrī Veṅkaṭeśvara Oriental institute* II, pp. 185-6. It deals with vocal and instrumental music and dance.
Divya-nāma-gīta-vivaraṇa	Do	Do	See *Journal of Music Academy*, Madras, XXV 11, pp 120 123-4, 130-50 (For a complete inded Upa. Bra. Mutt 10 (u)
Divya-nāma-saṃkīrtana	Do		

Nādadīpaka	Bhaṭṭācārya	L. 538	
Nṛtya-raṅganavī-karaṇa		Tirupati 268 Tra. Ad. Rep. 1110.34	
Prabandha-dīpikā	Gauranārya	Same as *Lakṣmaṇadī-pikā* (q.v.)	
Bālarā-mabharatam	Bālarā-mavarman		A treatise on music and dance in 18 chapters. It contains an introductory essay in prose on the interdependence of *bhāva, rāga* and *tāla*, followed by description of music, vocal and instru-mental, and the develop-ment of the sentiments by gasticulation.
Bījaturyā (tīta)-gīta-vivaraṇa		Upaniṣad Brahmendra-Yogin.	Up. Br. Mutt, 78
Bīja-bījā (tīta) gīta-vivaraṇa	Do	Do,	77
Bījasūtra (atīta)-gīta-vivaraṇa		Do	Do,75

Bharata-śāstra-grantha	Lakṣmīdhara	BRI(1916-18), No. 40	
Bharata-sāra-saṃgraha	Mummidi Cikkadevarāya III (Ruler of Mysore, 1672-1704)	*Mys.* 308	In 2,500 verses; incomplete. It lays down views of Bharata, Mataṅga and Vidyāraṇya.
Mataṅga-bharata	Lakṣmaṇa Bhāskara	Tanj XVI. 7231	Based on Mataṅga. In about 1,000 verses, deals mostly with dance.
Melādhikāra-lakṣaṇa		Tanj XVI. 7313	Of c.18th. cent. A.D. It enlarges Veṅkaṭa-makhin's system of *Melakartās.*
Ratnamālā			Another name of *Rāgamālā* (q.v.).
Rāga-tāla pārijātaprakāśa	Govinda	MS. in Andhra Sāhitya Pariṣad Library under name *Saṃgītaratnākara.*	*Deals with music tones and time.*
Rāgamañjarī	Puṇḍarīka Viṭṭhala,	Bik 575	
Rāgamālā	Jīvarāja	Mitra VII. 264 CC I. 499	

Rāgamālikā (or, Kalāṅkuranibandha)	Puruṣottama Kaviratna	T. C. IV. 4705	Author belonged to Orissa.
Rāgamālā (1570 A.D.)	Kṣemendra	1.0.II.319 Bik. 516	Author, son of Maheśa Pāṭhaka, and also known as Kṣemakarṇa or Meṣakarṇa. Written in 1570 A.D. at the instance of Jalava Bhūpati.
Rāgasāgara		DC, XXII, 8742	Written in Purāṇic style in the form of a dialogue between Nārada and Dattila on different kinds of *rāgas*, their forms and attributes. Some later theories adopted in it. Śārṅgadeva is mentioned. So, probably not earlier than 14th cent. A.D.
			Author, son of Ayamaprabhu,

			who was brother of Potana, Minister of Śiṅgaya Mādhava, king of Racakoṇḍa of Recarla dynasty, who ruled about 1422 A.D.
Lakṣaṇadīpikā or Prabandhadīpikā	Gaurāṅgārya	Part relating to music is found in Mys. 399. Part relating to dance is with M.R. Kavi, Madras. DC. XXII. 8692, 8694, Tanj. IX.4029	A general treatise on poetics, music and dance. He quotes from *Alaṃkāra-saṃgraha*. *Kavikaṇṭhapāśa*, *Camatkāra-candrikā*, *Sāhitya-candrodaya*, etc.
Viṭṭhalīya	Puṇḍarīka Viṭṭhala	Tanj. XVI. 7245	
Virāṭ-turya-gīta-vivaraṇa	Upaniṣad Brahmayogin	Up. Br. Mutt. 70(U)	
or Virāṭ-turyātīta-gīta-vivaraṇa	Do	Do	
Virāṭ-bījātīta-gīta	Do	Do	

SAMGĪTA-CŪḌĀMANI

By Jagadekamalla, son of Someśvara, **Cālukya king of Kalyāṇī** (C. 1127-38 A.D.). Someśvara **appears to have been referred to** as Someśa in the Svaragatā-**dhyāya (1.18) of the** *Saṃgītaratnākara.* So, Jagadekamalla, **perhaps, preceded** Śārṅgadeva.

The treatise comprises **four sections called respectively** *Prabandha, Tāla, Vādya* and *Rāga.* Of these, the *Tāla* section is quite lengthy. The author deals with both *Deśī-tāla* and *Mārga-saṃgīta* or *Mārga-tāla.*

Verses 65 to 79 of the **second section name 101** *tālas* most of which occur in the *Bharatārṇava* **and the** ***Saṃgītamakaranda.*** The *tāla* portion appears to have followed the above works. The originality of the *Cūḍāmaṇi* lies in the fact that it, at first, contains a list of 101 *Prabandha-tālas*: it differs from the earlier list in some respects, and mentions a few new names. The majority of the *Prabandha-tālas* has been included in five *Tālāṅgas,* and divided into five groups. These five *aṅgas* are named, in accordance with the names of *Mārgatālas,* as *Caccatpuṭa, Cācapuṭa Ṣaṭpitāputraka,* and *Udghaṭṭa.* The 101 *tālas,* enumerated earlier, have been divided, in accordance with *Jāti,* into two kinds, Viz. *Caturasra* and *Tryasra.* In respect of *Jāti,* the author has adopted the relative verse of the *Saṃgītamakaranda.* That is, mention has been made also of *Miśra Jāti* and *Khaṇḍa Jāti*; but, in grouping the *Tālas,* there is no mention of *Miśra* or *Khaṇḍa Jāti.* In this treatise, the following new *Tālas* are added: *Vardhāpana, Maḍḍa* and *Dvitīya Maḍḍa.* The following *tālas,* occurring in the earlier work, are missing in the present treatise: *Pratināṇṭha, Śrīnandana (Nandana,* however, is mentioned).

Sarvagrāsa-turya-turya-gīta	Upaniṣad Brahmayogin	Up. Br. Mutt, 225
Sarva-turyā (tīta)-gīta-vivaraṇa	Do	Do

Sāhitya-kallolinī	Bhāskarācārya	DC. XXII. 8706	Deal with poetics and dance.
Sūtra-turyā (tīta)-gīta-vivaraṇa	Upaniṣad brahmendra-yog in	Up. Br. Mutt. Do, 78(u)	
Sūtrabījā (tīta)-gīta-vivaraṇa	Do	Do, 73(u)	
Sūtra-virāṭ (atīta) gīta-vivaraṇa	Do	Do, 72(u)	
Svara-rāga-sudhā-rasa or Nāṭya-cuḍā-maṇi	Aṣṭāvadhānī Somanārya	Tāladaśa-prakaraṇa, included in it, with Telugu commentary, exists separately. In seven chapters, it deals with music and dance.	DC. XIII 8723, 8729. TC. I.R. No. 366 See newspaper, *Hindu* (Madras), Dec. 20, 26, 1932. Literary Supplements; V. Raghavan's paper read at Music Conference, Madras, 1933. The author quotes Rāvaṇa. He follows Nārada's school, and frequently differs from Bharata. He was probably the famous

			Telugu poet Nācana Somana, author of *Uttaraharivaṃśa*, and dance under the celebrated grant of 1344 A.D. of King Bukka I of Vijaynagar.

SUPPLEMENTARY LIST OF UNPUBLISHED WORKS
(English Alphabetical Order)

Abhinava-tāla-mañjarī	Jīvarāmopādhyāya		
Abhinavarāga-mañjarī	Do		
Ādibharata-prastāra		Opp. 4991	
Ānandasañjīvana	Madanapāla	Bik. 509	Author was son of Candradeva and King of Kanauj (12th. cent.) MS. dated Sam 1585
Aṅgahāra-lakṣaṇa		Trav.73	

Arjunabhāratam	Nāgārjuna	Tanjore XVI.7229	Treats of music. Several authors of this name are known The celebrated Buddhist philosopher Nāgārjuna, probably folurished in the latter part of the second century A.D.
Bharataśāstra	Raghunātha Prasāda	Tanj. XVI. 7232	
Gītadoṣavicāra		TC IV. 4707	
Lāsyapuṣpāñjali		Tanj.XVI.7268	
Melarāgamālikā	Mahā Vaidyanātha Śiva		See Krishnamachariar, *Hist. of Class. Skt. Lit.*, para 1060. Mṛdaṅgalakṣaṇa DC. XX11 874
Muralīprakāśa	Bhāvabhaṭṭa	Bik. 513	
Naṣṭoddiṣṭaprabodhaka	Bhāvabhaṭṭa	Bik. 514	
Rāgadhyānādikathanādhyāya		Bik.515	
Rāgādisvaranirṇaya	Rādhānātha		

Rāga-kalpadrumā-ṅkura	Appa Tulasī, alias Kāśīnātha	(1914)	
Rāgakautūhala			Same as *Saṃgīta-sāroddhāra* of Rāmakṛṣṇa Bhaṭṭa.
Rāganārāyaṇa	Puṇḍarīka Viṭṭhala		See Krishnamachariar *Hist. of Class. Skt. Lit*,. Para 1028
Rāgapradīpa		TC II. 2447	
Rāgaratnākara of Gandharvarāja		Tanj. XVI. 7302	
Tulajarāja		Tanj XVI7304	
Rāgārohā-varohaṇa-paṭṭikā		Tanj. XVI. 7349	
Rāgatāla-pāri-jāta-prakāśa	Govinda		The MS. is in Andhra Sāhitya Pariṣad Library, Madras, under the title *Saṃgīta-ratnākara*. See Krishnamachariar, *Hist. of. Class. Skt. Lit.*, para 1030, f.n. 1. It describes music tones and time.

Rāgavarṇa-nirūpaṇa		DC, *XXII* 8742	
Saṃgītacandra	*Abhilāṣa*	Nepal 260	In a verse of the work, it is stated that Jagajjyotirmalla, ruler of Nepal, got this work from South India, and had a commentary, *Saṃgīta-bhāskara*, written on it by Vaṅgamaṇi of Mithilā.
Saṃgītacintāmaṇi	Kamalalocana	CC.I.686	
Saṃgīta-cūḍāmaṇi	Jagadekamalla Pratāpa Cakravartin	MS. in Andhra Sāhitya Pariṣat Library Madras, Tanj. XVI. 7266.	On musio and dance. In five chapters. A work of this title is mentioned in Gajapati Vīraśrī Nārāyaṇadeva in his *Saṃgīta-nārāyaṇa*.
Saṃgīta-darpaṇa	Haribhaṭṭa		
Saṃgītakalānidhi	Haribhaṭṭa	CC.I.685	
Saṃgītakalikā			

Saṃgīta-kalpadruma	Kṛṣṇānanda Vyāsa	CC.I.685	
Saṃgīta-kramadīpikā	Kumbha	See List of B.O.R.I., V. Raghavan, Miscellanies in *ABORI*, XVI, Pts. iii, iv.	
Saṃgīta-lakṣaṇa	Candraśekhara	Mys-307	
Saṃgīta-makaranda	Veda	S.R. Bhandarkar's *Cat.of MSS.*, Raj, CI (1904-6), P.54 Bik 520	It treats of *Rasasṛṣṭi, Gati, Cārī, Hasta, Nṛtta* and *Rasas.*
Saṃgīta-maṇidarpaṇa			
Saṃgītamuktāvalī	Devaṇācārya	Bik 521	It deals mainly with dance, and contains a chapter on music.
		Tanj.XVI.7272	Author's name Devendra. It appears to have been another name of Devaṇācārya. It mentions Rudraṭa as a writer on *Saṃgīta* and *Nṛtta*. A Rudraṭa of C.9th

			cent. A.D. is known as author of *Kāvyālaṃkāra*, a well-known work on poetics.
Saṃgītanārāyaṇa	Nārāyaṇadeva	TC.V-6227	It deals, in four chapters, with music, dance, musical instruments and musical compositions. The author refers to his own work *Alaṃkāra-candra (or, Candrikā)* Among other works and authors, mentioned by him, are the *Saṃgītasāra* (probably of Vidyāraṇya), *Saṃgīta-ratnamālā* (of Mammaṭa), Gītaprakāśa, *Saṃgīta-candrikā*,

			Saṃgīta-kalpataru and Harināyaka.
Saṃgītanārā-yaṇa	King Gajapati Vīraśrī Nārā-vaṇadeva.	See Krishna-machariar. *Hist. of Class. Skt. Lit.*, para 1048.	Author was son of Padmanābha and ruled at Parlakimedi (Orissa) about 1700 A.D.). Belonging to the race of Uttuṅgagaṅga, he learnt music from Kaviratna Puruṣottama. The work deals, in four chapters, with music, dance, musical instruments and musical compositions. The illus-trations glorify the author himself. Besides his own work, *Alamkāra-candra*, he cites, *inter alia*, the following works and authors; *Saṃgī-*

			taśiromaṇi, *Saṃgīta-sāra* (of Vidyāranya?) *Saṃgīta-candrikā Saṃgītacūḍamaṇi*, *Saṃgīta-kalpataru*, Harināyaka, Kṛṣṇadatta
Saṃgīta-prakāśa	Raghunātha (18th cent.)		
Saṃgīta-puṣpāñjali	Veda	Tanj. XVI 7268	
Saṃgītarāja	Kumbhakarṇa	We quote below an excerpt quoted by Krishna-machariar in his *Hist. of Class. Skt. Lit.*, para 1022:- "About 1440 Kumbhakarna, king of Mewar, completed his *Saṃgīta-mīmāṃsā* alias *Saṃgītarāja* in five sections of *pāṭhya, gīta, vādya, nṛtya* and rasa. The whole work is	

not available to us. Each of the five sections is further classfied into four chapters of minor divisons. The work extends over 16,000 *ślokas.* His treatment is thorough in *gī-ta* and *vādya.* He sifts all the material then available to him and possessing high Sāstric proficiency, discusses theories very intelligently, For example, we cite the theory of *rasa* and use of the word *sattva*, etc. He did not quote from Kohala or Kāśyapa, though he says he studied them. He mentions

Dattila rarely. He had with him Rāhula's and Kīrti-dhara's *Vārtikas* on Bharata's *Nāṭyaśāstra*. He examined the treatises of Kshetrarāja. Modern research cannot be complete without a thorough study of this grand work. The author was a profound scholar in Mīmāṃsā and Vedic rites, and thus scarcely misunderstands the arguments of Mataṅga, Dattila and Abhinavagupta whom he closely follows. His section on musical prosody was borrowed from the later writers of North India. In the construction of *vīṇās* and *vaṃśas*, he gives all possible details. He touches upon chiefly *Nakula*, *Pinākī*, *Svaramaṇḍala* *Mattakokila*, *Kinnarī* of medium and higher sorts, Someśvara treats of only *Ekatantrī*, *Ālāpinī*, and *Kinnarī* of two kinds. Nānyadeva elaborates *Rudravīṇā*, and *Kinnarī*. He accidentally mentions that Nārada used *Vīṇā* of 21 strings and Mataṅga practised upon *Chaitrika* and *Svāti* on a lute of 9 strings.

Saṃgīta-ratnāvalī	Somarājadeva	See list of authors on music in *Saṃgīta-makaranda*, GOS, Baroda, pp.72.5	Author may or may not be identical with Someśvara, author of the *Mānasollāsa*, According to some, author was a *Pratihāra* of the Cālukya King Ajayapāla of Gujarat, 1174 A.D.
Saṃgītasāgara	Pratāpasiṃha	Is it the same as CCI 1686?	
Saṃgīta-saṃgraha-cintāmaṇi	Appalācārya	Adyar, 46	We reproduce below a quotation given by Krishnamachariar (*Hist. of Class. Skt. Lit.*, Para 1019 f.n.) "There is a manuscript in the Mahārājās Library at Bikaner called *Saṃgitasāra* which consists of about 160 *ślokas* without its author's name. The work maintains the theory of

Nandikeśvara, who, we know from *Aumāpata*, enumerates 264 *rāgas*. Whether the work is a summary or a fragment of Vidyāraṇya's production has yet to be decided. But some of the points, dealt with in it, appear to be developments in music attained in the 16th or the 17th century, and lacks in the grandeur that we usually find in Vidyāraṇya's works."

The work is quoted by name by Cikkadevarāya of Mysore in

			Nārāyaṇadeva in his *Saṃgītanārāyaṇa*, by Raghunātha in his *Saṃgītasudhā*.
Saṃgītasāra	Vidyāraṇya	Anonymous MS. of this title is in Mahārājā's Library at Bikaner	A *Saṃgītasāra* is mentioned by Gajapati Vīraśrī Nārāyaṇadeva in his *Saṃgītanārāyaṇa*. It contains about 160 verses. It supports the theory of Nandikeśvara who, we learn from the *Aumāpata*, enumerates 264 *Rāgas*. It is not yet known for certain whether it is a summary or fragment of Vidyāraṇya's work. It should however, be pointed out that the points, dealt

			appear to be developments in music as late as 16th. or 17th. cent., and lack the usual grandeur of Vidyāraṇya's works. Vidyāraṇya's *Saṃgītasāra* is quoted by name by Cikkadevarāya of Mysore in the *Bharata-sāra-saṃgraha* and by Nārāyaṇadeva in his *Saṃgīta-nārāyana.* King Raghunātha of Tanjore mentions, in his *Saṃgīta-sudhā,* both *Vidyāraṇya and his Saṃgītasāra.*
Saṃgītasārāmṛta (Also see under Published works)	Tulajāji	Tanj. XVI 7288	Author, also called Tukkoji, was King of Tanjore (1929-35)
Saṃgītasaraṇi	Nārāyaṇa	Miśra Kaviratna	See Krishnamachariar,

			Hist. of Class. Skt. Lit., para 1047.
Saṃgītasāra-saṃgraha	Anonymous	Rice 292 Opp.I.1052	
Saṃgītasāra-saṃgraha	Jagajjyotir-malla	Nepal, 262	Nepal Era 799
Saṃgītasā-roddhāra	Rāmakṛṣṇa Bhaṭṭa	Bik 518	
Saṃgītasā-roddhāra	Haribhaṭṭa	Bik 527	Another work of the same title is by Kikarāja (q.v.).
Saṃgītasā-roddhāra	Kikarāja	PR IV.32 Ex 42	Author known as Śāradā-nandana BORI.1886-92 No.832.
Saṃgītaśāstra-dugdha-vāridhi		Mys. Sup.51	
Saṃgītaśāstra		Tanj.XVI 7306	
Saṃgītaśāstra-saṃkṣepa	Govinda	Adyar, 45	See under Govinda in the list of Authors.
Saṃgīta-siddhānta	Rāmānanda Tīrtha		
Saṃgīta-śṛṅgārahāra	Hammīra	S.R. Bhan-darkar's Rep. of Raj. and C.I.MSS, 54, 92-3	
Saṃgītasudhā	Raghunātha Nāyaka of Tan-	TC.IV.4568	Appears to have been

jore (accession 1614)

actually written by his Minister, Govinda Dīkṣita, and dedicated to his patron King. It is a fairly exhaustive work on music, vocal and instrumental, and dance. In the introductory portion, there is much historical information. We reproduce below an excerpt quoted by Krishnamachariar *(Hist. of Class. Skt. Lit.*, para 1037) about the work. "Raghunātha treats at length of only 50 *rāgas* which he says were in use. Older writers simply gave *aṃsá*, *nyā-*

			sa and *graha* to each of the *rāgas*; but, Raghunātha gives in detail the number of the *śrutis* in each *svara* with *ālaptika*. He arranged 50 *rāgas* under 15 *melakartās*, the details given against each of them are full and useful for *vīṇā*. The third and fourth chapters of the work are devoted to musical compositions known as *prabandhas* then in vogue and to minor trophes in music."
Saṃgītasudhā	Bhīmanarendra	Oudh	X.12
Saṃgītasudhākara	Haripāladeva	Tanj.7293 IC.I.1025 IV.4570	In six chapters it deals with *Nāṭya, Tāla, Vādya, Rasa*

			and *Prabandha* with an appendix on *Gāyakalakṣaṇa*.
Saṃgītasūryodaya	Lakṣmīnārāyaṇa		Krishnamachariar mentions this title (*Hist. of Class Skt. Lit.*, para 1030), and notes his source of information as follows: M.R. Kavi, *Bhāratī*, 1925, 64.
Saṃgītavaralakṣaṇa		Mys 641	
Saṃgītavinoda	Bhāvabhaṭṭa		
Saṃgītavṛttaratnākara	Puṇḍarīka Viṭṭhala		Tanj XVI.7244
Saṃgītasvaralakṣaṇa		Trav. 73	
Saṃgītopaniṣat (Sam. 1380-1323 A.D.)	Sudhākalasa	Bik. 528	In six chapters, on music and dance. Author himself wrote a commentary (Saṁ. 1406=1340 A.D.) and the whole is called *Saṃgītopanisat*. The dates of the

			work and its commentary are as given by Krishnamachariar. Author is stated to have been a disciple of Rājaśekhara whose idendity has been desribed under Saṃgīta-sāroddhāra in connection with published works.
Saṃgrahacūḍāmaṇi	Ṣanmukha	MS, in Andhra Sāhitya pariṣat Library (See Krishnamāchariar *Hist. of Class Skt. Lit.*, para 992 f.n. 1)	Purported to form part of *Skandapurāna*. It must be later than the 13th cent. So, it could not have possibly formed part of the lost views of Ṣanmukha. It deals, in three chapters, with the origin of music and musical tones.
Tāladaśaprāṇaprakaraṇa			*DC.* XXII. 8723

Tālalakṣaṇa of Kohala			DC. XXII, 8725 see *Tanj*- XVI 7312
Tālamālikā	Veṅkaṭa Vaidyanātha Dīkṣita		See Krishnamachariar, *Hist. of Class Skt. Lit.*, para 1052.
Tālaprastāra			*Tanj* XVI 7329
Varṇapada			Tanj XVI. 7328
Varṇalaghu-vyākhyāna of Rāma			

WORKS KNOWN FROM REFERENCES ONLY

Title	Author	Reference	Remarks
Caturasabhā-vilāsa		Quoted in Nārāyaṇa Śivayogin's *Nāṭyasarvasva-dīpikā*	
Gītaprakāśa		BR 1916, No. 41 Quoted in *Saṃgītanārā-yaṇa.*	
Gītaratnāvalī	Jāyasenāpati		Mentioned in author's *Nṛttaratnāvalī* (p. 172 of the ed. pub. by Govt. Oriental MSS. Library).

Rāgadīpikā		Mentioned by Lakṣmīdhara in his comm. on the *Gītagovinda*.
Rāgakutūhala		Quoted by Bhāvabhaṭṭa.
Saṃgīta-candrikā	Mādhava-bhaṭṭa	Quoted in *Saṃgītasudhā*. A work of this title is quoted in *Saṃgīta-nārāyaṇa*. TC, V, 6227; IV. 4804
Saṃgīta-candrodaya		Quoted by Gaṅgārāma
Saṃgītakalikā		Quoted by Hemādri (1250-1300 A.D.) in his comm. on *Raghuvaṃśa*.
Saṃgīta-kalpataru		Quoted by Rucipati and Raṅganātha. There is a comm. on it by Roya Gaṇeśa (Bik.512). Raṅganātha wrote a comm. (1655) on the *Śakuntalā*. A work of this

		title is mentioned by Gajapati Vīraśrī Nārāyaṇadeva in his *Saṃgītanārāyaṇa.*
Saṃgītakaumudī		Quoted in *Saṃgītanārāyaṇa.* TC., V. 6127
Saṃgītaratnamālā	Mammaṭa	Mentioned by Gajapati Vīraśrī Nārāyaṇadeva in his *Saṃgītanārāyaṇa.*
Saṃgītasarvasva	Jagaddhara	Quoted copiously by Rucipati and Rāghavabhaṭṭa. Quoted by Jagaddhara in his comm. on *Veṇīsaṃhāra.* CC. 1687.
Saṃgītaśiromaṇi		Mentioned by Gajapati Vīraśrī Nārāyaṇadeva in his *Saṃgītanārāyaṇa.*
Saṃgītasudhānidhi		Quoted by Rāghavabhaṭṭa.

Sāradīya	Śāradātanaya	
Tāla-kalāvilāsa		Quoted in Nārāyaṇa Śivayogin's *Nāṭya-sarvasva-dīpikā*. BR. 1916, No. 41
Viṭṭhalīya	Puṇḍarīka-viṭṭhala	Tanj. XVI. 7245.

VI

MUSIC IN PURĀṆAS

Elements of music are mentioned in some major and minor Purāṇas. The Purāṇas, dealing with such elements, are as follows.

AGNIPURĀṆA (c.9th.cent.A.D.) (Chaps.328 ff, 336, 341)

This Purāṇa contains certain matters which are relevant for music and dance. In it, there is discussion on Metre(*Chandas*). The metres *Gāyatrī, Anuṣṭubh, Bṛhatī,* etc. are especially useful for *Sāmagāna*.. In connexion with metres, *Gaṇas* have been discussed. These are constituted by short and long vowels, and play a great part in music too. The *Saṃgītaratnākara* discusses *Gaṇa* in connexion with music. This Purāṇa deals, *inter alia,* with *Varṇa* which forms a foundation of music.

This Purāṇa deals exhaustively with *Aṅgakarman*, the action of different limbs in dance and drama. For example, it mentions 13 kinds of head, three types of hand, six kinds of nose, nine sorts of inhalation and exhalation, six modes of lip-movement, seven kinds of chin, 13 modes of hands joined together, 24 different positions of single hand, 5 modes of chest-position, three kinds of belly, 5 types of the action of the sides, 5 actions of shanks, many kinds of foot-action.

BRAHMAVAIVARTA PURĀṆA

Believed to be originally composed c.8th century. A.D. and finally recast in the 16th, it mentions 36 *Rāgiṇīs* and 6*Rāgas* with various *Tālas.*

BṚHADDHARMA PURĀṆA (C.13th.cent.A.D.)

This Purāṇa insists that the aspirant should practise *Saṃgīta* as a spiritual pursuit. It states that, of the two essentials of songs, one is sweet voice and the other is knowledge of the music lore.

It mentions 22 Śrutis. 22 *Srutimaṇḍalas* (spheres of *Śruti*) are supposed to exist within the body from the navel to head. The seven *Svaras* in order consist of 4, 2, 3, 4, 3, 2, and 6 *śrutis* respectively. The *Svaras* are threefold according as they are *Ghora, Mandra* and *Ucca.*

Three kinds of movements of *Svaras* are known as *Arohī* (ascending), *Avarohi* (descending) and *Saṃcārī (flitting). Such movements of Svaras* are stated to give rise to 5 crores, 5 lacs and 1000 *Rāgas* and *Rāgīṇīs* (consorts) and handmaids (*Uparāgiṇī*). The principal *Rāgas* are six, viz. *Kāmoda. Vasanta, Mallāra, Vibhāsa, Gandhāra and Dīpaka*

Each of them has 6 consorts (*Rāgiṇīs*) which, in their turn, have 6 handmaids (*Uparāgiṇīs*) each. The male *Rāgas*, the females and the maids, all taken together, number 6+36+36 =78[1]. *Dīpaka* Rāga has a male servant called *Pradīpanābha.*

It may be noted that the names of the consorts of *rāgas* differ from those found in the *Skandapurāna.*

In practice, the division of *Rāgas* of north -Indian music into male and female probably came into vogue in the 18th. cent. A.D

LINGAPURĀṆA

The extant work, believed to be a recast of the original *Liṅgapurāṇa*, appears to have been written not later than 1000 A.D.

Chapter I—there are references to songs relating to Viṣṇu having been sung with suitable *Tāla, Varṇa, Laya, Mūrchanā, Akṣara,* distinct Śrutis. The *Rāgas*, as found in works on musicology, were in vogue. The prevalence of *Sāmagāna* is also indicated in this work.

Chapter II requires one to worship Viṣṇu, sing and dance to the accompaniment of instrumental music; *Tāla* must be there.

1. The Bibliotheca Indica ed. and the Vaṅgavāsī ed. differ from each other in the names of the *Rāgas* and *Rāgiṇīs.*

Verses 10-16 of the third chapter clearly contain some material relating to *Saṃgīta*. Verses 64-70 deserve special mention in this connexion. The habits to be avoided, at the time to singing, are: laughing, expression of anger, shaking of the body, thought about things other than song. One is prohibited to beat time (*tāla*) with one hand. One should not sing before those who are hungry, thirsty or alarmed. None should sing in the dark.

Stanzas 68-70 speak of *Gīta-prastāra*, number of *Gītas* and instruments called *Vipañcī (Vīṇā)*, etc. *Svara-vibhāga* (division of *Svaras*) has also been referred to.

It is clear from this Purāṇa that music was practised as a religious pursuit. There is a spiritual overtone in the musical matter contained in this work.

From an anecdote, contained in this Purāṇa, we learn that Nārada learnt music from Ulūkas on a mountain to the north of Mānasasarovara. Ulūka, generally denoting the owl, is stated , by Kṣitimohan Sen[1], to refer to a non-Aryan race; may be that the people of this race used the owl as a totem.

MĀRKAṆḌEYA PURĀṆA (Probably earlier than 6th.cent. A.D.)

The following pieces of information are scattered in it. The verse 61.57 refers to charming song accompained by the lute and the flute.68.26 mentions the instruments *Vīṇā*, *Veṇu* and *Mṛdaṅga*, and refers to song and dance. Besides the above, the following instruments are mentioned in 106.61:

Dardura, Paṇava, Puṣkara, Paṭaha, Ānaka, Dundubhi, Śaṃkha.

In the following verse, we have the expression *turyavāditra*. It is not clear whether *Vāditra* denotes instrumental music in general or a particular instrument; according to dictionaries, the word has been used in both these senses in different contexts. For example, in the *Naiṣadha-carita* XXII.22, *Vāditra* denotes an instrument.

1. *Vedottara Saṃgīta, p.25.*

The word *tūrya* also appears to be used to denote both instrumental music in general as in Manu VII.225 (*Vāditra*, according to Kullūka), and a particular instrument as in *Kumārasambhava*, VII.10.

Some of the above instruments are mentioned also in 128.24. From 10.93 we learn that dancing girls used to put on ornaments like necklace and anklets. 106.60 refers to dancing in a dramatic performance.

It is in chapter 13 that we get some information which is valuable for the history of musicology. Verses 51 and 52 of this chapter mention the following: Seven *svaras*, seven *grāmarāgas*, seven kinds of *gītas* (songs), seven *mūrchanās*, forty-nine *tālas*, three *grāmas*. Svāmī Prajñānānanda thinks that, by seven *mūrchanās, the author intends the seven mūrchanās* of only the *Ṣaḍja-grāma* which is the chief of the *grāmas*.

Verse 23.52 mentions four kinds of *Pada*, three kinds of *Tāla* and three kinds of *Laya*.

This Purāṇa mentions also three *yatis* and four kinds of instruments.

SKANDAPURĀṆA

This Purāṇa regards Śiva as *Nāda*. The *Rāgas*, emanating from Śiva, are stated to be formless (*amūrta*); they are possessed of *līlāvapu* (body assumed as a sport).

The Kāśīkhaṇḍa part of this Purāṇa contains glorification of music. Tumburu and Nārada are stated to have attained greatness through this art. It is declared as a medium of worshipping Hari and Hara.

The Nāgarakhaṇḍa section of this Purāṇa contains considerable information on music, thus testifying to the high degree of its development. Each of the following *Rāgas* is stated to have six consorts: Śrī-Gaurī (Gauḍī?), Kolāhalī, Dhira, Draviḍī Māla(va?) Kauśikī, Devagāndhārī; Vasanta-Āndolā, Kauśikī, Caramañjarī, Gaṇḍagiri, Devaśākhā, Rāmagiri.

Pañcama-Triguṇā, Stambhatīrthā, Āhīrī.

Kuṅkumā, Vairāṭī, Sāmanerī

Bhairava-Bhairvaī, Gurjarī, Bhāṣā, Velāvalī, Devagiri, Devālī.

Naṭṭanārāyaṇa-Troṭakī, Narādumbī, Malhārī, Sindhumalhārī

This Purāṇa refers also to three *grāmas*, seven *svaras* and various modes of singing.

VĀYUPURĀṆA (c.between 3rd. cent. and 5th. cent. A.D.)

Chapters 86 (Verse 3 onward) and 87 of the *Vāyupurāṇa* are devoted exclusively to music. It should be noted that the portion on music is not found in some manuscripts of this work. This tends to indicate that this portion was a later interpolation. This inference is corroborated by the fact that the portion, dealing with music, is irrelevant where it occurs.

It deserves notice that the above portion is singularly lacking in references to Bharata and his *Nāṭyaśāstra*. From this fact some think that this portion originated before the *Nāṭyaśāstra*. This surmise seems to be justified in view of the fact that this portion of the Purāṇa reveals similarity, in certain matters, with the *Nāradīya Śikṣā. As we shall see later, one verse of the Purana is identical with a verse of the Nāradīya Śikṣā.* It is, perhaps, significant that the names of the *Tānas*, mentioned in this Purāṇa, are different in comparison with those usually mentioned in the works on musicology.

Gāndharva-vidyā is stated to be one of 18 *Vidyās* (61.78-80). *Sāmaveda* has been mentioned (65.22:26) as *śarva-geya-purahsara*' (the best of all songs). *Saṃgīta* has been associated with Śiva (eg.,30.198ff). Śiva has been described as *mukhavāditrakārī* (30.198ff) i.e., maker of that kind of musical instruments which can be played with the mouth. He is *gītaśīla* (24.142-43), i.e., accustomed to songs; *tumbavīṇāpriya* (30.203) i.e., fond of the lute of the *Tumba* type (Vide *SR.* VI.29-53), *Kiṃkiṇika* (24.148), ie., one who dances and sings wearing anklets. Śiva is stated to play the instrument called *Ghaṇṭā.* The ghosts are said to give him delight with dance and song accompanied by various instruments. (40.24-25). The *Siddhas* also are stated to serve him with *saṃgīta.* There is mention (30.119) of prayer to Śiva with *Rathantara Sāman.*

In connexion with *Svaramaṇḍala (86.36), mention has been made of seven svaras.* three *grāmas,* twenty-one *Mūrchanās* and forty-nine *tālas..*

There are references (e.g., 62.137-8, 68.37 etc.) to *Sāman* songs sung at sacrifices. There is mention (80.10-15) of the glorification, to the accompaniment of vocal and instrumental music, of those who make gifts in *Śrāddhas.*

The three *grāmas,* mentioned in it, are *Madhyama, Ṣaḍja* and *Gāndhāra.* They are of 20, 14 and 15 varieties respectively.

The number of *Mūrchanās* differs in different *grāmas.* The *Mūrchanās* of the *Madhyama grāma* are (86.38-39): *Sauvīrī, Hariṇāsyā, Kalopa-natā, Śuddhamadhyamā, Śāriṅgī, Pāvanī* and *Dṛṣṭakā,* etc.

The *Mūrchanās* of the *Gāndhāragrāma* are (86.39-41); *Uttaramandrā, Rajanī, Uttarāyaṭā. Śuddha-ṣaḍjā,* etc.

The *Mūrchanās* of the Gāndhāragrāma are (86.4.49: *Āgniṣṭomikā, Vājapeyikā, Pauṇḍrakā, Aśvamedhikā, Rājasūyā, Cakrasuvarṇakā, Gosava, Mahāvṛṣṭika, Brahmadāna, Prājāpatya, Nāgapakṣāśraya. Gotara, Hayakrānta, Mṛgakrānta, Viṣṇukrānta, Sūryakrānta, Sāvitra, Ardhasāvitra, Sarvato-bhadra, Suvarṇa, Sutantra, Viṣṇu, Viṣṇuvara, Sāgara, Vijaya, Haṃsa, Aghātra, Vikala, Upanīta, Vinata, Śrī, Abhiramya, Puṇyāraka.*

In connexion with songs, three *Sthānas* have been mentioned; viz., *Vakṣaḥ* (chest), *Kaṇṭha* (throat) and *Mastaka* (head). The *Svaras,* arising from these places (known respectively as *Mandra, Madhya* and *Tāra)* are the best.

In songs, *Varṇas* are of four kinds, viz., *Sthāyī, Saṃcārī, Ārohī* and *Avarohī.*

This Purāṇa speaks of *Gītālaṅkāras* (embellishments of songs). As misplaced ornaments in the body (e.g. earrings on the feet, girdle over throat) cause loss of grace to it, so also improper use of *gītālaṃkāras* detract from the charm of songs instead of enhancing it.

For *gītālaṃkāras* the following four are stated to be necessary; viz. *Saṃsthāna, Pramāṇa, Vikāra and Lakṣaṇa.*

The basic *gītālaṃkāras* are four—*Sthāpanī, Krama-rejinī, Pramāda* and *Apramāda.* The total number of primary and secondary *Alaṃkāras* is 300 (87.1).

That part of *Saṃgīta,* containing incomplete *pada,* in which *Tālas* are not arranged in accordance with *Mātrās,* is called *Mativīraṇā (87.39). The part, which is lacking in the fixed number of Mātrās,* is called *Yāna* (87.39). The reducing of two or more *Svaras* into one is called *Patākāhariṇa* (87.44). The combination of the threefold *Vrttis* of *Saṃgīta* is called *Dakṣiṇa* (87.45).

The discussion on the fundamental facts of *Saṃgīta,* contained in chapter 86 of this Purāṇa, appears to follow the *Nāradīya Śikṣā.* The *Śikṣā* verse I.2.4 occurs verbatim in 86.36 of this Purāṇa (Vaṅgavāsī ed.).

There is one difference between the two. In place of the term *tāna* in the *Śikṣā, the Purāṇa has tāla.* There is, however, the possiblity of confusion between *La* and *Na* in Devanāgarī script. The points of similarity between the above two works clearly indicate that one borrowed from the other. The Śikṣā cannot possibly be the borrower, because being a Vedāṅga it must have preceded the Purāṇa. So, it is the Purāṇa which may be taken as the borrower.

The Purāṇas testify to the fact that some musical instruments are included among military equipments and appurtenances. For example, the *Agnipurāṇa* (269-35-37) states that the rumbling of the war-drum, while spurring the army of one party to action, strikes terror in the hearts of the adversaries. In the *Mārkaṇḍeya* (ch.82), it is stated that the gods used *ghaṇṭā* (bell) in order to terrorise the demons in battle. The *Matsya* (ch.136) mentions the *Rauravī Bherī*. There is a hell called Raurava. The above type of *bherī(drum) was, perhaps, used to cause hellish fear to the enemies. Among the other musical instruments, included in the Purāṇic list of military equippage,are the following: ḍamaru, Paṭaha, Vīṇā, Ānaka, Paṇava, Gomukha, Mṛdaṅga, Mardala* and Tūrya.

There is, however, no information about their shape and methods of construction.

VIṢṆUDHARMOTTARA PURĀṆA (Sometime between C.450 and 650 A.D.)

Of all the Purāṇic treatises, this Purāṇa (Vol.III) appears to contain the largest amount of material on music and dance. The burden of the discussion on fine arts is that these are interdependent. True knowledge of the one is not possible without a sound knowledge of the other. It is stated that the art of painting is very difficult to master (*sudurvida) without the knowledge of the dance-lore which, in its turn, is difficult to know without Ātodya* (instrumental music) which again is beyond the ken of one devoid of the knowledge of vocal music.

In volume three of this treatise, chapter XVIII is devoted to *Gītalakṣaṇa* and the following chapter to *Ātodya* (musical instruments). By and large, the author or compiler follows the *Nāṭya-śāstra* and the *Dattilam.*

Vocal music (chap.18)

Gīta (song) is stated to be twofold, viz. *Saṃskṛta* and *Prākṛta.* The broad topics, dealt with in this treatise, are briefly as follows:

Three *Sthānas*, viz. *Mandra, Madhya* and *Tāra*, three *Grāmas* called *Ṣaḍja, Madhyama and Gāndhāra,* seven *Svaras,* 21 *Mūrchaṇās*, 49 *Tānas*, 10 *Jātis*, 4 *Alaṃkāras*, songs with *Svara, Pada, Laya, etc.,* 22 *Śrutis.*

According to this treatise, the different *Svaras* manifest *Rasas* in the following way:

Name of *Svara*	Name of *Rasa*
Ṣaḍja and *Pañcama*	Hāsya
Ṣaḍja and Ṛṣabha	Vīra, Adbhuta and Raudra
Niṣāda and Gāndhāra	Karuṇa
Dhaivata	Bībhatsa and Bhayānaka
Madhyama	Śānta

This work mentions also *Tālas* of four and eight *mātrās*, *Śamya tāla* and the three kinds of *laya*.

The notable departures in the Purāṇa from the traditional ideas, are breifly as follows.

While Bharata mentions two *grāmas*, viz. *Ṣaḍja* and *Madhyama*, the Purāṇa adds *Gāndhāra*. The fact seems to be that though, at the time of the Purāṇa, *Gāndhāra* passed out of vogue, yet, the author mentions it just as a matter of form or in consonance with the academic practice.

Bharata mentions eight *Rāgas*, but this Purāṇa adds *Sānta* as the ninth.

Considerable divergence between this Purāṇa and the *Saṃgitamakaranda* of Nārada is noticeable in the names of the *Tānas*.

Instrumental music

It has been dealt with in chapter 19. The Purāṇa mentions the instruments belonging to all the four classes of *Tata*, *Suṣira*, *Avanaddha* and *Ghana*.

The author specifies the ways in which the male and female artistes should sit with their instruments on the stage.

Dance

It has been dealt with in III. 20,24,25,218.

In connexion with dance, the Purāna mentions *Aingahāra*, *Karaṇa*, *Maṇḍala*, *Mudrā*.

VII

TANTRA AND MUSIC

Tantra originated (C. 5th. or 6th. cent.A.D.) as a protest against the conventional Brāhmaṇical religion and sacerdotalism. It sought to show the path for attaining liberation (*mukti*) through enjoyment (*bhukti*) in contrast to the traditional religion whcih advocated austerities and self-moritification as the means of attaining the goal. It gave considerable freedom to women and Śūdras in religious observances. Thus, Tantra became very popular. Its influences was pervasive. Its impact on Purāṇas and Smṛti-śāstra was tremendous. The musical lore also came within the ambit of its influence. We shall briefly state, on the basis of the *Saṃgitaratnākara* of Śārṅgadeva, how Tāntric ideas were adopted in the musicology of ancient and medieval India.

CAKRA

Like Tantra, musicology recognises *Cakras*(nerve-plexuses or mystical circles) within the body, which are fancied as lotuses of varying number of petals. It may be noted that, instead of the usual six Tāntric *Cakras* Śārṅgaideva recognises nine principal ones. The *Viśuddhi-cakra* (in tne throat) is stated to be the resort of *Svaras.* This *Cakra is conceived as a lotus with sixteen petals. The soul, residing in the eighth and some other petals, wants success in music. The sixth and some other petals mar songs, etc. Resort to eight petals, beginning with the eighth, brings about success in vocal music, etc. Its sixteenth petal spoils them. The tenth and eleventh petals of Lalanā-cakra* (in the forehead) cause success. The first and some other petals of it are destroyers. The soul in the *brahmarandhra* (a passage in the cerebal region) seems to be contented being soaked with nectar, and leads to the accomplishent of the best kinds of songs, etc.

According to Śārṅgadeva, the area two *aṅgulas* above

Ādhā
racakra (generally called *Mūlādhāra* in between the anus and the genital organ) is called *dehamadhya* measuring one *aṅgugla*. In it, there is a slender flame of fire. Nine *aṅgulas* away from it, there is the body-root, called *brahmagranthi*, measuring four *aṅgulas* in height and width. In it, there is *nābhicakra* with twelve petals. In it, the soul moves about like a spider in the cobweb.

NĀḌĪ

Nāḍis (nerves) are innumerable. Of them, thirteen including the three principal ones, *called Iḍā, Piṅgalā, Suṣumnā*, are important.

VĀYU

Ten kinds of winds are supposed to be within the body. Of these, *Prāṇa* is the chief being the source of inhalation and exhalation. *Apāna* generates sound.

NĀDA

Nāda or sound is twofold, *āhata*(struck) and *anāhata* (non-struck, spontaneous). *Anāhata* is changeless and inaudible, and is a subject of meditation. *Āhata nāda*, giving rise to *Śruti* and the like, expands songs, and is ever-changing. Twenty-two *nāḍis* are supposed to be united with the upward artery. These exist in an oblique manner. When the wind strikes against them, twenty-two *Śrutis* arise. In the same way, twenty-two *Śrutis* are admitted in the throat and the head.

MUDRĀ

It is the Tāntric name of certain positions of hands or fingers in connexion with *saṃgīta*, particularly with dance.

ŚIVA-ŚAKTI

Tāntric philosophy revolves around the dual principle of Śiva-Śaki. In musical lore, too, *Rāgas* and *Rāgiṇīs* are traditionally supposed to have issued from the mouths of Śiva and Śakti respectively. According to a tradition, one *Rāga* came out of each of the five mouths of Śiva, and the sixth emanated from the mouth of Pārvatī.

The influence of Tantra was pervasive. It was very popular. No wonder, therefore, that the populist Tantra included, within its ambit, music also the appeal of which was universal.

The influence of Tantra on music, however, was not a one-way traffic. Music, in its turn, also influenced Tantra.

Some works among the thirty-two *Yāmala-tantras* deal with music, as we shall presently see. These are valuable also as referring to the earlier authorities on music, eg. Umāmaheśvara, Bharata, Nandin, Vāsuki, Nārada, Durgā, Yāṣṭika, Dattila. In this connexion, the *Yamalāṣṭaka-tantra* deserves special mention. It states that *Gāndharvaveda* (science of music) consists of 36,000 works (*ṣaṭ-triṃśat-sahasra-grantha*). It mentions the following matters relating to music.

Saptasvara, Vīṇā, Kalā, Rāga, Tāla, Gīta, Lāsikā (female dancer), Ullāsikā(?), Mela, Jāti, Graha, Laya, Sthāna, Mārga, Aṅgaprakriyā, Kāla, Vādya, Aṅgahāra, etc.

Of the 32 *Yāmalatantras*, the ninth, *Kalātantra*, deals with *Rasa, Bhāva, Nāṭya* and Kāmaśāstra; these have a bearing on music and dance. The nineteenth, the *Vīṇātantra* comprehends the entire domain of music; it prescribes means to the attainment of the highest bliss of the realisation of Supreme Being in the form of *Nāda* or Sound (*nāda-brahmānanda-siddhi*). The highlights of its contents are as follows:

Niṣādādi-svarotpatti, Gītotpatti, Rāgabheda, Rāgakāla, Dhvanibheda, Miśra, Amiśra (i.e., Śuddha), *Tāla, Śruti, Laya, Caturvidha-vīṇā-lakṣaṇa, Tantrilakṣaṇa, Kinnara-svara-yantra, Mela, Ṣaḍgīta*, etc.

The twenty-eighth *Yāmalatantra*, viz. the *Trotāla* , deals with:

Tāla, Aṅgulonmāna, Mārgakriyā, Jāti, Kalā, Graha, Laya, Sapta-tāla Vaināyikānām Aiśānāṃ Vāgbhavānāṃ lakṣaṇa, Tālakoṭi, Tribhinna (name of a measure), *Līlā (a kind of metre?)* etc.

UḌḌĪŚA-MAHĀMANTRODAYA[1]

Among the Tantras, it deals most elaborately with musical instruments. In sixteen separate chapters, it discusses sixteen different instruments which are as follows:

Tālanilaya, Sallari, Patana, Maddala, Bherī-vignā(?), *Himila, Thuthuka, Mitha.* (?), *Ḍamaru, Murava, Aṅgulisphoṭa, Vīṇā, Ālamani*(?), Rāvaṇa-hastaka, Udyanta, Ghoṣavatī, Brahmaka[2](?).

Krishnamachariar informs us that the *Kāśyapatantra* also has similar chapters on the subject.

---

1. T.C.III. 3987. Reference taken from Krishnamachariar's *Hist. of Class, Skt.Lit.*, p.842. He observes, "The name *Tālavidhāna*, there given, does not seem to be correct."

2. Query marks are put against the names which are not legible in the above work of Krishnamachariar. The names of 17, instead of 16, instruments are given.

VIII

RĀGAS AND RĀGIṆĪS[1]

The term *Rāga* is very old. For instance, it occurs in the *Nāradīya Śikṣā*. I. ii. 2. But, the term *Rāgiṇī* is very late. It does not occur even in such a late work as the *Saṃgītaratnākara* (13th. cent.). Instead, we find the terms *Bhāṣā*, *Vibhāṣā* and Antarabhāṣā.

Rāga, derived from the root *Rañj* (to please), denotes something that pleases the listeners. Mataṅga (probably of the Gupta period) defines it as *rañjako janacittānāṃ sa ca rāga udāhṛtaḥ*: that is called *Rāga* which delights the hearts of the people. Generally, it is defined as a sound, consisting of *svara* and *varṇa*, which pleases the mind of the people. In this sense, it is hardly different from the western harmony. The chord, expressive of harmony, is also a sound, consisting of *svara* and *varṇa*, which attracts the mind of the people. The question arises—how does *Rāga-saṃgīta* differ from harmony-song? The difference lies in the fact that *Rāga* is an arrangement of *svaras* in which the order or succession of *svaras* predominates, and is subject to a principle; in harmony, there is a harmonious or simultaneous sound of *svaras*.

The origin of *Rāga* is obscure. Where history is silent, mythology speaks. Dāmodara (C. 17th. cent. A.D.) records the tradition that *Rāga* owes its origin to the union of Śiva and Śakti. One *Rāga* is said to have emanated from each of the five mouths of Śiva,

---

1. For a fairly exhaustive enumeration of *Rāgas* and *Rāgiṇīs*, see the *Sarasvatī-hṛdayālaṃkāra*, otherwise called *Bharata-bhāṣya* or *Bharatavārtika*, of Nānyadeva. For general information about *Rāgas* and *Rāgiṇīs*, see O.C. Ganguly, *Rāgas* and *Rāgiṇis*.

Also see Rāga under Select Technical Terms.

while the sixth one emerged form the mouth of *Pārvatī*. This is how the idea of six *Rāgas* originated.

As a matter of fact, however, we come across a number of *Rāgas*, besides the traditional six. For example, Śārṅgadeva mentions (*Saṃgītaratnākara*, II.16-18) the following twenty *Rāgas*: Śrī, Naṭṭa, Vaṅgāla (2), Bhāṣā, Madhyma-ṣāḍava, Raktahaṃsa, Kolhahāsa, Prasava, Bhairava, Dhvani, Megha, Soma, Kāmoda (2), Āmrapañcama, Kandarpa, Deśa, Kaiśikakakubha, Naṭṭanārāyaṇa. Besides, he mentions the following eight *Uparāgas.*[1] Śakatilaka, Ṭakkasaindhava, Kokilāpañcama, Revagupta, Pañcamaṣāḍava, Bhāvanāpañcama, Nāgagāndhāra, and Nāgapañcama. The following fifteen are, on the authority of Yāṣṭika, stated to be the *janaka* (begetter or source) of Bhāṣās[2].

The *Rāgas*, with their respective *Bhāṣās*, according to Sārṅgadeva, are given below:

Janaka Rāga	Bhāsā, Vibhāṣā and Antarabhāṣā.
Sauvīra	Bhāṣās are; Sauvīrī, Vegamadhyamā, Sādhāritā, Gāndhārī.
Kakubha	Bhinnapañcamī, Kāmbhojī, Madhyamagrāmā, Ragantī, Madhurī, Śakamiśra Vibhāṣās are Bhogavardhanī, Ābhīrikā, Madhukarī, Antarabhāṣā, Śālavāhanikā
Ṭakka	Bhāṣās are—Śravaṇā, Śravaṇoddhavī, Vairañjī, Madhyama-Grāmadehā, Mālavavesarī, Chevāṭī, Saindhavī, Kolāhalā, Pañcamalakṣitā, Saurāṣṭrī, Pañcamī, Vegarañjī, Gāndhārapañcamī, Mālavī, Tānavalitā, Lalitā, Ravicandrikā, Tānā, Ambā-

1. Though arising from *Jātis*, yet so called as they emanate from near *Grāmarāga*.

2. What is known as *Rāgiṇī*, in later times, appears to have been termed *Bhāṣā*, *Vibhāṣā* and *Antarabhāsā* in earlier times.

	herikā, Dohyā, Vesarī, Vibhāṣās Devāravardhanī, Āndhrī, Gurjarī, Bhāvanī.
Pañcama	Bhāṣās—Kaiśikī, Trāvaṇī, Tānodbhavā, Ābhīrī, Gurjarī, Saindhavī, Dākṣiṇātyā, Āndhrī, Māṅgalī, Bhāvanī, Vibhāṣās-Bhāmānī, Āndhālikā.
Bhinnapañcama	Bhāṣās—Dhaivatabhūṣitā, Suddhabhinnā, Vārāṭī, Viśālā. Vibhāṣā-Kauśalī.
Ṭakkakaiśka	Bhāṣās—Mālavā, Bhinnavalitā, Vibhāṣā-Drāviḍī
Hindola (Preṅkhaka)	Bhāṣās—Vesarī, Cūtamañjarī, Ṣaḍjamadhyamā, Madhurī, Bhinnapaurālī, Gauḍī, Mālavavesarī, Chevāṭī, Piñjarī.
Boṭṭa	Bhāsā—Māṅgalī
Mālavakaiśika	Bhāṣās—Vāṅgālī, Māṅgalī, Harṣapurī, Mālava-vesarī, Khañjanī, Gurjarī, Gauḍī, Paurālī, Ardhavesarī, Śuddhā, Mālavarūpā Saindhavī, Ābhīrikā. Vibhāṣās—Kāmbhojī, Devāravardhanī.
Gāndhārapañcama	Bhāṣā Gāndhārī
Bhinnaṣaḍja	Bhāṣās—Gāndhāravallī Kacchellī, Svaravallī, Nivādinī, Travaṇā Madhyamā, Śuddhā, Dākṣiṇātyā, Pulindakā, Tumburā, Ṣaḍjabhāṣā, Kālindī, Lalitā, Śrī-Kaṇṭhikā, Vāṅgālī, Gāndhārī, Saindhavī, Vibhāṣās—Paurālī, Mālavā, Kālindī, Devāravardhanī.
Vesaraṣāḍava	Bhāṣās—Nādyā, Bāhyaṣāḍavā. Vibhāṣās—Pārvatī, Śrīkaṇṭhī.
Mālavapañcama	Bhāṣās—Vedavatī, Bhāvanī, Vibhāvanī.
Tāna	Bhāṣā-Tānodbhavā.
Pañcamaṣāḍava	Bhāṣā-Potā

Revagupta — Bhāṣā (according to some) Śakā, Vibhāṣā—Pallavī. Antarabhāṣā—Bhāsavalitā, Kiranāvalī, Śakavalitā.

Note: Pallavī—Śakavalitā are mentioned in the *Bṛhaddeśī* without Janaka.

Mataṅga is stated, by Śārṅgadeva, to have declared *Bhāṣās* of four kinds; viz. *Mukhyā, Svarākhyā, Deśākhyā* and *Uparāgajā.* That is called *Mukhyā* which does not depend on anything else. That which is named after a *svara* is called *Svarākhyā* (e.g., *Gāndhārī*). That which takes its name from a *deśa* (country) is called *Deśākhyā* (e.g. *Āndhrī*). Different from these there is the *Uparāgadeva* (arising from *Uparāga* state above.). According to commentator, Siṃhabhūpāla, it originated from the above three. The above four classes are stated, by Śārṅgadeva, to have been named by *Yāṣṭika,* as *Saṃkīrṇā, Deśajā, Mūlā, Chāyāmātrā.* According to commentator Kallinātha, *Mukhyā,* etc. are called respectively *Mūlā, Saṃkīrṇā, Deśajā* and *Chāyāmātrā.*

The following twenty are regarded as fundamental or basic *Rāgas:*

Kānāḍā, Kāfi, Kāmodā, Khāmbāj, Gauḍasāraṅg, Naṭa, Vṛndāvanī-sāraṅg, Velāval, Vehāg, Bhairava, Mālkoṣ, Mālaśrī, Megha, Lalita, Śaṃtarā, Śuddha Kalyāṇa, Śuddha Mallāra, Śrī, Sindhu, Hindola.

Besides the four classes of *Bhāṣās,* etc. we find another class which derives names from different classes of aborigines. In later times, some *Rāgiṇīs* are named after aborigines; eg Bhairavī, Sāverī (same as Śābarī), Ābhīrī.

Some prominent *Rāgas* and *Rāgiṇīs,* named after different regions, are as follows:

Mālava or Mālavī, Dakṣiṇī or Dākṣīṇātyā, Karṇāṭī or Kānāḍā, Saurāṣṭrī, Gauḍī, Vāṅgāli, Gurjarī.

From Armenia comes Hārmāna.

Some notable *Rāgas* and *Rāgiṇīs*, named after different races, are:

Gurjara and Gurjarī, Drāviḍī, Āndhrī.

From foreign races some Rāgas and Rāgiṇīs have taken their names; e.g. Śaka, Turuṣka-toḍi, Turuska-gauḍa.

Śrīkaṇṭha, in his *Rasakaumudī* (C. 16th. cent., first quarter), gives us *Dhyānas* or poetical *mantras* relating to *Rāgas* and *Rāgiṇīs*. Somanātha (c.1609 A.D.), in his *Rāgavibodha*, introduced the pictorical concept of *Rāgas* and *Rāgiṇīs*. He deals with both the Nādamaya and Devatāmaya aspects of *Rāgas*. The Indian musicologists did not rest content with the body or external aspect of melodies; they were concerned with their soul or the inner element too. It may be added that paintings of *Rāgas* and *Rāgiṇīs* started being drawn in Rajputana (Rājasthan) in the 13th. century. We find specimens of this art in the extensive tract of land form Bikaner to Gujarat and from Jodhpur to Gwalior and Ujjain. There are many specimens of such paintings among Pāhā ri Paintings; this art developed, to a great extent, in the area from Jammu to Almora..The contribution of Jammu and Kangra is oustanding. The art of painting *Rāgas* and *Rāgiṇīs* flourished considerably under the Mughals, and also in the post-Mughal period. In this respect, the contribution of Mursidabad in Bengal (now West Bengal) deserves special mention. The Mursidabad paintings reveal a mixture of Rajput and Mughal styles with a distinctive Bengali touch. Of these, the representations of the *Rāgas Hindola, Kakubha* and Śyāmaguñjarī, all dated 1755 A.D., were painted during the time of Nawab Siraj-ud-daula of Bengal (1756-1757).

It should be noted that the conception of the forms of *Rāgas* and *Rāgiṇīs* is highly sensuous and evocative. They are imbued with *Rasa*(sentiment) and *Bhāva* (emotion) of which we hear so much in *Alaṃkāra-śāstra*. The later rhetoricians emphasised

Rasa as the essential element of poetry[1], *Rasa* was considered to be the indispensable substratum of the different forms of *Rāgas* and *Rāgiṇīs* that were conceived. The *dhyānas* of *Rāgas* and *Rāgiṇīs* reveal different moods and sentiments[2]. We have reproduced some such *dhyānas* in Appendix IV. The *Rasas*, generally recognised in poetics, are eight, viz. *Śṛṅgāra* (erotic), *Hāsya* (comic), *Karuṇa* (pathetic), *Raudra* (furious), *Vīra* (heroic), *Bhayānaka* (terrible), *Bībhatsa* (disgusting), *Adbhuta*(marvellous), To these some add the *Sānta* (quietistic) sentiment. The permanent feelings of emotions (*sthāyibhāva*), underlying the above sentiments, are respectively *Rati* (love), Hāsa (mirth), *Śoka* (sorrow), *Krodha* (anger), *Utsāha* (courage), *Bhaya* (fear), *Jugupsā* (aversion), *Vismaya* (wonder).

Rāgas have been classified form different points of view. These are generally threefold, viz.

Saṃpūrṇa—Complete in all the *svaras*.

Ṣāḍava—consisting of six *svaras*.

Auḍava—comprising five *svaras*. In another way, these are divided as

Śuddha—pure.

Sālaga or

Chāyālaga—a *rāga* containing the *Chayā* (shadow, i.e., faint likeness) of another *rāga*. In other words, it is a *rāga* constituted of two *rāgas*.

Saṃkīrṇa—consisting of an admixture of *Śuddha* and *Chāyālaga* *rāgas*.

Divāgeya—to be sung by day.

Sandhyāgeya—fit for being sung in the evening.

---

1. *C.f.vākyaṃ rasātmakaṃ kāvyam—Sāhityadarpaṇa.*

2. See Svāmī Prajñānānanda, *Cultural Heritage of Indian Fine Arts*, 1983; pp.110-117, and his work in Bengali, *Rāg O Rūp*, Pūrvabhāga, Uttarārdha, pp 212-226.

or

Ūṣogeya—fit to be sung at dawn.

Rātrigeya—to be sung by night.

There has been a seasonal division also according to some Sanskrit works on musicology, as we shall see hereafter.

According to Bhātkhaṇḍe, a division of the current Hindustānī songs into three classes is as follows:

1. *Rāga* with *Śuddha RA* and *Śuddha DHA.*
2. *Rāga* with *Komala RA* with *Komala DHA.*
3. *Rāga* with *Komala GA* and *Komala NA.*

Some writers have declared different hours of the day and the night as suitable for different *Rāgas* and *Rāgiṇīs*. For instance, according to *Dāmodara, Megharāga, Bhairavī* and *Velāvalī* are to be sung from morning. *Śrīrāga, Karṇāṭī* and *Kedārī* are fit to be sung from after the third *prahara* up to midnight.

Dāmodara, however, adds that any *rāga* may be sung at any time at the behest of the king. According to him, the *Rāgas Śrī, Vasanta, Bhairava, Pañ*cama, Megha and *Naṭṭanārāyaṇa* are fit for being sung respectively in winter, spring, summer, autumn, rainy season and dewy season. This rule is also not rigid. The author ordains that any *rāga* may be sung in any season, if it proves to be pleasant.

IX

SELECT TECHNICAL TERMS

(Mainly based on the *Nāṭyaśāstra* and *Saṃgīta-ratnākara*)

Abbreviations used

DR — Daśarūpaka

Nṛtyādhyāya—a work by Aśokamalla.

NS — Nāṭyaśāstra

SR — Saṃgītaratnākara

Y — Yājñavalkya-smṛti

(In Devanāgarī alphabetical order)

AṄGAPĀṬAKA

SR. II. 1016

A kind of *Yati* (q.v.).

AṄGAHĀRA

NS.I.44, IV. 175-1213

SR VII. 790,797 etc.,

102-888, 1206, 1213

1) Graceful posture or movement of the body in dancing or acting.

2) A kind of *lāsyāṅga* (q.v.) in which there is gradual graceful bending of the two parts of the body,

accompained by beating of time (*tāla*), like a bow.

AṄGHRITĀḌITA

SR.VII. 1007-8

A kind of *Deśī Cārī* (q.v.).

of the aerial type.

AÑCITA

SR.VII.340

A particular posture of the arms.

VII.312-14

A particular position of feet.

VII.594-95

A kind of *Karaṇa* (q.v.).

in dance.

VII. 757

A kind of *Utpluti-karaṇa*

(q.v.). See *Karaṇa.*

AÑCITABHRAMARĪ

SR.VII. 780

A kind of *Utplutikaraṇa* (q.v.).

See *Karaṇa.*

AḌḌAKHALĪ

SR. Just below VI.851a.

A kind of *Pāṭa* (q.v.).

AḌḌASKHALITA

SR.VII.1000

A kind of terrestrial Deśī Cārī (q.v.).

AḌḌĀVAJA

SR.VI.824

A kind of *Pāṭaha* (q.v.).

AḌḌITA

NS. XII.58

SR.VII.1160-63

A kind of terrestrial *Maṇḍala* (q.v.).

ADDITĀ
NS.XI.23, 32.11
SR.VII.934
1) A kind of *Cārī* (q.v.).
2) A kind of *Dhruva* (q.v.).

ATIKRĀNTA
NS.XII.9
SR.VII.1174-77
A kind of *Maṇḍala* (q.v.).

ATIKRĀNTĀ
NS.XI.30
SR.VII.942-44
A kind of *Cārī* (q.v.).

ATIVĀDITA
NS.XXVIII.56
See under *Vādya.*

ADBHUTA
SR.VII.392-93
1494-1504
A kind of gaze or a kind of sentiment.

ADHYARDHA
NS.XII.62
SR.VII.1167-68
A kind of *Maṇḍala* (q.v.).

ADHYARADHIKA
NS.XI.17
SR.VII.923-24
A kind of *Cārī* (q.v.).

ANIBADDHA
SR.IV.4,18,24
A kind of song devoid of words. Also called *Ālapti* (q.v.). or *Ālāpa.*

ANUCCHALLA

SR.VI.839,below 851 (a)
A kind of *Pāṭa* (q.v.).

ANUBANDHA
SR.VI.127,148, 150
152,161
A kind of *Dhātu* (q.v.).

ANUBHĀVA
SR.VII.1399-91
Activity, glance, movement of brows, complexion, etc. indicating love, etc. One of the elements in the manifestation of *Rasa* (sentiment).

ANUVĀDĪ
NS.XXVIII.22
SR.I.3.48,50 etc.
A *Svara* (q.v.) which serves to manifest clearly the *Saṃvādī* (q.v.) *Svara*. For example, the *Anuvādī svaras* of Śaḍja are Ṛṣabha, Gāndhāra, Dhaivata, Niṣāda. According to some modern musicologists, all the *svaras* of a *Rāga*, excepting *Vādī* and *Saṃvādī*, are *Anuvādi*.

ANUVĀDITA
NS.XXXIII.57
See under *Vādya*.

ANTARAPĀṬA
SR.VI.947,1001
A kind of *Vādyaprabandha*.

ANTARABHĀṢĀ
SR.II.1.23.ff
A sort of minor *Bhāṣā* (q.v.). Four *Antarabhāṣās* have been mentioned by Śārṅgadeva.

ANTARĀLAGA
SR.VII.762-63
A kind of *Utpluti-karaṇa* (q.v.).
See *Karaṇa*.

ANTARBHRAMARĪ
SR.VII.776
A kind of *Utplutikaraṇa* (q.v.).
See *Karaṇa.*

APAKRĀNTA
SR.VII.713
A kind of *Nṛttakaraṇa* (q.v.).
See *Karaṇa.*

APAKRĀNTĀ
NS.XI.31
SR.VII.944-45
A kind of *Cārī* (q.v.).

APAKṢEPĀ
SR.VII.1005
A kind of terrestrial Dèśī Cārī (q.v.).

APAḌAPA
SR.VII.1304-6
A kind of *Gharghara* (q.v.).

APARĀJITA
SR.VII.810-11
A kind of *Aṅgahāra* (q.v.).

APARĀNTAKA
NS.XXXI.220
Y III.113
A kind of song included,
in the *Mitākṣarā* commentary,
among the seven kinds of songs called
Prakara. (q.v.).

APAVIDDHA
SR.VII.845-47
A kind of *Aṅgahāra* (q.v.).
VII.339
A particular position

of the arms. [VII,595-97
A kind of *Nṛttakaraṇa.*
See *Karaṇa.*

APASARPITA
SR.VII.831-33
A kind of *Aṅgahāra* (q.v.).

ABHITAPTA
SR.VII.416-17
A kind of glance.

ARAṆYAGĀNA
Book of forest-song, attached
to the *Āreīka* (q.v.).

ARĀLA
NS.XXVI.12
SR.VII.122-28
A particular position
of the palm or fingers.
Name of a *Vartanā* (q.v.).

ARĀLAKHAṬAKĀMUKHA
SR.VII.224-29
A particular position
of the hands or fingers
in dance.

ARGALA
SR.VII.664-66
A kind of *Nṛttakaraṇa.*
See *Karaṇa.*

ARDHAKARTARĪ
SR.VI.67,81,92,845
A particular position of the hands.

ARDHACANDRA
SR.VII.117-19.
VI.68,86

A particular position of the single palm in dance.
Name of a particular position of the hands in dance.

ARDHANIKUṬṬAKA
SR.VII.98,135
A kind of *Nṛttakaraṇa* and a kind of *Aṅgahāra* (q.v.).
See *Karaṇa.*

ARDHAPURĀṬĪKĀ
SR. VII.996-7
A kind of terrestrial *Deśī Cārī* (q.v.).

ARDHAMAṆḌALA
Name of a *Vartanā* (q.v.).

ARDHAMAṆḌALIKĀ
SR.VII.985
A kind of terrestrial *Deśī Cārī* (q.v.).

ARDHAMATTALLI
SR..VII.631-32
A kind of *Nṛttakaraṇa.*
See *Karaṇa.*

ARDHAMUKULA
SR.VII.237
A particular position of the hand in dance.
VII.628-29
A Kind of *Nṛttakarana.*
See *Karaṇa.*

ARDHASAÑCA
SR.VI.848,891

A kind of *hastapāṭa* (q.v.).

ARDHASAMA

SR.VI.840

A kind of *hastapāṭa* (q.v.).

ARDHASŪCĪ

SR.VI.100

A kind of *Nṛttakaraṇa*.

See *Karaṇa*.

ARDHASVASTIKA

SR.VI.595-87

A kind of *Nṛttakaraṇa*.

See *Karaṇa*.

ARDHĀRDHAPĀṆI

SR.VI. 842,861

A kind of *hastapāṭa* (q.v.).

ALAṂKĀRA

NS.XXIX.23

Qualities contributing to the beauty of songs. Generally these are 33 in number according to Bharata; e.g., *Prasannādi, Prasannānta, Prasannādyanta*, etc.

Śārṅgadeva speaks of 63 *Alaṃkāras*. He defines *Alaṃkāra* as *Viśiṣṭa-varṇa-sandarbha* I.6.3), as a concatenation of letters of special qualities.

Gītālaṃkāras are different from *Kāvyā-laṃkāras* like *Upamā*. etc.

ALAGA

SR.VII 760-61

A kind of *Utplutikarṇa* (q.v.).

See *Karaṇa.*

ALAGABHRAMARĪ

SR.VII.778-79

A kind of *Utplutikaraṇa* (q.v.).

See *Karaṇa.*

ALAGAPĀṬA

SR.VII.1304-6,

1309

A kind of *Gharghara* (q.v.).

SR.VI.849,894

A Kind of

Hastapāṭa (q.v.).

ALAPADMAKA

SR.VII.276-77

A particular position

of hands or fingers in dance.

Name of a *Vartanā* (q.v.).

ALAPALLAVA

NS.XXVI.13

SR.VII.144-46

A particular position of the palm or fingers.

ALĀTA

NS.XII.29

SR.VII.1199-1202

A kind of *Maṇḍala* (q.v.).

ALĀTAKA

SR.VII.871-72

A kind of *Aṅgahāra* (q.v.).

ALĀTĀ

NS.XI.41

SR.VII.950-51

A kind of *Cārī* (q.v.).

AVAKUÑCITĀ

SR.VII.992
A kind of terrestrial Deśī Cārī (q.v.).

AVAGHAṬA
SR.VI.837,843, below
851m (a), 869, 914
A kind of *hastapāṭa* (q.v.).

AVANADDHA
NS.VI.27-29
XXVIII.1
XXXIII.1 etc.
SR.VI.4,6
Percussion instrument whose two
sides are covered with leather.

AVAROHA
SR.VI.200,255 etc.
Descent of a *Svara* to a
lower scale.

AVASPANDITĀ
SR.VII.936
A kind of terrestrial *Cārī* (q.v.).

AVAHITTHA
SR.VII.208-9
A particular position of the united hands.
VII.1063-65
A kind of *sthāna* (q.v.). for
woman in dance.

AVAHITTHAKA
SR.VI.720-23
A kind of *Nṛttakaraṇa*.
See *Karaṇa*.

AṂŚA
SR.U.7.34.,
V.62 VI.123

NS. XXVIII.76

The note that manifests the *Rañ*jakatva (quality of causing delight) of a song. The notę whose *Saṃvādī* and *Anūvādī* are largely perceived, and, being used as *Graha* (q.v.) and *Nyāsa* (q.v.) in singing, is abundantly felt. Abundance and pervasion in *Rāgas* are its characteristics. According to Mataṅga, it is the *Vādī* or principal *Svara*. One view is that *Aṃśa* is the name of those *Svaras* in which the full form of a *Rāgas* becomes *aṃśita* or *khaṇḍita* (divided). In this opinion, there cannot be more *Vā dī svaras* than one in a *Rāga*, whereas there may be more than one *Aṃśa*.

ASVAKRĀNTA

SR.VII.1065-68

A kind of *Sthāna* (q.v.) for women in dance.

ĀKĀŚIKĪ CĀRĪ

NS.XI.13

The *Cārī* (q.v.) that is performed in the air.

ĀKUÑCITA

SR.VII.1107

A kind of lying posture.

ĀKṢIPTA

SR.VII.663-4

A kind of *Nṛttakaraṇa*.

See *Karaṇa*.

ĀKṢIPTAKA

SR.VII.818-20

A kind of *Aṅgahāra* (q.v.).

ĀKṢIPARECITA

SR.VII.583-5,

850-58

A kind of *Nṛttakaraṇa* or an *Aṅgahāra* (q.v.).

ĀKṢIPTĀ

NS.XI.37

SR.VII.961-62
A kind of *Cārī* (q.v.).

ĀḌILLA
SR.III.40
A kind of voice in songs.
Khāhula (q.v.), expanding in *Mandra*- and *Madhya-sthānas*, is so called.

ĀDIKĀMODĪ
SR.VI.730
Name of a *Rāga* (q.v.).

ĀBHUGNA
SR.VII.298-99
A particular position of the chest in dance.

ĀNADDHA
Same as *Avanaddha* (q.v.).

ĀBHOGA
SR.IV.8,9.V.233
VII.1294 etc.
That part of the song-composition in which there is the name of the composer.

ĀYATA
NS. XXVI.45
SR.VII.1055-56
A kind of *Sthāna* (q.v.).

ĀRĀTRIKA
SR.VII.76-77
A particular position of the head in dance.

ĀROHA
SR.VI.200,222 etc.
Rising or ascent of a *svara* to a higher scale.

ĀRCIKA
Nāradīyaśikṣā
I.1.2

Name of the earlier part of the *Sāmaveda* of the Kauthuma-śākhā.

It consists of verses meant for singing.

ĀLAPTI

SR.VI.1048; III

189

Also called Ālāpa, it is a method of spreading out a *Rāga* by some meaningless sounds without any composition and *tāla*.

ĀLĀPINĪ

SR.VI.10

A kind of *Svara-viṇā.*

ĀLĪḌHA

SR.VII. 825-27

A kind of *Aṅgahāra* (q.v.).

SR.VII.1049-51

A kind of posture of males.

In it, a man has his left thigh in the air, the right foot is stretched forward, and both the feet remain in the *Tryasra* form.

ĀVARTA

SR.VII.1154-57

A kind of terrestrial *Maṇḍala* (q.v.).

SR.VII.673-74

A kind of *nṛtta-karaṇa* (q.v.). See *Karaṇa.*

ĀVĀPA

SR.V.7

A kind of *Kalā* (q.v.).

In it, the fingers of an upturned hand are contracted.

NS.XXX.31,34.

A kind of *Niḥśabda tāla* (q.v.).

It is shown by raising a finger upward.

ĀVIDDHA

NS.XXXIX.93

SR.VI.126,133 etc.

A particular mode of lute-playing is called *Āviddha Dhātu.* Name of a *Vartanā* (q.v.).

ĀVIDDHAVAKTRA

SR.VII.230-31

A particular position of the hand in dance.

AVIḌḌHĀ

NS.XI.38

SR.VII.963-64

A kind of *Cārī* (q.v.).

ĀŚRĀVAṆĀ

NS.XXIX.126

SR.VI.179,186,200,648

A kind of *Śuṣkavādya,* i.e., lute-play without song; an element of *Pūrvaraṅga* (preliminaries of a Sanskrit drama).

ĀSĀRITA

NS.31.62

Y III.113 *Mitākṣarā* (comm.)

Stated, in the *Mitākṣarā,* to be a kind of *Mahāgīta.*

ĀSKANDITA

NS.XII.47

SR.VII.1151-53

A kind of *Maṇḍala* (q.v.).

ĀHAVANĪ

SR.VI.962

A kind of *Vādya-khaṇḍa* (q.v.).

UṬṬAVAṆA (ṆI)

SR.VI.949,950,965,969,1015

A kind of *Vādya-prabandha.*

UḌUVA (UḌAVA)

SR.VI.900,910,949,1013

A kind of *Vādya* produced by drum and the like.

UTKUÑCITĀ

SR.VII.986

A kind of terrestrial *Deśī Cārī* (q.v.).

UTKṢEPA

SR.VII.1012-13

A kind of aerial *Deśī Cārī* (q.v.)

UTTĀNAVAÑCITA

SR.VII.244-46

A particular position of the hand in dance.

UTTARA

Y III.113

NS.XXXI.220

Included, in the *Mitākṣarā* commentary, among the seven kinds of songs, called *Prakara*. (q.v.).

UTTARĀRCIKA

The latter part of the *Sāmaveda* of the Kauthuma-śākhā. It consists of verses to be sung.

UTPLUTIKARAṆA

SR.VII. 749-57

Nṛtyādhyāya, 1306-82

It is a kind of *Karaṇa* (q.v.) in which the dancer jumps. Śārṅgadeva describes 36 such *Karaṇas*. The *Nṛtyādhyāya* describes 38 such *Karaṇas* of which 27 are the same as in *SR*. The *Bhramarīs*, as types of *Utplutikaraṇas*, mentioned in *SR*, are absent in it; instead, it describes 11 new types.

UTSYANDITA (Utspandita?)

I.24

SR.VII.921-33

A kind of *Cārī* (q.v.).

UDGRĀHA

SR.VI.944,946 etc.,

Name of the first *dhātu* (q.v.);

an element of *Prabandha.* (q.v.). In it, a song commences.

UDGHAṬṬAKA

A kind of *tāla* (q.v.)..

UDGHAṬṬITA

SR.VII.321

To keep standing with a particular position of the feet.

SR.VII.740

A kind of *Nṛttakaraṇa.* See *Karaṇa.*

SR.VII.849-50

A kind of *Aṅghāra* (q.v.).

UDVĀHITA

NS.XXVI.2

SR.VII.1109-10

A particular posture of the head in dance.

UDVṚTTA

SR.VII.731

A kind of *nṛttakaraṇa.*

See *Karaṇa.* For other meanings of the word, see VII.218-20, 494.

UDVṚTTAKA

SR.VII.881-83

A kind of *Aṅgahāra* (q.v.).

UDVṚTTĀ

NS.XI.39

SR.VII.964-65

A kind of *Cārī* (q.v.)..

UDVEṢṬANA

SR.VII.1012

A kind of Deśī Cārī (q.v.).

UDVEṢṬITA

NS.IX.204
XXVI.16
A kind of *Karaṇa* (q.v.)..

UNMATTA
SR.VII.599
A kind of *nṛttakaraṇa*.
See *Karaṇa*.

UPARĀGA
SR.II.1.15
Though originating from *Jātis*, yet so called as it arises from near *Grāmarāga* (q.v.).
Uparāgas are eight in number; viz. *Śakatilaka*, *Ṭakka-saindhava*, *Kokilāpañcama*, Revagupta, *Pañcamaṣaḍava*, *Nāgagāndhāra*, *Nāgapañcama*.

UPASṚTA
SR.VII.727-28
A kind of *Nṛttakaraṇa*.
See *Ka*[illegible]*a*.

UROṄGAṆA
SR.VII.1206,1211-12
A kind of *Lāsyāṅga* (q.v.) in which there are graceful movements, fast or delayed, of the pair of breasts and the shoulders.

ULVAṆA
SR.VII.277-78
A particular position of hands in dance.

UHAGĀṆA
Book of songs connected with *Grāmageya-gāna* (q.v.).

UHYAGĀNA
Book of songs connected with *Āraṇyagāna* (q.v.).

ŪRUTĀḌITA
SR.VII.981
A kind of terrestrial *Deśī Cārī* (q.v.).

ŪRUVEṆĪ

SR.VII.982

A kind of terrestrial Deśī Cārī (q.v.).

ŪRŪDVṚTTĀ

NS.XI.22

SR.VII.939-41

A single-handed pose in dance.

ŪRDHVA

A kind of *Vartanā(q.v.).*

ŪRDHVAJĀNU

NS.XI.33

SR.VII.626-27

A kind of Cārī (q.v.).

VII.949-50

A kind of aerial *Cārī* (q.v.).

ŪRDHVMAṆḌALĪ

SR.VII.260-61

A particular hand-pose in dance.

ŪRDHVĀLAGA

SR.VII.742

A kind of *Utplutikaraṇa.*

See *Karaṇa.*

GĀTHĀ

Y III.144

A kind of song.

ṚṢABHA

The second of the seven notes in a song. It is so called as it is supposed to have been obtained from the bellow of a bull (*ṛṣabha*). It is indicated by *RA.*

EKAPĀDALOHAḌĪ

SR.VII.765

A kind of *Utplutikaraṇa* (q.v.).

EKALA

SR.III.23

A solo singer.

EDAKĀRĪḌITA

SR.VII.1169-71

NS.XII.54 (pīḍita?)

A kind of *Maṇḍala* (q.v.).

EḌAKĀKRĪḌITĀ

NS.XI.20

SR.VII.927

A kind of *Cārī* (q.v.).

OYĀRAKA

SR.VII. 1206,1214

A kind of *Lāsyāṅga* (q.v.) in which the head moves downward a little obliquely.

OVENAKA OR AUVEṆAKA

NS.XXXI.220

Y III.113

A kind of song included. in the *Mitākṣarā* commentary, among the seven kinds of songs called *Prakara*.

OHĀṬĪ

SR.II.51.5

A kind of song. It takes place when the chin in placed on the heart, and there is a combination of *HA-kāra* and *AU-kāra* with *Svara*, which is *Mandra*(low, deep) and very swift (*atidruta*) and is joined with *Gamaka* (q.v.). called *Kampita*.

AUḌAVA (AUḌUVA)

SR.II.224,IV 362

A *Rāga* consisting of five *svaras* instead of the usual number. In it, the *Ṣaḍja-svara* is always present.

The word is derived from *Uḍu* denoting star. Stars remain in the sky which is the fifth of the five gross elements of *Kṣiti* (earth), *Ap* (water), *Tejas* (fire), *Marut* (air), and *Vyoman* (sky). So, *Auḍuva* indicated the number five.

KAKṢAVARTANIKĀ

SR.VII.262-63

A kind of hand-pose in dance.

KAKṢA is the name of a *Vartanā* (q.v.).

KAṬAKĀMUKHA

NS.IX.60

XXVI.19

A particular position of the palm or fingers.

KAṬKĀVARDHAMĀNA

NS.IX.136

XXVI.71

A particular position of the palm or fingers.

KAṬICCHINNA

SR.VIII.608-9

A kind of *Nṛttakaraṇa.*

See *Karaṇa*

KAṬIBHRĀNTA

SR.VII.649-52

A kind of *Nṛttakaraṇa.*

See *Karaṇa.*

KAṬISAMA

SR.VII.610-12

A kind of *Nṛtta-karaṇa.*

See *Karaṇa.*

KAPĀLACŪRṆANA

SR.VII.767-68

A kind of *Utplutikaraṇa.*(q.v.).

KAPITTHA

SR.VII.132-33

A single-hand pose in dance.

KAPITTHA-VARTANĀ

Nṛtyādhyāya,752

Done with *Kapittha* (q.v.) hand.

KAPOTA

NS.IX.129

XXVI.71

SR.VII.186-188

A particular position of the palm or fingers.

KARAṆA

NS.II.43

IV.30

VIII.15

XI.3

XXIX.91

SR VII.548-49

1) A mode of dance performed simultaneously with charming movements of hands and feet in consonance with *Rasa*. From different sources, *Karaṇas* appear to have been of 65 types.

2) Traversing with two feet in dance.

3) A particular mode of lute- playing is called *Karaṇadhātu*.

VII.899

A kind of *Cārī* (q.v.).

KARIHASTA

SR.VII. 710-11

A particular position of the hands joined together in dance.

KARTARĪMUKHA

S. VII.119-21

A particular pose of the single hand in dance.

KARTARĪMUKHA-VARTANĀ

Nṛtyādhyya, 750 the same action is done with the hands as in *Kartarīmukha*.

KARTARĪLOHAḌĪ

SR.VII.764

A kind of *Utplutikaraṇa*.
See *Karaṇa*.

KARTARYAÑCITA
SR.VII.760
A kind *Utplutikaraṇa*. See *Karaṇa*.

KALĀ
SR.V.6
An action of *Mārgatāla*; it may be soundless or with sound. The latter is known also as *Pāta*.

KALĀSA
SR.VII.
Occurs in the *Nṛtyādhyāya*. It means a special type of sequence. It is not defined as such, but its various forms are described. According to K.Ambrose (*Classical Dances*, P.68), the term is derived from the Arabic word *Xalāsa* denoting 'conclusion.' Amborse further states that *Kalāsa* occurs in *Kathākali*, and that it consists in vigorous movements characterising pure *Tāṇḍavas*. *Kalāsas* are sixfold: *Vidyutkalāsa*, *Khaḍgakalāsa*, *Mṛgakalāsa*, *Bakakalāsa*, *Plavakalāsa* and *Haṃsa-kalāsa*.

KĀṄGULA
SR.VII.132-33
A particular position of the single hand in dance.

KĀTARĀ
SR.VII.979
A kind of terrestrial Deśī
Cārī. (q.v.).

KĀLA
NS.III.6
Time, *tāla* (q.v.).

KĀHALA
Kullūka's commentary on Manu VII.196.

KUÑCITA

SR.VII.674-75
A kind of *Nṛttakaraṇa.*
See *Karaṇa.*

KUTAPA
NS.II.82
Orchestra.

KULĪRIKĀ
SR.VII.978
A kind of terrestrial Deśī Cārī (q.v.).

KUŚĪLAVA
NS. XXXV.106
One, who is a connoisseur, and can apply the rules of playing instruments.

KŪṬATĀNA
SR.I.4.32,33 etc.
Those complete and incomplete ***Mūrchanās*** (q.v.) in which the notes are uttered in an irregular order, e.g. SA,MA, GA,PA instead of SA,GA,MA, PA.

KŪRMAKA
SR.VII.186-188
A particular position of the hands joined together in dance.

KŪRMĀLAGA
SR.VII.761
A kind of *Utplutikaraṇa* (q.v.). See *Karaṇa.*

KŪRMĀSANA
SR.VII.1092
A kind of *Deśī Sthāna*(q.v.).

KEŚABANDHA
SR.VII.242-43
A particular position of the hand in dance.
Name of a *Vartanā* (q.v).

KRĀNTA

SR.VII.1180-82
A kind of aerial *Maṇḍala* (q.v.).
VII.655-57
A kind of *nṛttakaraṇa*
See *Karaṇa.*
VII.1097-98
A kind of sitting *sthāna* (q.v.).

KHAJA
NS.VII.134-37
A particular position of a single hand in dance
Name of a *Vartanā* (q.v.).

ḲHAṬAKĀVARDHAMĀNAKA
SR.VII.202-4
A particular position of the hands, joined together, in dance.

KHAḌGA
Name of a *Vartanā* (q.v.).

KHAṆḌA
NS.XI.4.
SR.VII.899,901
A combination of *Karaṇas* (q.v.).
A kind of *Cārī* (q.v.).

KHAṆḌASŪCĪ
SR.VII.1087
A kind of *Deśī sthāna* (q.v.).

KHALUHALA
SR.VII.1312-14
A kind of *Gharghara* (q.v.).

KHĀHULA
SR.III.40
A kind of voice in song. Arising from phlegm, it is soft and sweet.

KHUTTĀ

SR.VII.994

A kind of terrestrial *Deśī Cārī* (q.v.).

GAṄGĀVATARAṆA

SR.VII.747-48

A kind of *nṛttakarana*.

See *Karaṇa*.

GAJADANTA

SR.VII.204-7

A particular position of the hand. joined together, in dance.

GAJAVIKRĪḌITA

SR.VII.689-90

A kind of *nṛttakaraṇa*.

See *Karaṇa*.

GAṆḌASŪCĪ

SR.VII.690-92

A kind of *nṛttakaraṇa*.

See *Karaṇa*.

GATĀGATA

SR.VII.1069

A kind of *sthāna* (q.v.). for women.

GATI

A particular mode of gait in drama and dance. From the different sources, the following list of gaits can be made out: *Kaukkuṭī* (moving the feet together like an excited cock), *Khañjanī* (moving round qucikly like the *Khañjana* bird which is a species of the wagtail), *Khañjarīṭa* (moving like a wagtail) *Gajalīlā* or *Gajagāminī* (moving like an elephant in a slow and dignified manner). *Turaṅgiṇī* or *Hayalīlā* (raising the right foot and jumping repeatedly,) *Bhānavī* (moving the hands upward describing a circle or the dancer moving like the *Bhujaṅgī* (repeating the movement of the *Siṃhī gati*, q.v), *Mānavī* (moving in circles and coming forward repeatedly), *Māṇḍukī* (meaning not clear), *Māyurī(moving hands gradually upwards, slowly raising the feet standing on toes and shaking both knees alternately), Mṛgī* (looking with straight eyes like a deer; moving quickly to the front or side ways like a deer), *Mainavī* (moving without rest like a fish in a well), *Vīrā* (coming forward from a distance), *Siṃhī* (standing on toes and jumping quickly to the front), *Haṃsī* (walking like a goose with feet placed half a cubit apart from each other and bending body on both sides alternately).

GATIMAṆḌALA

SR.VII.843-45

A kind of *Aṅgahāra* (q.v.).

GAMAKA

SR.II.144;III.87, etc.

Designation of the trembling of a *svara*. It is of fifteen kinds, viz. *Tiripa, Sphurita, Kampita, Līna, Āndolita, Bali, Tribhinna, Kurula, Āhata, Ullāsita, Plāvita, Humphita, Mudrita, Nāmita, Miśra.*

GARUḌAPAÑCAKA

SR.VII.259-60

A particular position of the hand in dance.

GARUḌAPLUTA

SR.VII.693

A kind of *nṛttakaraṇa*.

See *Karaṇa*.

GĀTRA

Name of a *Varaṭanā* (q.v.).

GĀNDHARVA

NS.XXVIII.8

SR.III.12

Formed by stringed instruments, dependent on other instruments and with *Svara, Tāla* and *Pada*. According to the *SR*, it denotes a person who is versed in both *Mārga* and

Deśī songs. (q.v.).

GĀNDHĀRA

SR.VIII.12

The third of the seven notes in the heptatonic system. It is indicated by *GA*.

GĀRUḌA

SR.VII.1091

A kind of *Deśī Sthāna* (q.v.).

GṚDHRĀVALĪNAKA

SR.VII.697

A kind of *nṛttakaraṇa*. See *Karaṇa*.

GAUḌĪ

SR.II.4

A kind of song.

GAUṆḌALĪ

SR.VII.1273-77

Name of a class of female dancers. Their dance is also so called.

GRAHA

NS.XXVIII.75

SR.I.7.2,8,31;II.33.90, V.50 etc.

1) The *Svara* (q.v.) that is adopted at the commencement of a song. Same as *Aṃśa* according to Bharaṭa. Later writers take it to denote the secondary note in a *Raga*.

2) *Grahaṇa* or beginning of a *tāla*.

GRĀMA

NS.XX.5,XXVIII.23 etc

SR.I.4.1; II.109,172 etc. A gamut, scale in music. The *Svaras* (q.v.) on which are based *Mūrchanā* (q.v.). *Krama* (q.v.), *Tāla* (q.v.), *Varṇa* (q.v.), *Alaṃkāra* (q.v.) and *Jāti* (q.v.). According to Bharata and *Śārṅgadeva*, *Grāmas* are twofold, viz. *Ṣaḍja* and *Madhyama*. The *Nāradīya Śikṣā* mentions also *Gāndhāra-grāma*.

GRĀMAGEYA GĀNA

Book of songs to be sung in the village, attached to the *Ārcika.* (q.v.)

GRĀMARĀGA

SR.II.1.2,3,14

It is of five kinds according as it is the resort of five songs. The five kinds of *Grāmarāgas* are:

Śuddhā,Bhinnā, Gauḍī Vesarā, and *Sādhāraṇī.*

Their number respectively is 7,5,3,8 and 7. The total number of *Grāmarāgas* is 30. Some well-known *Grāmarāgas* are also called *Deśī.*

GHAṬA

Name of a *Vartanā* (q.v.).

GHAṆṬĀ

SR.VI.15

A metallic instrument, usually a bell.

GHANA

NS.VI.27,28 etc.

SR.II.4,6, etc.

Metallic musical instrument, e.g. *Karatāla.*

GHARGHARA

SR.VII.1304-6

A kind of jingling of the anklets by a dancer called *Peraṇī.*

GHŪRṆITA

SR.VII.624-25

A kind of *nṛttakaraṇa.* See *Karaṇa.*

CAKRABHRAMARĪ

SR.VII.779

A kind of *Nṛttakaraṇa.* See *Karaṇa.*

CAKRAMAṆḌALA

SR.VII.671-72

A kind of *Nṛttakaraṇa.* See *Karaṇa.*

CACCATPUṬA OR CĀCATPUṬA

SR.VI.18
NS.XXXI.60
A kind of *tāla* (q.v.).

CATURA
SR.VII.648-69
A kind of *Nṛttakaraṇa*. See *Karaṇa*.

CATURAŚRA
NS.XI.93
SR.VII.216-17
When, in a *Vaiṣṇava-sthāna* (q.v.), the two hands move in the hip and the navel, and the chest is raised, it is so called.
SR.VII.1039-40
A kind of *Sthāna* (q.v.) of males.
SR.VII.1080
A kind of *Deśī Sthāna* (q.v.).

CATURASRĀKHYA-VARTANĀ
SR
Nṛtyādhyāya, 744
The *Caturaśra* hands are moved with the shoulders and elbows. The arms at first assume *Udveṣṭita*, and are then placed on the chest.

CĀCAPUṬA
SR.V.18
NS.XXXI.60
A kind of *Tāla* (q.v.).

CĀRĪ
NS.XI.1
SR.VII.897
Simultaneous movement of the feet, shanks, thighs and the hip is so called. *Cārīs* are of 32 kinds. Of these 16 are *Bhaumī* (terrestrial, i.e., performed on the ground) and 16 *Ākāśikī* (aerial, i.e., performed in the sky). Each of the above two major types can be *Deśī (regional) and General.*

CĀLAKA

SR.VII.50

Nṛtyādhyāya of Aśokamalla. Also described by Kohala as quoted in Kallinātha's commentary on the *SR.*

A kind of movement of the arms in dance or drama. Fifty varieties of *Cālakas* have been mentioned. The following entirely new *Cālakas* are described in the *Nṛtyādhyāya, Digvarṣābhidha-cālana, Anaṅgāṅgamoṭana, Toraṇa-cālaka, Anaṅgoddīpana, Murajakartarī-cālaka.*

CĀLĪ

SR.VII.120-6-1207

A kind of Lāsyāṅga (q.v.). It means the simultaneous movements of feet, thighs, hip and the arms in dance. It is neither too fast nor too slow.

CĀLIVAḌA

SR.VII.1206

It is the name of *Cālī* (q.v.) performed very fast, in which there is forward movement.

CĀṢAGATA

NS.XII.65

SR.VII.1173

A kind of *Maṇḍala*(q. v.)

CĀṢAGATI

NS.IX.18

SR.VII.925-26

A kind of *Cārī* (q.v.).

CHATRBHRAMARĪ

SR.VII.777

A kind of *Utplutikaraṇa.*

See *Karaṇa*

CHĀYĀLAGA

SR.III.16,37, 311 etc.

A kind of *Rāga*, Also called *Sālaga.* So called as it is manifested after being attached to the shadow of another *Rāga.*

CHALIKA

Mālavikāgnimitra I. 3/4 (Prākrit) and 18/9(V.L. Chalitika). A song consisting of four parts. Stated to be an orchestra in which five persons used to sing to the accompaniment of lutes and flutes.

CHĀLIKYAGĀNA

Mahābhārata, Harivaṃśa, Viṣṇuparvan, ch.148 Perhaps same as *Chalika* (q.v.).

JAṄGHĀLAṄGHANIKĀ

SR.VII.1008-9

A kind of aerial *Deśī Cārī* (q.v.).

JAṄGHĀVARTĀ

SR.VII.1010

A kind of aerial *Deśī Cārī* (q.v.).

JANITA

SR.VII.726-27

A kind of *Nṛttakaraṇa*.

See *Karaṇa*.

JANITĀ

NS.XI.25

SR.VII.938-39

A kind of *Cārī* (q.v.).

JALAŚAYANA

SR.VII.766

A kind of *Utplutikaraṇa*.

See *Karaṇa*.

ṆS.XX.5; XXVIII.37 etc.

SR.I.5.1; VI.172,422 etc VIII. 115

A song with *Varṇa* (q.v.). and *Alaṃkāra* (q.v.). *Jāti* is twofold, *Śuddha* and *Vikṛta*.

ḌAMARĪ

SR.VII.1006

A kind of aerial Deśī Cārī (q. v.).

ḌOLA

SR.VII.195-96

A particular position of the hand joined together in dance.

ḌOLĀPĀDA

SR.VII.676

A kind of *nṛttakaraṇa.*

See *Karaṇa.*

ḌOLĀPĀDĀ

SR.VII.954-55

NS.XI.37

A kind of aerial *Cārī* (q.v.).

ḌHAKKĀ

Kullūka's commentary on Mannu VII.196. A kind of drum.

TATA

SR.VI.4,7 etc.

NS.VI.27; XXVIII etc.

Stringed instruments; e.g. lute (*Vīṇā*).

TALADARŚINĪ

SR.VII.995

A kind of terrestrial *Deśī*

Cārī (q.v.).

TALAPUṢPAPUṬA

SR.VII.568-70

A kind of *nṛttakaraṇa.*, See Karaṇa.

TALAMUKHA-VARTANĀ

SR.

Nṛtyādhyāya.

The *Talamukha* hands are moved with *Sauṣṭhava.*

TALAVILĀSITA

SR.VII.667-68

A kind of *nṛttakaraṇa.*

See *Karaṇa.*

TALASAṂGHAṬṬA

SR.VII.729-30

A kind of *nṛttakaraṇa.*

See *Karaṇa*

TALASAṂSPHOṬITA

SR.VII.664-95

A kind of *nṛttakaraṇa.*

See *Karaṇa.*

TALODVṚTTĀ

SR.VII.983

A kind of terrestrial *Deśī Cārī* (q.v.).

TĀṆḌVA

NS.4,13,261

According to a tradition, recorded in the NS., it is so called as it is believed to have been initiated by Taṇḍu. According to this work, it is dance consisting of forceful *Karaṇas* (q.v.). and *Aṅgahāras* (q.v.).

TĀNA

SR.I. 4.27,28 etc

Designation of *Śuddha Mūrchanā* (q.v.).

TĀMRACŪḌA

SR.VII.181-84

A particular single-hand pose in dance.

TĀLA

Y III.115

NS.ch.31

SR.ch.V.39

IV.13

VII.089

1. Derived dfrom root *tal*(meaning foundation) with the affix *ghañ*, it means that on which are founded dance and music, vocal and instrumental. It is regarded as essential in songs, so much so that, according to the *Saṃgīta-ratnākara* (ch.5),

a song without *tāla* is like a face without the nose. Beating time in music, usually by striking a *ghana* (q.v.) instrument, flapping of the two outstretched palms or striking the knee with the palm.

2. A musical instrument made of bell-metal, generally called *karatāla*. See *Raghuvaṃśa*, ix.71.
3. A kind of *Kalā* (q.v.).
4. A kind of *prabandhāṅga*. The following five are known as *Mārgatāla: Caccatpuṭa, Cācapuṭa Ṣaṭpitā-putraka, Saṃpakveṣṭaka, Udghaṭṭaka.* In the NS (31.30). *tāla is declared to be twofold; viz., Niḥśabda* (soundless). The former is tha which is indicated by the movement of fingers., It is of four kinds, viz., *Āvāpa. Niṣkrāma, Vikṣepa* and *Praveśaka. Śabdavān tāla* is fourfold; viz. *Śamyā, Tāla, Dhruva, Sannipāta.*
5. A kind of *tāla* in which the left palm is struck.
Tāla is again twofold; viz. Caturaśa and *Tryaśra.*

TIRIPABHRAMARĪ
SR.VIII.778
A kind of *Utplutikaraṇa.*
See *Karaṇa.*

TIRYAKKARAṆA
SR.VII.772-73
A kind of *Utpluti-karaṇa.*
See *Karaṇa.*

TIRYAKKUÑCITA
SR.VII.986
A kind of terrestrial
Deśī Cārī (q.v.).

TIRYAKSVASTIKA
SR.VII.774
A kind of *Utplutikaraṇa*
See *Karaṇa.*

TIRYAGAÑCITA

SR.VII.773

A kind of *Utplutikaraṇa*.

See *Karaṇa*.

TIRYAṄMUKHĪ

SR.VII.975

A kind of terrestrial

Deśī Cārī (q.v.).

TRIPATĀKA

NS.IX.27; XXVI.19

SR.VII.109-16

A particular position of the palm or fingers.

DAKṢAVIHITĀ

Y.III.114

A kind of song.

DAṆḌA

Name of a *Vartanā* (q.v.).

DAṆḌAPAKṢA

SR.VII.257-58

A particular position of hands in dance.

VII.836-37

A kind of *Nṛttakaraṇa*.

See *Karaṇa*.

DAṆḌAPADA

NS.XII.22

A kind of *Maṇḍala* (q.v.).

DAṆḌAPĀDĀ

NS.XII.44.SR.III.

955-56

A kind of *Cārī* (q.v.).

DAṆḌAPRAṆĀMĀÑCITA

SR.VII.759

A kind of *Utplutikaraṇa*.

See *Karaṇa.*

DAṆḌARECITA

SR.VII.646-47

A kind of *nṛttakaraṇa.*

See *Karaṇa.*

DARPASARAṆA

SR.VII.765-66

A kind of *Utplutikaraṇa.*

See *Karaṇa.*

DIKSVASTIKA

SR.VII.587-89

A kind of *nṛttakaraṇa.*

See *Karaṇa.*

DIGBHRAMARĪ

SR.VII.782

A kind of *Utplutikaraṇa.*

See *Karaṇa.*

DEŚĪ

SR.I.1.22,24,4

1) The song, instrumental music or dance which pleases the people of particular regions according to their taste.

2) A kind of *Tāla.*

It indicates distinction from *Mārga* (q.v.).

DEŚĪ-RĀGA

SR.II.2.2

Regional melody.

Name of some *Grāmarāgas,* etc. Some well-known *Deśī Rāgas* are: *Mālavakaiśika, Toḍī, Hindola,* etc.

DVISIKHARA

SR.VII.284-85

A particular position of hands in dance.

DHASAKA

SR.VII.1206,1212

It is a kind of *Lāsyāṅga* (q.v.). in which there is rhythmic and graceful lowering of the breasts.

DHĀTU

SR.IV.7.VI.125 etc.

Element of a song. There are four principal *Dhātus*, viz, *Udgrāha, Melāpaka, Dhruva* and *Ābhoga*. A fifth, *Antara* or *Antarā* is also added.

DHAIVATA

The sixth note of the Indian gamut, indicated by *Dha.*

DHRUVA

SR.V.9;IV.7.317 etc

1) A kind of *Kalā* (q.v.).

2) A kind of *Dhātu* (q.v.).

3) A kind of *Prabandha* (q.v.).

NS.31.32

A Kind of *Śabdavān tāla* (q.v.).

DHRUVĀGĀNA

NS.VI.29-30

Chap.32

A kind of song used in dramatic representation. The significance of *dhruva* is that in it, *Pada, Varṇa, Alaṃkāra, Laya, Jāti* and *Pāṇi* become united with one another firmly. The following kinds of songs are known as *Dhruvā, ṚK, Pāṇikā, Gāthā*, and seven kiṇds of traditional songs.

Dhruvā is of five kinds; viz., *Praveśa, Ākṣepa, Niṣkrāma, Prāsādika, Āntara.* It is chiefly of three kinds, viz., *Uttama, Madhyama* and *Adhama.*

According to Bharata, *Dhruvā* songs contain *rasa* and *hāva*(NS.32/330).

NATAPṚṢṬ HA

SR.VII.768-69

A kind of *Utplutikarṇa.*

See *Karaṇa.*

NANDYĀVARTA

SR.VII.1075

A kind of *Deśī Sthāna* (q.v.).

NALINĪ-PADMAKOṢA

SR.VII.272-76

A particular position of the hands in dance.

NARKUṬAKA

NS.IV. 323

A kind of song.

NARTAKĪ

SR.VII.1224 ff.

Female dancer. Such dancers may be of three kinds; viz., *Mugdhā*, *Madhyā* and *Pragalbhā*. They are respectively in the first three stages of youth. In the first, a girl becomes eager for such sexual union in which she, out of bashfulness, keeps her lips, breasts, cheeks, buttocks and thighs covered. In the second stage, the thighs and buttocks become heavy, and the breasts become plump, heaving and hard, signs which are the very life of Cupid. In the third stage, the woman has ravishing charm, and possesses skill in complete sex-act and proper emotions.

NĀGABANDHA

SR.VII 1093

A kind of *Deśī*

Sthāna (q.v.).

SR.VII.767

A kind of *Utplutikaraṇa*.

See *Karaṇa*.

NĀGĀPASARPITA

SR.VII.745-46

A kind of *nṛttakaraṇa*.

See *Karaṇa*.

NĀDA

SR.1,3.1, 2,5,6,11 etc.
A kind of sound which becomes manifest by the contact of fire and breath, within the body.

NĀRĀṬA
SR.III.61
A kind of sound in vocal music.

NIKUÑCAKA
SR.VII.283
A particular position of the hands in dance.

NIKUÑCITA
SR.VII.621-23
A kind of *Nṛttakaraṇa*
See *Karaṇa*.

NIKUṬṬAKA
SR.VII.873-75
A kind of *Aṅgahāra* (q.v.).
VII.603-6
A kind of *Nṛttakaraṇa* (q.v.).

NIKUṬṬIKĀ
SR.VII.998
A kind of terrestrial *Deśī Cārī* (q.v.).

NITAMBA
SR.VII.238-39
A particular position of the hands in dance.
Name of a *Vartanā* (q.v.).

NIBADDHA
SR.III.4
A musical composition, a song set in words.

NIVEŚA
SR.VII.724
A kind of *Nṛttakaraṇa* (q.v.).

NIŚUMBHITA
SR.VII.682-83

A kind of *nṛttakaraṇa*. See *Karaṇa*.

NIṢĀDA

The seventh note of the Indian gamut, indicated by *NI*.

NIṢKRĀMA

SR.V.7

A kind of *Kalā* (q.v.).

NS.31. 31,35

A kind of *Niḥśabda tāla* (q.v.). It takes place when a palm, with outstreched fingers, is half lowered.

NŪPURA

SR.VII.639-40

A kind of *nṛttakaraṇa*.

See *Karaṇa*.

NŪPURAPADIKĀ

NS.XI.35

SR.VII.953-54

A kind of *Cārī* (q.v.).

NŪPURABIDDHĀ

SR.VII.974

A kind of terrestrial *Deśī Cārī* (q.v.).

NṚTTA

SR.VII.3,4,14,28,35 etc.

Dance which, according to the *Daśarūpaka*, is based on *tāla* (q.v.). and *laya* (q.v.).

NṚTYA

SR.VII.3,4,14,27, etc.

Pantomime, tableau which, according to the *Daśarūpaka*, is based on *bhāva* (condition, feeling, emotion).

NYĀSA

SR.II.21,28 etc.

V.62,73 etc.

The *svara* marking the end of a song or *Rāga*.

PAKṢAPRADYOTAKA

SR.VII.255-56

A particular position of the hands in dance.

PAKṢAVAÑCITA

SR.VII.255

A particular position of the hands in dance.

PAÑCAPĀṆĪ

NS.XXXI.60

A kind of *Tāla* (q.v.).

PAÑCAMA

The fifth note of the Indian gamut, indicated by *PA*.

PAṬAHA

Me. 36.R.IX.71

A kettle -drum or tabour.

PAḌIVĀṬA

SR.VII.1306-7

A kind of *Gharghara* (q.v.).

PATĀKĀ

SR.VII.102-8

A single-handed pose in dance.

Name of a *Vartanā* (q.v.).

PATĀKĀ

NS.XXVI.2

A particular position of the palm or fingers.

PADMA

Name of a *Vartanā* (q.v.).

PADMAKOŚA

NS.IX.80; XXVI;18

SR.VII.142-43

A particular position of the palm or fingers.

PARĀVṚTTA (Parivartita)

NS.IX.206;XXVI.16

SR.VII.873-75

A kind of *Karaṇa* (q.v.).

PARĀVṚTTATALĀ

SR.VII.973

A kind of terrestrial *Deśī Cārī* (q.v.).

PARICCHINNA

SR.VII.820-22

A kind of *Aṅgahāra* (q.v.).

PARIMAṆḌALA

NS.XXVI.74

Two palms positioned like a circle, According to some, palms positioned like *Uromaṇḍalī*.

(NS.IX.192).

PARIVṚTTA

SR.VII.703

A kind of *Nṛttakaraṇa*.

See *Karaṇa*.

PARIVṚTTARECITA

SR.875-80

A kind of *Aṅgahāra* (q.v.).

ṖARYASTAKA

SR.VII.806-7

A kind of *Aṅgahāra* (q.v.).

PALLAVA

SR.VII.249-42

A particular position of hands in dance.

Name of a *Vartanā* (q.v.).

PĀṬ A

SR.IV.13,257. VI,828 etc.

An element of *Prabandha* (q.v.). Syllable of *Vādya*; e.g. *Dhigi*.

PĀTA

SR.V.6

See *Kalā*.

PĀDĀPAVIDDHAKA
SR.VII.638-39
A kind of *nṛttakaraṇa*.
See *Karaṇa*.

PĀṬA
SR.IV.13,257
An element of *Prabandha* (q.v.).

PĀRŚVAKRĀNTA
SR.VII.680-81
A kind of *nṛttakaraṇa*.
See *Karaṇa*.

PĀRŚVAKRĀNTĀ
NS.XI.32
SR.VII.945-47
A kind of *Cārī* (q.v.).

PĀRŚVANIKUṬṬAKA
SR.VII.669-70
A kind of *nṛttakaraṇa*.
See *Karaṇa*.

PĀRŚVAMAṆḌALĪ
SR.VII.262-63
A particular position of the hands in dance.

PĀRŚVASVASTIKA
SR.VII.814-16
A kind of *Aṅgahāra* (q.v.).

PĀRṢṆIRECITĀ
SR.VII.980
A kind of terrestrial *Deśī Cārī* (q.v.).

PIṢṬAKUṬṬA
NS.XII.64
SR.VII.1171-72
A kind of *Maṇḍala* (q.v.).

PURAḤKṢEPĀ

SR.VII.1002-3

A kind of aerial *Deśī Cārī* (q.v.).

PURĀṬIKĀ

SR.VII.996

A kind of terrestrial *Deśī Cārī* (q.v.).

PUṢPAPUṬA

SR.VII.196-97

A particular position of the hands together in dance.

PUṢPAPUṬA-VARTANĀ

Nṛtyādhyāya, 748. One hand in Puṣpapuṭa is moved in *Pārivartanā* and then placed on the chest after moving it in *Vyāvartanā*.

PṚṢṬHASVASTIKA

SR.VII.589-92

A kind of *Nṛttakaraṇa* (q.v.).

PṚṢṬHOTKṢEPA

SR.VII.1013

A kind of aerial *Deśī Cārī* (q.v.).

PṚṢṬHOTTĀNATALA

SR.VII.1079

A kind of *Deśī Sthāna* (q.v.).

PERAṆĪ

SR.VII.1301

Designation of a dancer who is specially dressed, and is specially qualified.

PRAKARA

Mitākṣarā commentary under Y.III. 113

Appears to denote a class of songs.

It takes place when the palm is turned downward.

PRAKARI

Y.III.113

included in the *Mitākṣarā* commentary, among the seven kinds of songs called *Prakarī* (q.v.).

PRATIVARTANIKĀ

Name of a *Vartanā*.

PRATYĀLĪḌHA

NS.XI.71

SR.VII.1052-53

A kind of Sthāna (q.v.).

PRATYĀHĀRA

NS.V.9

A kind of song. An element of *Pūrvaraṅga* (preliminaries) of a Sanskrit drama). A posture reverese of that in *Ālīḍha* (q.v.)

PRABANDHA

SR.IV.6,12,20, 21

VI.952,1261 etc.

A kind of *Nibaddha* (q.v.)-

gāna. At first, divided threefold (viz.*Dvidhātu*, *Tridhātu* and *Caturdhātu*), it is again divided as *Niryukta* and *Aniryukta*. It has been further divided as *Sūḍastha*, *Ālisaṃśraya* and *Viprakīrṇā*.

Also see under Nārāyaṇa Miśra.

There is *Vādya-prabandha* too; e.g. *Melāpaka*, etc.

PRAVEŚA

SR.V.8

A kind of *Kalā* (q.v.).

NS.31.31,36 (Praveśaka)

A kind of *Niḥśabda tāla* (q.v.).

PRASARPITA

SR.VII.711-12

A kind of *Nṛttakaraṇa*.

See *Karaṇa*.

PRASTĀRA

SR.V.314,317 etc.

Spreading out. The way of arranging the seven *Svaras* in an irregular order.

PRĀVṚTA

SR.VII.1016

A kind of aerial *Deśī Cārī* (q.v.) See *Cārī.*

PREṄKHOLITA

SR.VII.706-7

A kind of *nṛttakaraṇa.*

See *Karaṇa.*

PLUTA

Nāradīya Sikṣā I.iii.8

Protracted or prolated vowel. *dūrāhvāneca gāne ca rodane ca pluto mataḥ* A vowel, requiring a longer time to pronounce than a long vowel, used in calling from afar, singing and weeping. Such a vowel has three *mātrās* (units of measure).

PHĀLA

Name of a *Vartanā* (q.v.).

BADDHĀ

NS.XI.21

A kind of *Cārī* (q.v.).

BĀHYABHRAMARĪ

SR.VII.775-76

A kind of *Utplutikaraṇa.*

See *Karaṇa.*

BRAHMAGĪTIKĀ

Y.III.114

A kind of song.

BHĀṆḌA

(V.L.Bheṇḍa)

NS.XXII.201,206,210

A musical instrument.

BHĀṢĀ

SR.II.1.19 ff.

It appears to have been the name of what came to be called *Rāgiṇī* in later times. Fifteen *Rāgas* have been stated as *Janakas* (progenitor) of the *Bhāṣās* the total number of which is 90. Mataṅga is stated, by Śārṅgadeva, to have mentioned four kinds of *Bhāṣās*; viz. *Mukhya*, *Svarākhya*, *Deśākhya* and *Uparāgaja*.

BHUJAṄGATRĀSITA

NS.XI.42

SR.VII.959-61

A kind of *Cārī* (q.v.).

BHAUMĪ CĀRĪ

NS.XI.10

That kind of *Cārī* (q.v.). which is performed on the ground.

BHRAMARA

NS.XII.44

SR.VII.817-18

A kind of *Maṇḍala* (q.v.).

BHRAMARĪ

NS.XI.45

SR.VII.958-59

A kind of *Cārī* (q.v.).

MAKARA

SR.VII.212-13

A particular position of the hands joined together in dance. Name of a *Vartanā* (q.v.).

MAṆḌALA

NS.XI.65

SR.VII.1142 ff.

A particular position of the feet in dance. It is twofold; viz., *Ākāśika* (aerial) and Bhauma (terrestrial). Connected with three or four *Khaṇḍas* (q.v.).

SR.VII.899,901,1142-45

A kind of *Cārī* (q.v.).

SR.VII.1040-48

A kind of *Sthāna* (q.v.) for males.

MAṆḌALASVASTIKA
SR.VII.579-80
A kind of *Nṛttakaraṇa*.
See *Karaṇa*.

MATTALLI
NS.XI.28
SR.VII.630-31
A kind of *Cārī* (q.v.).

MATTALLĪ
SR.VII.930-31
A kind of *Deśī Cārī* (q.v.).

MATTASKHALITA
SR.VII.841-43
A kind of *Aṅgahāra* (q.v.).

MATTĀKRĪḌA
SR.VII.833-36
A kind of *Aṅgahāra* (q.v.).

MATSYAKARAṆA
SR.VII.769-70
A kind of *Utplutikaraṇa*.
See *Karaṇa*.

MADAVILASITA
SR.VII.822-25
A kind of *aṅgahāra* (q.v.).

MADAṢKHALITA
SR.VII.734-35
A kind of *nṛttakaraṇa*.
See *Karaṇa*.

MADĀLASA
SR.VII.1096-97
A kind of *Upaveśana-sthāna* or sitting posture.
See *Sthāna*.

MADĀLASĀ

SR.VII.987

A kind of terrestrial *Deśī Cārī.* (q.v.).

MADRAKA

NS.XXXI.220

Y III.113

A kind of song included, in the *Mitākṣarā* comm. on Yājñavalkya, among the seven kinds of songs called *Prakara* (q.v.)

MADHYAMA

The fourth of the seven *Svaras* of the Indian gamut; it is indicated by *MA*.

MANA

SR.VII.1206,1215

A kind of *Lāsyāṅga*, which has *sthāya* (q.v.). and *Laya* (q.v.). derived from song etc.

MAYŪRLALITA

SR.VII.705-6

A kind of *Nṛttakaraṇa* (q.v.).

See *Karaṇa*.

MĀTU

SR.III.2

Language of a song.

MĀRGA

SR.I.22; III.1, 12,V. 4,10.VII.27.

1) A kind of *Rāga* (q.v.).

2) Derived from the root *mṛg* (to seek).

A kind of music said to be have been sought and found by god Brahmā, etc. and performed by sages Bharata, etc. The word also means path, ie., the path shown by the sages. The term is used to denote that kind of music which is performed in strict conformity with the rules laid down in authoritative works.

3) A kind of dance.

As qualifying *Saṃgita*, it means the classical style as distinguished from *Deśī or regional style.*

MĀRGATĀLA

See Tāla.

MUḌUPACĀRĪ

Described in the *Nṛtyādhyāya*. According to P. Shah, the editor, the term is another name of *Madhupacārī*, an *Ākāśki Cārī* stated by Kallinātha, in his commenatary on the SR, to have been mentioned by Kohala.

According to M.Bose (*Classical Indian Dancing*, P.170), *muḍupa* denotes the upper side of a toe, and the *Cārī* (q.v.)., done with it, is called *Muḍupacārī*. It involves *Nikuṭṭana* (pounding by the feet.).

MUDRĀ

NS.IX.4 ff; XIV.62

A particular position of the fingers in the hand. Such positions may be in a single palm or in both palms joined together.

MURAJA

ME.58,66; K VI.40; Mal.

I.22

A kind of drum.

MUṢṬIKASVASTIKA

SR.VII.270-71

A particular position of the hands in dance.

MUṢṬIVARTANA

Nṛtyādyāya, 751.

The *Muṣṭi* hands are moved to the right and to the left in *Vyāvartanā*.

MŪRCHANĀ

SR.XXVIII.28

SR.I.4.1,9.12 etc

Name of the gradual ascent and descent of the *Svaras* (q.v.). The rising of sounds, an intonation duly regulated rise and fall of sounds, conducting the air and the harmony through the keys in a pleasing manner, changing the key or passing from one key to another.

SR.VI.67,96 Chap

A kind of action of hand (Karakriyā) in *Vādya.*

MṚGAPLUTĀ

SR.VII.948-49

A kind of aerial *Cārī* (q.v.).

MṚGAŚĪRṢA

NS.IX.6; XXVI.77

SR.VII.159-60

A kind of position of the palm or fingers.

MELA

See Appendix V

MOṬITA

SR.VII.1071-72

A kind of *Sthāna* (q.v.). for females.

YATI

SR.V.46

Pause in a song.

YAMALA

SR.III.23

A duet singer.

RATHACAKRA

SR.VII.972

A kind of terrestrial *Deśī Cārī* (q.v.).

RASA

This term is often used in connexion with the enjoyment of poetical compositions, dramas, dance and music. Generally rendered as sentiment, it is, in fact, such a word as defies an exact rendering into English. It is unexpressible inward experience of a connoisseur, a sort of supernatural delight.

According to the *Nāṭyaśāstra*, its *niṣpatti* follows from a combination of *Vibhāvas* (excitants), *Anubhāvas* (ensuants) and *Vyabhicārī* or *Saṃcārī Bhāvas* (flitting emotions) with the *Sthāyī Bhāvas* (permanent moods). The term *niṣpatti* has been interpreted by different scholars as (i) *Utpatti* (production), (ii) *Anumiti* (inference), (iii) *Bhukti* (enjoyment) and (iv) *Abhivyakti* (manifestation or revelation).

The following eight *Rasas* are generally recognised: *Śṛṅgāra* (erotic), *Vīra*(heroic) *Raudra*(furious), *Bībhatsa* (disgustful), *Hāsya*(comic), *Adbhuta*(marvellous), *Karuṇa* (pathetic) and *Bhayānaka* (terrible). *Śānta* (quietistic) is recognised by some as the ninth *Rasa*.

In the literature of the Bengal Vaiṣṇavas, *Bhakti*, regarded as a *Bhāva* (mood in the earlier works on poetics), came to be regarded as a *Rasa*.

RĀGA

Nāradīya Sikṣā I.ii.2

SR.II.2,18 etc. III.14.IV.362

VI.399-401 etc.

See ch.VIII on Rāgas and Rāgiṇīs.

Derived from root *Rañj* (to please), it means a musical mode, possesed of particular *Svaras* and *Varṇas*, which please a person.

The *Saṃgīta-ratnākara* mentions the following 20 *Rāgas*: *Śrīrāga*, *Naṭṭa*, *Vaṅgāla* (2), *Bhāsā*, *Madhyamaṣādava*, *Raktahaṃsa*, *Kolhahāsa*, *Prasava*, *Bhairava*, *Dhvani*, *Megharāga*, *Somarāga*, *Kāmoda* (2), *Āmrapañ*cama, Kandarpa, Deśa, Kaiśikakakubha, Naṭṭanārāyaṇa.

The above *Rāgas* are, perhaps, regarded as principal by Śārṅgadeva. He says (Rāgavivekādhyāya, ii.19) that the total number of *Rāgas* is 264.

The names of *Rāgas* differ in different works. For example Rāgas appear to be broadly divided into two classes; viz., *Grā-*

marāga and *Deśī Rāga*. The former is so called a s it arises from *grāma* (not in the sense of village) which has been defined as a group of *svaras* which are the resort of *mūrchanā*, etc. *Grāma-rāga* and *Deśī-rāga* may be rendered as classical *rāga* and regional *rāga* respectively.

Rāgas are divided into three classes in accordance with the number of *Svaras* constituting them. These are *Saṃpūrṇa* comprising all the seven *Svaras*, *Ṣāḍava* containing six *svaras* and *Auḍava* or *Auḍuva* consisting of five *svaras* only; the first or *Ṣaḍja svara* being ever present in it.

Rāgas may again be divided as *Śuddha* (pure or unmixed) and *Chāyālaga* or *Sālaga*, *Chāyālaga* is so called as it has the shadow (*Chāyā*) of another Rāga. Some take *Saṃkīrṇa* as another class of *Rāgas*. Samkīrṇa-rāga arises when there is an admixture of more *Rāgas* than *Śuddha* and *Chāyālaga*.

In accordance with the suitability of different *Rāgas* in different seasons, (*Ṛtu*), *Rāgas* are classified as follows:

Season	Rāga
Grīṣma	Dīpaka
Varṣā	Megha
Śarat	Bhairava
Hemanta	Mālavakauśika
Śiśira	Śrī
Vasanta	Hindola

Bhātkhaṇḍe classifies *Rāgas* as follows:

A. *Divāgeya* - to be sung by day.

B. *Sandhyāgeya* and *Ūṣogeya*- worthy of being sung in the evening and dawn.

V. *Rātrigeya*- to be sung at night.

In some later works, e.g. *Pañ*cama-sāra saṃhitā, Saṃgita-darpaṇa, Rāgas or principal *Rāgaṣ* are stated to be six on the names of which *authorities differ. According to the Saṃgīta-darpaṇa, the following five Rāgas* are supposed to have emerged from the five mouths of Śiva: *Śrī, Vasantaka, Bhairava, Pañcama* and *Megha. Rāga Naṭṭanārāyaṇa* is stated to have come out of the mouth of Pārvatī. According to some authorities, the six principal *Rāgas* are: *Bhairava, Kauśika, Hindola, Dīpaka, Śrī* and *Megha.* Others regard the following as principal *Rāgas*: *Bhairava, Pañ*cama, Nāṭa, Mallāra, Gauḍamallarā, Deśākhya.

In some comparatively late works, *Rāgas* have been fancied as possessed of anthropomorphic features. There are *Dhyānas* of different *Rāgas.*

RĀGĀṄGA

SR.II.2.4-5

Accessory of *Rāga.* According to the ancient authorities, cited by Śārṅgadeva, the following are *Rāgāṅgas*:

Śaṃkarābharaṇa, Ghaṇṭārava, Haṃsaka, Dīpaka, Rīti, Karṇāṭikā, Lāṭī, Pāñcālī.

RĀGĀLAPTI

SR.III.190

Same as *Rāgālāpa* (q.v.).

RĀGĀLAPA

SR.II.24

The demonstration or spreading out of a *Rāga* (q.v.). without any wording and *Tāla.*

RĀGIṆĪ

It occurs in such late works as the *Saṃgita-darpaṇa* and *Pañcamasārasaṃhiā.*

The term *Rāgiṇī* appears to have come into vogue in the post-Śārṅgadeva period. In the voluminous *Saṃgitaratnākara, Rāgiṇī* does not occur anywhere; instead, the term *Bhāṣā* has been used.

Later writers conceive of *Rāgiṇīs* as consorts of *Rāgas.*

On the names and number of *Rāgiṇīs* authorities differ.

Like *Rāgas*, *Rāgiṇīs* also have been fancied as having anthropomorphic features, and *Dhyānas* depict their images.

RŪPAKĀLAPTI

SR.III. 197

A kind of *Rāgālāpa* (q.v.).

REKHĀ

SR.VI.1216

Name of a position of the body, which pleases the mind and the eyes, and in which there is a combination of the different postures of the head, eyes, hands, etc.

RECAKA

NS.IV. 248

SR.VII.892ff

Particular movements relating to the hands, feet, hips and neck.

RECITA

SR.VII.858-65

A kind of *Aṅgahāra* (q.v.).

SR.VII.235-37

A particular position of the hands in dance.

Name of a *Vartanā*(q.v).

LAṂGHITAJAMGHIKĀ

SR.VII.991

A kind of terrestrial *Deśī Cārī*.

See *Cārī*.

LAḌHI

SR.VII.1206-120-10

A kind of *Lāsyāṅga* (q.v.). in which there is simultaneous graceful, delicate and oblique movements of the hip and the arms accompanied by dalliance.

LATĀKARA
SR.VII.246-47
A particular position of hands in dance.

LATĀKṢEPĀ
SR.VII.999
A kind of terrestrial *Deśī Cārī* (q.v.).

LATĀVṚŚCIKA
SR.VII.662-63
A kind of *Nṛttakaraṇa.*
See *Karaṇa.*

LAYA
SR.V.44
Pause after action. Tempo or time in between two *Mātrās. Laya* may be of three major kinds; viz. *Druta* (fast), *Madhya*(medium) and *Vilambita* (delayed). Some Sanskrit works on musicology mention many *layas.* For example, the *Saṃgīta-dāmodara* of Subhaṃkara enumerates 40 kinds of *layas.*

LALĀṬ ATILAKA
SR.VII.668-69
A kind of *nṛttakaraṇa* (q.v.).
See *Karaṇa.*

LALITA
SR.VII.1202-5
A kind of *Maṇḍala* (q.v.).
SR.VII.278-80
A particular position of the hands in dance.
SR.VII.634
A kind of *nṛttakaraṇa.* See *Karaṇa.*
Name of a *Vartanā* (q.v.).

LALITASÑCARA
NS.XII.17.SR.VII.1182-86
A kind of *Maṇḍala* (q.v.).

LĀSYA

SR.VII.30, DR.I.10

In the opinion of Śārṅgadeva, it is a kind of dance consisting of delicate movements exciting the erotic sentiment. It is a form of *Nṛtta* according to the *VDP*. A *Dar*. refers to it as the dance of the mythical Pārvatī. The *DR* refers to it as a division of *Nṛtta* and *Nṛtya*.

The *Mānas*. describes it as a graceful style of dance consisting of *Aṅgahāras* (q.v.).

Lāsya, according to the *BhP*, is a form of dance consisting of delicate *Karaṇas* (q.v.). and *Aṅgahāras* (q.v.), accompanied by songs. It is of four types; viz.

Śṛṅkhalā, *Latā*, *Piṇḍī* and *Bhedyaka*. The following four *Nṛtyabhedas* also, according to the *Bh.P*, appear to be among the constituents of *Lāsya*.

LĀSYĀṄGA

SR.VII.1206-1215

Nṛtyādhyāya 1519 ff. Particular movements of the limbs in dance. The ten *Deśī Lāsyāṅgas* are *Cālī*, *Cālīvaḍa*, *Laḍhi*, *Sūka*, *Uro'ṅgana*, *Dhasaka*, *Aṅgahāra*, *Oyāraka*, *Vihasi* and *Mana*. The *Nṛtyādhyāya* describes 37 *Deśī* Lāsyāṅgas of which 10 are identical, with minor variations, with those mentioned in the *SR*.

LĪNA

SR.VII.572-73

A kind of *nṛttakaraṇa*.

See *Karaṇa*.

LUṬHITA

SR.VII.764

Another name of *Lohaḍī* (q.v.).

LOLITA

SR.VII.733-34

A kind of *nṛttakaraṇa* (q.v.).

See *Karaṇa*.

LOHAḌĪ

SR.VII.763-64

A kind of *Utplutikaraṇa.*

See *Karaṇa.*

VAKṢAḤ SVASTIKA

SR.VII.581-82

A kind of *nṛttakaraṇa.*

See *Karaṇa.*

VAṄKOLA

SR.VII.768-69

A kind of *Utplutinkaraṇa.*

See *Karaṇa.* Also called *Natapṛṣtha.*

VARADĀBHAYA

SR.VII.285-86

A particular position of the hands in dance.

VARṆA

NS.III.6

24,181, etc.V.270

VI.172 etc.

1) Act of singing.

2) A kind of *tāla* (q.v.).

3) A kind of *prabandha* (q.v.).

VARTANĀ

SR.VII.348

Occurs in the *Nṛtyādhyāya* of Aśokamalla.

In his commentary on the *SR.*, Kallinātha quotes Kohala to describe it as a kind of movement of the arms.

24 varieties of *Vartanās* are mentioned.

11 kinds of *Vartanās* are mentioned in the *Nṛtyādhyāya.*

VARTITA

SR.VII.573-76

A kind of *nṛttakaraṇa.*

See *Karaṇa.*

VARDHAMĀNA

NS.XXXI.98

Mitākṣarā on Y III.113

A kind of song stated,in the *Mitākṣarā,* to be a kind of *Mahāgīta.*

VALANA

Another name of *Veṣṭana* (q.v.).

VALITA

SR.VII.280-82

A particular position of the hand in dance.

VII.635-36

A kind of *Nṛttakaraṇa.*

See *Karaṇa.*

VII.1070-71

A kind of *Sthāna* (q.v.) for woman.

Name of a *Vartanā* (q.v.).

VALITORU

SR.VII.576-76

A kind of *nṛttakaraṇa.*

See *Karaṇa.*

VĀGA

SR.III.97

Name of *Gamaka* (q.v.).

VĀGGEYAKĀRAKA

SR.III.2

A writer of sentences and of compositions that can be sung.

VĀDĪ

NS.XXVIII.22

SR.I.3.47,48.50 etc.VI 216 etc.

That *Svara*, which is sometimes *Aṃśa* (q.v.)., is called ***Vādī***. It manifests the form of a *Rāga*.

The principal note in relation to which other notes are determined.

VĀDYA'

NS.XXXIII.4-8,56-57

SR.Chap.VI

One of the three constituents of *Saṃgīta*. It may mean instrumental music in general or musical instruments. The instruments are generally divided into four classes; viz.

Tata—stringed instruments—*Ghana*; metallic instruments.

Suṣira—instruments with holes, wind-instruments.

Avanaddha or Ānaddha—percussion instruments.

The following tentative list of musical instruments, prevailing in different periods, can be made out from the results of modern researach: (Vide M.S.Chakrabarti, *Tālattver Kramavikāś*, p.p. 253f:

A. From the earliest times up to second centuray A.D.

Mṛdaṅga, *Paṇava, Dardura, Muraja, Āliṅgya, Āṅkika,* ***Ūrddhvavaka***, *Vāmaka, Madhyaka, Sabhyaka, Dakṣiṇa,* ***Bherī, Paṭaha***, *Bhambhā, Dundubhi, Ḍiṇḍima.*

B. From the third century A.D. to the eighth

Tuṅga, Jharjhara, *Śambhu-vādya, Mukharikā, Ḍhakkā,* ***Madda, Jharjhara***, *Ḍamaru.*

C. From the ninth century, A.D. to the thirteenth

Mardala, Huḍukkā, Karaṭā, *Ghaṭa, Ghadasa, Ḍhavasa,* ***Kuḍukkā, Kuḍuvā, Ruñjā***, *Ḍakkā, Maṇḍiḍakkā, Ḍukkuli,* ***Sellukā, Jhallarī, Bhāna, Trivalī***, *Niḥsāna, Tumbakī.*

D. From the fourteenth century to the fifteenth

Muraja, Bimbaka, Darpavādya, Ghanaśa, Lāvajākṣa, Karaṭha, Kamaṭha, Muralivādya, Jhallī, Dukkali, Dauṇḍiśālā, Ṭamakī, Kuṇḍalī, Guṅgu, Raṇaghaṭa, Āvaja, Dudukī,

Upāṅga, Ghaṇṭāvādya.

In accodance with their use for various purposes, the musical instruments can be grouped as

A. Sāṃgrāmika

Used as military equipage. These instruments were used at the time of march or expedition, in action or to intimidate the enemy; e.g. *Dundubhi, Ānaka, Bherī*, etc.

B. Bahirdvārika

Placed at the entrace and exit of the palace, it was used to indicate the coming in or going out of the king or to sound warning about impending attack by the enemy; e.g. *Ḍiṇḍima, Ḍakkā, Ghaṇṭāvādya*, etc.

C. Māṅgalika

Usually played on an auspicious occasion, especially on the occasion of waving lights, etc, before the images of deities, worship, invocation and immersion of images; e.g. *Mṛdaṅga, Muraja, Mardala, Ḍhakkā, Paṭaha*, etc.

D. Ānuṣṭhānika

Generally used as accompaniments; e.g. *Jhallarī, Ḍakkulī, Ṭamakī.*

In ancient times, the percussion instruments were played before, to the accompaniment and after a musical performance or dance. Played before function, these were called *Ativādita.* When played to the accompaniment of a performance, they were termed *Samavādita.* Played after a performance, they were designated as *Anuvādita.*

VĀMAVIDDHA

NS.XII.33

SR.VII.1188-91

A kind of *Maṇḍala* (q.v.).

VIKAṬA

SR.VII.31.32

A kind of dance.

VIKṢIPTA

SR.VII.686-88

A kind of *nṛttakaraṇa*.

See *Karaṇa*.

VIKṢIPTĀKṢIPTAKA

SR.VII.616-18

A kind of *nṛttakaraṇa*.

See *Karaṇa*.

VIKṢEPA

SR.V.8

A kind of *Kalā* (q.v.).

NS.31.31,35

A kind of Niḥśabda *tāla* (q.v.).

It takes place when a *mātrā* (unit of measure) is indicated by swinging the hand a little towards the right.

VIKṢEPĀ

SR.VII.1003-4

A kind of aerial *Deśī Cārī* (q.v.).

VICITRA

NS.XII.13

SR.VII.1192-95

A kind of *Maṇḍala* (q.v.).

VICYAVĀ

NS.XI.19

A kind of *Cārī* (q.v.).

VIDĀRĪ

SR.V.75-77

VI.120 etc.

That which rends. It may be of two kinds. viz, *Gīta-vidārī* (song-rending) and *Padavidārī* (word-rending).

The first is *Gīta-khaṇḍa*. For example, *Lalita*, lavaṅgalatā, *pariśīlana-komala-malaya-samīre*. Each of the above parts is a *Gītavidārī*.

If a *Vidārī* becomes complete in the *Aṃśa svara* (q.v.). of a *Rāga* and in its *Saṃvādi svara* (q.v.). or *Anuvādī svara* (q.v.). and in its *Nyāsa-svara* then it iṣ called *Padavidārī*. See B.KRoychaudhuri, *Bhāratīya Saṃgīt-koṣ* (in Bengali), p.107.

VIBHĀṢĀ

SR.II.1.22 ff.

A sort of minor *Bhāṣā* (q.v) *Vibhāṣās* are mentioned by Sārṅgadeva.

VIDDHĀ

SR.VII.1015

A kind of aerial *Deśī Cārī* (q.v.).

VIDYUDBHRĀNTA

SR.VII.837-39

A kind of *Aṅgahāra* (q.v.).

VII.684-85

A kind of *nṛttakaraṇa*.

See *Karaṇa*.

VIDYUDBHRĀNTĀ

NS.XI.40

SR.VII.957

A kind of *Cārī* (q.v.).

VINIVṚTTA

SR.VII.678-80

A kind of *nṛttakaraṇa*.

See *Karaṇa*.

VIPRAKĪRṆA

SR.VII.223-24

A particular position of hands in dance.

VIPRAKĪRṆA-VARTANĀ

Nṛtyādhyāya,747 The hands are moved in *Udveṣṭita* and are separated. The left hand is then placed on the left side, the right on the right.

VIVĀDĪ

NS.XXVIII.22
SR.I.3.47,51 etc.
If one *śruti* intervenes between two *svaras* (q.v.)., then those *Svaras* are *Vivādī* (discordant) of each other.

Vivādī *Svara* detracts from the charm of a *Rāga* (q.v.).
SR.VII.1109
A kind of *Sthāna* (q.v.).

VIVṚTTA
SR.VII.677-78
A kind of *nṛttakaraṇa* .
See *Karaṇa.*

VIŚLIṢṬA
SR.VII.978-79
A kind of terrestrial *Deśī Cārī* (q.v.).

VIṢAMA
SR.VII.31-32
A kind of dance.

VIṢAMASŪCĪ
SR.VII.1085-86
A kind of *Deśī Sthāna* (q.v.).

VIṢKAMBHA
SR.VII.847-49
A kind of *Aṅgahāra* (q.v.).
VII.737-39
A kind of *nṛttakaraṇa.*
See *Karaṇa.*

VIṢKAMBHĀPASṚTA
SR.VII.839-1100
A kind of *Aṅgahāra* (q.v.).

VIṢKAMBHITA
SR.VII.1099-1100
A kind of *Upaveśana-sthāna*
(sitting posture).

See *Sthāna.*

VIṢṆUKRĀNTA

SR.VII.732

A kind of *nṛttakaraṇa.*

See *Karaṇa.*

VIHASĪ

SR.VII.1206,1214-15

A kind of *Lāsyāṅga,* consisting in laughter which, unlike the wonted laughter, is suffused with the erotic sentiment, is very subtle and, is accompanied by novel gestures.

VIHṚTA

NS. XII.26

SR.VII.1195-98

A kind of *Maṇḍala* (q.v.).

VĪṆĀ

Y III.115.R.VIII

33, XIV.35

Me.91

Lute

VṚNDA

SR.III.203

A band of vocalists

and instrumentalists.

VṚNDAGĀYANA

SR.III.23

One who sings in a chorus.

VṚŚCIKA

SR.VII.658-59

A kind of *nṛttakaraṇa.*

See *Karaṇa.*

VṚŚCIKAKUṬṬITA

SR.VII.660-61

A kind of *nṛttakaraṇa.*

See *Karaṇa.*

VṚŚCIKANIKUṬṬAKA
Another name of *Vṛścikakuṭṭita.*

VṚŚCIKARECITA
SR.VII.661-62
A kind of *nṛttakaraṇa.*
See *Karaṇa.*

VṚŚCIKĀPASṚTA
SR.VII.869-70
A kind of *Aṅgahāra* (q.v.).

VṚṢABHAKRĪḌITA
SR.VII.744-45
A kind of *nṛttakaraṇa.*
See *Karaṇa.*

VṚṢABHĀSANA
SR.VII.1091
A kind of *Deśī sthāna* (q.v.).

VEṢṬANA
SR.VII.1011
A kind of aerial *Deśī Cārī* (q.v.).

VESARA
SR.II.6
A kind of song.

VAIŚĀKHA
NS.XI.632
SR.VII.1043-45
A kind of *Sthāna* (q.v.).

VAIŚĀKHA-RECITA
SR.VII.812-14
A kind of *Aṅgahāra* (q.v.).
SR.VII.657-58
A kind of *nṛttakaraṇa.*
See *Karaṇa.*

VAIṢṆAVA
NS.XI.53;XXVI.45
SR.VII.1089
A kind of *Sthāna* (q.v.).

VOMBAKA
SR.III.41
A kind of sound.

VYAṂSITA
SR.VII.652-54
A kind of *nṛttakaraṇa.*
See *Karaṇa.*

VYĀYĀMA
Another name of *Cārī* (q.v.).

ŚAKAṬĀSYA
NS.XII.60
SR.VII.1158-59
A kind of *Maṇḍala* (q.v.).

ŚAKAṬĀSYĀ
NS.XI.16
SR.VII.920-21
A kind of *Cārī* (q.v.).

ŚAMYĀ
SR.V.9
A kind of *Kalā* (q.v.).
NS.31.32,39
A kind of *Śabdavāin tāla* in which the right palm is struck.

ŚĀRĪRA
SR.III.82
The inherent capacity of a singer for manifesting a *Rāga* (q.v.) without practice.

ŚIKHARA
SR.VII.130-31
A particular single-hand pose in dance.

ŚIKHARA-VARTANĀ

Nṛtyādhyāya, 752.

Done like *Muṣṭivartanā* with *Śikhara* hand.

ŚIROBHRAMARĪ

SR.VII.781

A kind of *Utplutikaraṇa*.

See *Karaṇa*.

ŚUKATUṆḌA

SR.VII.137-39

A particular single-hand pose in dance.

Name of a *Vartanā*. (q.v.).

ŚAIVA

SR.VII.1090

A kind of *Deśī sthāna* (q.v.).

ŚUṢKAGĀNA

NS.XX. 136

A song composed in words conveying no sense.

ŚRUTI

NS.XX.SR.I.3.8,9,10 etc.

Y.III.115

Name of 22 sounds in the heptatonic system of *Svaras* (q.v.). These are heard (śruta). The difference between *Svara* and *Śruti* lies in the fact that, while the former has resonance, the latter has not. It is a unit of measurement of the gradual rise of the notes of the Indian gamut.

ṢAṬPITĀPUTRAKA

SR.V.22 and many other places.

A kind of *tāla* (q.v.).

ṢAḌJA

The first of the seven notes in the Indian gamut. It is so called as it is supposed to have originated from six notes. Some think, the name means 'that which has given birth to the other six notes'. It is indicated by *SA*.

ṢĀDAVA

SR.II.9 *passim.*

A *Rāga* (q.v.). consisting of six *Svaras* (q.v.). in it, the initial *Ṣadja* is never given up.

SAṂGHAṬṬITĀ

SR.VII.993

A kind of terrestiral *Deśī Cārī* (q.v.).

SADASA

SR.VII.175.81

A particular single-hand pose in dance.

SANNATA

SR.VII.707-8

A kind of *nṛttakarana.*

See *Karaṇa.*

SAṂNIPĀTA

SR.VI.10

A kind of *Kalā* (q.v.). NS.31.32,39

A kind of *Śabdavān tāla* in which sound is produced bt striking both the palms equally.

SAMANAKHA

SR.VII.598

A kind of *nṛttakaraṇa.*

See *Karaṇa.*

SAMAPĀDĀ

SR.VII.917-18

A kind of terrestrial *Cārī* (q.v.).

SAMAPĀDĀCITA

SR.VII.783-84

A kind of *Utplutikaraṇa.*

See *Karaṇa.*

SAMAVĀDITA

NS.XXXIII.56

See under *Vādya.*

SAMASŪCĪ
SR.VII.1084-85
A kind of *Deśī sthāna* (q.v.).

SAMASKHALITIKĀ
SR.VII.1000-1
A kind of terrestrial *Deśī Cārī* (q.v.).

SAMOTSĀRITA
SR.VIII.1164-66
A kind of *Maṇḍala* (q.v.).

SAMOTSĀRITA-MATALLĪ
NS.XI.27
SR.VII.928-29
A kind of *Cārī* (q.v.).

SAPAKVEṢṬAKA
A kind of *tāla* (q.v.).

SAṂBHRĀNTA
SR.VII.883-86
A kind of *Aṅgahāra* (q.v.).
VII.736-37
A kind of *nṛttakaraṇa*.
See *Karaṇa*.

SĀRIKĀ
SR.VII.997
A kind of terrestrial
Deśī Cārī (q.v.).

SAROBINDU
Y III.113
Included, in the *Mitākṣarā* commentary, among the seven kinds of songs.

SARPAŚIRAS
SR.VII.152-53
A single-hand pose in dance.

SARPITA

SR.VII.708-9
A kind of *nṛttakaraṇa* (q.v.).
See *Karaṇa.*

SAṂVĀDĪ
NS.XXVIII.22
SR.I,3.47, 49, 50 etc. V.74.VI.123 etc.
Two *Svaras* are *Saṃvādī* of each other if nine or thirteen *Śrutis* intervene between them. It is a note that helps develop a *Rāga* manifested by the *Vādisvara.* (q.v.).

SAṂHATA
SR.VII.1076
A kind of *Deśī Sthāna* (q.v.).

SĀRAṆĀ
SR.I.3.19ff
The act of making *Svaras* ascend and descend.

SĀLAGA
Same as *Chāyālaga* (q.v.).

SIṂHAVIKRĪḌITA
SR.VII.717-18
A kind of *nṛttakaraṇa.*
See *Karaṇa.*

SIṂHĀKARṢITA
SR.VII.718-19
A kind of *nṛttakarana.*
See *Karaṇa.*

SUṢIRA
NS.VI.27; XXVIII-1
SR.VI.4,5, etc.
A musical instrument with holes; eg. flute.

SŪKA
SR.VII.1206,1210-11
A kind of *Lāsyāṅga* (q.v.) in which there is rhythmic delayed or fast movement, with enough of feminine erotic feeling, of the

ears adorned with bright ornaments.

SŪCĪ

SR.VII.698-99

A kind of *nṛttakaraṇa*. See *Karaṇa*.

SŪCĪ

NS.XI.34

SR.VII.951-52

A kind of *Cārī* (q.v.).

ŚŪCĪVIDDHA

NS.XII.19

SR.VII.808-9

A kind of *Aṅgahāra* (q.v.). VII.1186-88

A kind of *Maṇḍala* (q.v.). VII.700-1

A kind of *nṛttakaraṇa*. See *Karaṇa*.

SŪCĪMUKHA

SR.VII.232-35

A particular position of hands in dance.

SŪCĪMUKHA-VARTANĀ

Nṛtyādhyāya ,752. Done with a *Sūcīmukha*. hand.

SŪCYANTA

SR.VII.774-75

A kind of *Utplutikaraṇa*. See *Karaṇa*.

SKANDHABHRĀNTA

SR.VII.786-88

A kind of *Utplutikaraṇa*. See *Karaṇa*.

SKHALITA

SR.VII.716

A kind of *nṛttakaraṇa*. See *Karaṇa*.

STAMBHAKRĪḌANIKĀ

SR.VII.990

A kind of terrestrial *DeśīCārī* (q.v.).

STHĀNA

NS.XI.51 XXVI.32

SR.VII.1029-31

1) *Status quo* before dance and *status quo ante* after dance.

Sthānas may be for males alone, for females only, some are sitting (*Upaviṣṭa*) postures, while others are sleeping (*Supta*) ones.

Some *sthānas* are called *Deśī*.

2) Place of origin of sound e.g. heart, throat, head.

STHĀYA

SR.III.97

A part or element of a *Rāga*.

STHITĀVARTĀ

NS.XI.15

SR.VII.919-20

A kind of *Cārī* (q.v.).

STHIRAHASTA

SR.VII.802-5

A kind of *Aṅgahāra* (q.v.).

SPANDITĀ

NS.XI.26

SR.VII.935

A kind of *Cārī* (q.v.).

SPHURITĀ

SR.VII.998

A kind of terrestrial *Deśī Cārī* (q.v.).

SPHURITA

SR.VII.992

A kind of terrestrial
Deśī Cārī (q.v.).

SVARA

SR.I. 3.25, 28 etc.

IV 12,15, etc.

A note of the musical scale. These are *Ṣaḍja, Ṛṣabha, Gāndhāra, Madhyama, Pañcama*, Dhaivata, Niṣāda.

In a work on music, the derivative meaning of the word is *svato rañjayati*, that which pleases (the listeners) on its own.

It has resonance.

SVASTIKA

NS.XXVI.2

SR.VII.192-94

A particular position of the hands joined together in dance.

SR.VII.1073-74

A kind of *Deśī Sthāna* (q.v.).

SR.VII.592-93

A kind of *nṛttakaraṇa*.

See *Karaṇa*.

SVASTIKARECITA

SR.VII.886-88

A kind of *Aṅgahāra* (q.v.).

VII.600-3

A kind of *nṛttakaraṇa*.

See *Karaṇa*.

SVASTIKA-VARTANĀ

Nṛtyādhyāya, 746

The hands are moved in *Vyāvartanā* and crossed as in *Svastika*.

SVASTIKĀ

SR.VII.994

A kind of terrestrial *Deśī Cārī* (q.v.).

SVASTHA

SR.VII.1095

A kind of *Upaveśana Sthāna* (q.v.). or sitting posture.

HARIṆAPLUTĀ
NS.XI.43
SR.VII.1004
A kind of *Cārī* (q.v.).

HARIṆAPLUTA
SR.VII.702
A kind of *nṛttakaraṇa.*
See *Karaṇa.*

HARIṆATRĀSIKĀ
SR.VII.984
A kind of terrestrial *Deśī Cārī* (q.v.).

HAṂSAPAKṢA
SR.VII.163-67
A single-hand pose in dance.

HAṂSĀSYA
SR.VII.161-63
A single-hand pose in dance.

APPENDICES

I

INDIAN AND FOREIGN MUSIC

— difference, similarity and the mutual relation

INDIAN AND WESTERN MUSIC

Among some Europeans there is a colonial attitude and imperialistic outlook. They think that India became civilized with the introduction of British rule. According to them, whatever India can boast of in her cultural life, is the result of gifts of the gracious rulers. Some Indians, too, nurtured by an alien culture, appear to share the above view.

Leaving aside all other things of cultural life, we find that, in the realm of music and dance, India forestalled them several centuries before the light of civilization entered into the British Isles. As a result, the Indians developed their indigenous arts quite independently. The intrusion of foreign elements into Indian music is a very recent event, dating back to the late nineteenth century A.D.

There are certain fundamental differences between Indian music and western music. We shall set forth the salient points after Popley, as stated in his *Music of India*:

1) The most prominent difference is that while the predominant factor of Indian music is melody, that of the western is harmony.

2) Indian melody is cast in one particular mood all along; both time and tune are made into one homogeneous whole. Variations are not allowed to change the mood which persists with *rāga*. The balance of the music is obtained partly by time-

variations and partly by grace. In western music, mood is used to articulate the balance of the whole piece. The specified times for singing the different *rāgas*, the *rāga-images* and the emotions, associated with them, fit into Indian melody.

3) In India, the relation of the individual notes with one another has been fixed by long tradition. In the western music, the salient notes are made by the momentary impulse of the harmony or of the counterpoint; the conglomearation of notes, rather than the individual one, has special value.

4) In Indian composition, melody depends upon the relation to certain fixed notes which vary with the variation of the *rāga*. It is indifferent to any progress through suggesting harmony. Western melodies tend to move around the notes harmonically related to the tonic. The effects that imitation at different levels, so common in western music, is seldom found in Indian music, and the two tetrachords are rarely identical in the character of their constituents.

5) In Indian music, grace and *gamaka* (trembling of sound) are not accidental ornaments as in western music, but essential parts of the melodic structure.

6) In Mrs. Mann's language, "Western music is music without microtones, as Indian music is music without harmony".

7) Western music greatly emphasises tone and timbre, but Indian music passes by these on the other side, and pays all attention to execution and accuracy. The melody is not determined by canons of charm or pleasure, but they comply with certain fixed norms; the quality of tone, in which the melody is sung or played, does not have the importance it does in the west.

D.P. *Singhal* says[1]—"The highly developed *tāla* or rhythmic system, with its avoidance of strict metre and its development by the use of an accumulating combination of beat sub-divisions,

---

1. *India and World Civilization, I, p,222.*

has no parallel in western music. On the other hand, the Indian system has no exact counterpart to the tone of the tempered system, except for the keynote of western music.

Thus, we find that there is no semblance of affinity between Indian and Western music. Some western scholars[1] themselves have averred that the great art of Indian music is absolutely free from western inspriation.

Rabindranath goes deep into the spirit, rather than the form, underlying Indian and western music. There cannot be a more fitting finale to this topic than the following observations of this savant: "Our music draws the listener away beyond the limits of everyday human joys and sorrows, and takes us to that lonely region of renunciation which lies at the root of the universe, while European music leads us to a variegated dance through the endless rise and fall of human grief and joy".

The above difference is rooted in the ethos of the people of the above two parts of the globe. While Indian civilization aims at *Śānti(peace), the western culture is based on Gati (dynamism).*

Some scholars think that the musical instruments like the harp, which resemble the Indian *Vīṇā*, were borrowed from India by such ancient lands as Greece, Egypt and by Alexander, etc. Certain parallelisms between the Indian and Greek systems of music are striking. For instance, the two earliest systems of Greece, called Mixolydic and Doric, resemble early Indian scales. Pythagoras' scheme of cycle of the fifth and cycle of the fourth in the musical system correspond to the *Ṣaḍja-pañcama* and *Ṣaḍja-madhyama bhāvas* of the *Nāṭyaśāstra*. Though mere similarity of the two systems does not *ipso facto* prove the one borrowing from the other, yet the probability of Greece having been influenced by India cannot be categorically ruled out. In this connexion, we should remember that Indian music, dating back to the Ṛgvedic

2. G.T. Garratt, *The Legacy of India, p.325.*

period, was older than the Greek. It is also noteworthy that, according to some ancient Greek writers, the greater part of Greek music was borrowed from Asia. Strabo the eminent classical historian, among others, shares the above view. Alexander's (4th. cent. B.C., earlier half) biographer, Arrian, records the Indians' love of music since early times.

Aristotle's (385-322B.C) description of lyre reminds one of the Indian *Ekatantrī Vīṇā* (single-stringed lute.) Curt Sachs thinks that the South Indian drum, *Tambattam*, was known in Babylon by the name of *Timbuti.* According to him, the South Indian *Kinnarī* was King David's *Kinnor.*

It is admitted by some western scholars that the occidental violin and flute have been derived from the Indian *vīṇā* and *vaṃśa* respectively.

INFILTRATION OF INDIAN MUSIC INTO CENTRAL AND SOUTH-EAST ASIA AND OTHER COUNTRIES

We have evidence of the prevalence of Indian music in parts of Central Asia, particularly Kashgarh and Khotan. Probably Indian artistes in Kuchi carried this art to China where it found an honoured place even in the royal courts of China. In 581 A.D., many Indians musicians went to that country at the invitation of the then Chinese Emperor. An Indian artiste, Sujīva by name, adorned the royal court of China in the period between 560 and 578 A.D. Himself an expert *Vīṇā*-player, he used to train the music-lovers of China in the modes of Indian *rāgas.* It appears that the Chinese used to cultivate Indian music down to the 9th - 10th cent. A.D. Old Chinese manuscripts reveal the familiarity of the Chinese with the heptatonic system, *grāmas, mūrchanās,* etc. of Indian musicology. It is, perhaps, not a mere accident that, at least three notes of the Chinese gamut correspond to the three *Svaras* of the Indian system, viz.*Ṣaḍja, Ṛṣabha* and *Pañcama.*

In the sixth century A.D., Korea was a seat of Indian music. From China and Korea it journeyed to Japan. Indian colonies in

Champā or Kamboja also probably played some part in the trans mission of Indian music to Japan. According to an ancient Japanese tradition, two chief types of music, called *Bodhisttva* and *Bairo*, were imported from China to Nippon by an Indian Brahmin, named Bodhi. The term Bodhi-sattva leaves no doubt about its Indian origin, *Baira* is, perhaps from the Indian *rāga Bhairava* which is still called *Bhairo* in Hindī.

Among the countries of South East Asia, Java, Bali, Sumatra and Cambodia respectfully cultivated Indian music.

Some Tibetan songs, especially of the devotional type, appear to contain elements in imitation of the songs of the *Sāmaveda.*

The Arabian writer, Jahiz, (d. 868 or 869) states that Indian music was popular in the Abbasid court. He mentions an Indian musical instrument, called Kankalah, containing a string stretched on a pumpkin. It appears to be the *Kingar* made with two gourds. Another Arabian source records a book on Indian tunes and melodies. A few technical terms of Arabian musicology appear to have been borrowed from Persia and India. The Arabic *maqa iqa* appears to be the Persian rendering of Indian melodic rhythmic system. Yehudi Menuhin is definite that some elements of Indian music became the mainstay of Arabian music.

II

NON -ARYAN INFLUENCE ON INDIAN MUSIC: ROLE OF MUSIC IN NATIONAL INTEGRATION

India has been a multiracial country through ages. It has been proved that mainly four groups of people live in this vast subcontinent. They are

A. Aryan or Indo-Aryan

B. Dravidian
C. Aborigines
D. Mongolian type

It is, therefore, natural that a composite culture evolved in this land. As early as in the Ṛgvedic period, we find the *dāsas* forming an integral part of the Vedic society. They were, perhaps, the primitive non-Aryan people who were vanquished and enslaved by the Aryans of superior culture and power.

Besides the native non-Aryans, hordes of outsiders invaded this country in different periods. From Persia, there was the influx at first of the Indo-Iranians who settled here, and spread throughout India excepting South India which was the stronghold of the Dravidians who constituted a bulwark against the onrush of the Aryans. At a subsequent period, Persia invaded the north-west of India, and established (6th.cent. B.C.) its sway over it. Then came Alexander the Great (327-26 B.C.) in the wake of whose invasion Greek principalities were established in different parts. Among other foreign invaders were mainly the Śakas (2nd cent. B.C.), Yueh-chi Kushānas (1st. cent. B.C.), Hūṇas (5th cent.A.D.) and the Arabs (7th cent. A.D.), the Mughals (16th cent.), Pāthāns (15th. cent.).

The foreigners could not stamp out the traditional Aryan culture. But, some of them left the indelible imprint of their respective cultural characteristics on the Indian society. The fact that they ruled facilitated the infiltration of foreign elements into Indian culture. A fertile field was provided by music which, having been popular, became a medium of transmission. We shall briefly refer to the foreign elements in Indian music.

The names of certain *Rāgas* and *Rāgiṇīs* indicate their origin among non-Aryan tribes and foreigners. *Śaka, Pulinidī*. *Ābhirī, Śāberikā* and *Bhairava* appear to have been derived respectively from Śakas, Pulindas, Ābhīras, Śabaras and Bhairavas. *Mālava* (with its derivatives *Mālavaśrī, Mālavakauśika* etc.), *Āndhrī* and

Gurjarī probably originated among the *Mālavas, Andhras* and Gurjaras. The name *Velāvalī* is taken by some to have been derived from *Vela-ullī*, a Dravidian term. *Toḍī*, derived from *Tuḍī*, *Āśāvarī* and Dhannāsikā have no Sanskrit base, and may have come from foreign sources. The names *Chevāṭī*, *Kaccolī* and Gerañ jī appear to be non-Aryan. *Kāmbojī, Khāmbāja or Khāmācī* was probably obtained from Kambuja which may have been the region of this name, situated in the north-west of India. Or, it may refer to Cambodia in South East Asia. According to Mataṅga (in the *Bṛhaddeśī*) Kāmbojī is a non-Aryan term.

The names *Turuṣka Toḍī, Turuṣka-gauḍī* betray a blend of the Turkish and Indian elements. The name *Boṭṭa* is considered by some to have been a derivative of *Bhoṭṭa* or *Bhoṭa* which refers to Tibet. *Bhommāṇa* is regarded by some as hinting at its Armenian source. There is ample evidence of commerical intercourse between India and Armenia. Some look upon *Ṭakkarāga* as a contribution by the non-Aryan *Ṭakka* race.

The authors of some Sanskrit works on musicology appear to have been conscious of the foreign elements in certain *Rāgas*. For example, Mataṅga says in his *Bṛhaddeśī: saṃkīrṇā ca matā nityaṃ jñ eyā vaideaś - sambhavā*; it is mixed, and originated in a foreign country.

III

INFLUENCE OF NATURE ON MUSIC AND DANCE

Man was born and nurtured in the cradle of nature. He got food and sustenance from nature. The meadows were his study and nature was his book. Among the ruins of the Indus Valley civilisation we find line-drawings of animals. The Vedic seer, awestruck at the mighty aspects of nature, sang their glory. Part of the *Ṛgveda* was incorporated into the *Sāmaveda*.

That vocal music was inspired by nature has been beautifully expressed by Rabīndranāth in the following words:

Yedin dharāy nāmila prathama kususma-van, sedin eseche ā
mār gāner nimantraṇ/

On the day, when the first flower-garden descended on earth, came to me the invitation to songs.

According to some authorities, the seven *Svaras*, the basic elements of the Indian gamut, have all been taken from different objects of nature in the following way;

Name of *Svara*	Source
Ṣaḍja	Peacock's cry
Ṛṣabha	Cry of *Cātaka* bird
Gāndhāra	Bleat of the goat
Madhyama	Cry of the curlew
Pañcama	Cooing of the cuckoo
Dhaivata	Frog's croak
Niṣāda	Trumpeting of the elephant

Some *Rāgiṇīs* also have been named after animals and birds, e.g. *Kuraṅgī*, *Mayūrī*, etc.

Some of the *Rāgas* and *Rāgiṇīs* bear the names of seasons. For example, *Vasantaka-rāga*. *Madhu-mādhavī-rāgiṇī (Madhu* denotes spring; *Mādhava may mean spring season or the month of Vaiśākha).*

The *Megharāga* is obviously named after *megha* or cloud. *Dīpaka* (illuminator)-*rāga* clearly indicates that it has been named after fire. There is a tradition that, if properly sung, the *Megharāga*, called *Meghamallāra*, induces rainfall, and that the *Dīpaka-rāga*, when sung in strict adherence to the requirements of the music-lore, kindles fire.

It is well known that the moods of human beings change with the change of seasons and time. Some musicologists have tried to determine the suitability of certain *Rāgas* and *Rāgiṇīs* in particular seasons or hours of the day. Here, we briefly inidcate the view of Dāmodara. *Megharāga* and the *Rāgiṇīs Bhairavī, Velāvalī,* etc. should be commenced in the morning. *Śrīrāga* and the *Rāgiṇīs Karṇāṭī, Kedārī,* etc. are to be sung from the third *Prahara* up to midnight. This rule was not universally observed in practice. Dāmodara himself says—*rājājñayā sadā geyā na tu kālaṃ vicārayet.*

At the behest of kings, a *Rāgiṇī (Rāga* also implied) may be sung always, and one should not consider the restriction about the time.

In all seasons, those *rāgas* which are pleasant should be sung at will. According ton Dāmodara, the *Rāgas Śrī, Vasanta, Bhairava, Pañcama, Megha* and *Naṭṭanārāyaṇa* should be sung respectively in winter, spring, summer, autumn, rainy season and dewy season. This is also not intended to be rigidly observed. He says *yathecchayā vā gātavyāḥ sarvartaṣu sukhapradāḥ.*

Coming to dance we find that many of the gestures, postures and dance-modes have been named after the various objects of nature, e.g. *Ardhacandra, Aśvakrānta, Eḍakākrīḍita (Eḍakā* denotes ewe), *Kapota, Karihasta, Gṛdhrāvalīnaka, Cāṣagata (Cāṣa* means the bird blue jay), *Tāmracūḍa (cock), Nalinīpadmakośa, Pallava, Puṣpapuṭa, Vidyudbhrānta, Vṛścika, Vṛṣabhakrīḍita. Bhujaṅga-trāsita, Bhramara, Makara, Matsyakaraṇa, Mayūralalita, Marālā, Mṛgaplutā, Latākara, Śukatuṇḍa, Siṃhavikrīḍita.*

IV

POETIC IMAGERIES IN MUSIC-LORE

Music and poetry are allied. In fact, there is no music without poetry and no poetry without music. Poesy is, indeed, the child of Muse. We notice delectable flight of fancy in the conception of some *Rāgas* and *Rāgiṇīs*. A few examples are given below.

ŚRĪ-RĀGA

Aṣṭādaśābadaḥ smara-cāru-mūrtiḥ, dhīro lasat-pallava-karṇapū raḥ/ṣaḍjādi-sevyo'ruṇa-vastradhārī śrīrāga eṣa kṣitipā-lamūrtiḥ//

[This Śrīrāga, aged eighteen years, is handsome like Cupid, steady shining with ear-ornaments of leaves; he is served by *Ṣaḍja*, etc., wears a scarlet cloth, and has the image of a king.]

VASANTĪ

(Rāgiṇī of *Śrīrāga)*

Śikhaṇḍi-varhoccaya-baddha-cūḍā, karṇāvataṃsa-kṛtaśo-bhanāmrā/

indīvara-śyāma-tanuḥ, sucitrā vasnatikā .syādali-mañjulaśrīḥ//

[Vasntikā, adorned by bees, exquisitely beautiful, having her body blue like the lotus, is wearing a crown of peacock's plumes and decked with ear-ornaments of mango-blossoms.]

KARṆĀṬA-RĀGA

kṛpāṇapāṇis-turagādhirūḍho, mayūra-kaṇṭhāti-sukaṇṭha-kāntiḥ/ sphurat-snigdha-rasaḥ praśāntaḥ/karṇaṭa-rāgo haritālavarṇaḥ.

[*Karṇāta-rāga*, sword in hand, with a complexion more radiant than the peacock's throat, is riding a horse; he is very quiet, scintillating, lovely and has the colour of *haritāla (yellow orpiment or the yellow pigeon).]*

VELĀVALĪ

(Rāgiṇi of *Hindola-rāga*)

saṃketa-dīkṣāṃ dayite ca datvā, vitanvatī bhūṣaṇamaṅgakeṣu/

muhuḥ smarantī smarami-ṣṭadevaṃ, velāvalī nīla-saroja-kā-ntiḥ//

[*Velāvalī*, possessed of a complexion like the blue lotus, having instructed the husband about assignation, while adorning her slim limbs with ornaments, is repeatedly remembering her desired deity, Cupid.]

BHAIRAVA-RĀGA

gaṅgādharaḥ śaśikalā-tilakas-trinetraḥ, sarpairbhūṣita-tanur-gaja-kṛttivāsāḥ/

bhāsvat-triśūlakara eṣa nṛmuṃḍadharī śubhrāmbaro jayati bhairava ādirāgaḥ//

[Victorious is this three-eyed original *Rāga, Bhairava*, with the Ganges on his head, a lunar digit as the mark on his forehead, possessed of body adorned with a serpent, wearing elephant-skin, holding a trident in hand and carrying a human skull.]

BHAIRAVĪ

(*Rāgiṇi* of Bhairava)

sphaṭika-racita-pīṭhe ramya-kailāsaśṛṅge, vikaca-kamala-patrair-arcayantī maheśam/

karadhṛta-ghana -vādyā pītavarṇā-yatākṣī, sukavibhir-iyamuktā bhairavī bhairava-strī//

[This consort of Bhairava, large-eyed, yellow-complexioned, holding a *ghana*(q.v) instrument in hand, worshipped, with petals of lotuses in bloom, Mahādeva, seated on a crystal-pedestal on charming Kailāsa peak, is called *Bhairavī* by good poets.]

V

A NOTE ON MELA

Mela, so called as it brings about the *milana* or union of *svaras*, is a technical term which is difficult to translate. *Melakartā* may be taken to mean *āśrayarāga* or primary *rāga*. *Mela* is commonly known as *Thāṭa* or *Ṭhāṭa*. This is what is called *Krama* in Sanskrit musicology. This arises when the seven *svaras* are pronounced in order. It may be of many kinds according as the *Svaras* are *Śuddha* and *Vikṛta*. In his *Caturdaṇḍiprakāśikā*, Veṅkaṭamakhin has named seventy-two *melas* in connexion which South Indian music. This division does not apply in the case of North Indian Music. V.N. Bhātkhaṇḍe, a renowned exponent of this school of music, has formulated a system in which all the current *Rāgas* and *Rāgiṇīs* have been included in only ten *Melas* or *Ṭhāṭas*. His arrangement has, however, not been accepted by many distinguished musicologists. At present, *Śuddhasvara* means the seven *svaras* in order starting from *Ṣaḍja*. This heptatonic system has been designated by Bhātkhaṇḍe as *Vilāval Ṭhāṭa*. According to the modification *(Vikṛti)* of the *Svaras*, the *Ṭhāṭas* have been distinguished.

The ten *Ṭhāṭas* in North Indian system, according to *Bhātkhaṇḍe*, with the corresponding names in South Indian system, are as follows:

North Indian	South Indian
1. Kalyāṇa	Kalyāṇa
2. Vilāval	Śaṃkarābharaṇa
3. Khāmbāj	Kāmbhojī
4. Bhairava	Mālavagauḍa
5. Pūrvī	Kāmavardhanī
6. Māroyā	Gamanaśrama
7. Kāphi	Harapriyā
8. Āśāvarī	Naṭabhairava
9. Bhairavī	Toḍī
10. Todī	Varāṭī

Each of the above *Ṭhāṭas* may give rise to many *Ṭhāṭas* according as it is *Saṃpūrṇa, Ṣāḍava or Auḍava*. In every *Ṭhāṭa, all the rāgas,* excepting the *Āśraya-rāga* or *Janaka-rāga*, are called *Janyarāgas*.

VI

NORTH INDIAN MUSIC *VIS-A-VIS* SOUTH INDIAN MUSIC

The historians by and large think that the Aryans penetrated into India through the north-western frontier. They are believed to have settled in the north-western region from where they migrated towards the east. South India was mostly peopled by the Dravidians with a distinct culture and language of their own. The Aryans could not penetrate deep into the south. As a result, the Aryan civilisation was not widesprread in that region. The Dravidians maintained the distinctive cultural characteristics of their own. This is noticeable also in the domain of music and dance. Now-a-days, South Indian music is generally known as Carnatic or *Karṇātakasaṃgīta.* Time was when Indian music used to mean North Indian Music. From some ancient works like the *Cilappatikāram,* we learn of an ancient music tradition of the Tamils. That the Vedic tradition of music prevailed in the south too is proved by the discovery of a stone inscription of Pallava king Mahendravarman (c.600-625 A.D.). It mentions seven *Grāmarāgas* with notation. This corresponds with those mentioned in the *Nāradīya Śikṣā.* Several south Indian works on musicology, e.g. *Abhilaṣitārtha-cintāmaṇi* or *Mānasollāsa* of Someśvara (12th. century), *Saṃgītaratnākara* of *Śārṅgadeva* (13th. cent., first half), *Saṃgītasāra* of Vidyāraṇya (1320-1380), etc. reveal the same Indian music tradition that characterises the musicological works of North India.

Practically no demarcation between the northern and southern systems of music appears to have emerged before the 16th. or 17th. century when Rāmāmātya composed his *Svaramela-kalānidhi* and *Somanātha* wrote his *Rāgavibodha.*

After the bifurcation of Indian music into two distinct schools,

Northern and South Indian, certain features distinguished the one from the other. The salient characteristics of South Indian music are as follows:

Rāga is denoted by the word *Isāi*. *Śruti* is called *Alaku*. The seven *Svaras* of Carnatic music, corresponding to the traditional heptatonic system, are *Kurāla*, *Tuttam*, *Kaikikalāi*, *Ujhai*, *illi*, *Vilari* and *Taram*. In the *Cilappatikāram* (ch.3), there is mention of the terms *Kaṭṭe*, *Asāi*, *Tukaku*, *Alaku*, *Cīra* to denote Sanskrit *Druta*, *Laya*, *Guru*, *Pluta*, *Anudruta* respectively.

We have dealt with the *Mela* or *Melakartā* system, conceived in South India, in the appendix.

The ancient Dhātus of the Sanskrit musicologists, called *Udgrāha*, *Antarā*, *Dhruvā*, *Melāpaka* (modern *Sthāyī*, *Antarā*, *Saṃcārī*, *Bhoga*, *(Ābhoga)* correspond to *Pallavi*,*Anupallavi*, *Caraṇam*, *Muktāyi* and *Citteśvaram* in the Carnatic system.

South Indian music is marked by certain characteristic forms of songs and *Prabandha-saṃgīta*.. These are *Kṛti Kīrtanam*, *Gītam*, *Prabandham*, *Varṇam*, *Padam*, *Rāgamālikā*, *Svarāvalī*, *Alaṃkārā*, *Jātisvaram*, *Tillanā*, *Jāvalī*, etc. Of these, *Kīrtanam* and *Rāgamālikā* are almost similar to North Indian *Kheyāl* and *Tārāṇā* are virtually the same as Carnatic *Kṛti* and *Tillāna*. There is similarity in substance between the two systems in the above matters; but the mode of singing shows divergence. *Vilambita*, *Madhya* and *Druta layas* of the north correspond to the Carnatic *Caukākalā*, *Madhya* or *Madhyamākalā* or *Laghu*, *Druta*, *Anudruta layas*.. Similarity exists also in the application of *Tāna*, *Gamaka*, *Svaragrāma*, *Alaṃkāra* and *Mūrchanā*. Despite similarity in the division and number of *Śrutis* in both the systems, some difference is noticeable in their application. This is why there is difference in the *Svaragrāma* of the south. For example, in this system, besides *Śuddha Ṛṣabha*, there is the practice of *Ṛṣabha* of four and six *Śrutis* (in instruments like the *Vīṇā*).

In spite of some similarties, the two systems reveal wide divergence in certain respects. The divergences are marked in the manifestation of form, in the creation of *rasa* and in effecting the diversity of forms. The most remarkable characteristic that distinguishes the Carnatic music from its northern counterpart is almost the total absence of Muslim and foreign influence in the former. The reason is historical. Hordes of foreigners, Persain, Greek, Śakas, Parthians, Graeco-Scythians, etc. invaded northern India from time to time ever since pre-Christian times. Some of them settled in this country resulting in a sort of culltural symbiosis. The Muslims came to India as invaders as early as seventh century. A.D. Gradually they establised imperial sway throughout norlthern India. Despite occasional forays, the foreigners, including the Muslims, could not make a dent into the heart of South India. Thus, there was no foreign acculturation in that region, and the culture of the South Indians did not lose its pristine characteristics. A marked difference between the two systems is that the mixture of *Rāgas* and *Rāgiṇīs*, prevailing int he north, is absent in the south.

VII
CONTRIBUTION OF PERFORMING ARTISTES

Besides musicologists, some of whom composed treatises on music, some performing artistes made noteworthy contributions to the development of this art. We shall give brief accounts of a few eminent artistes who left indelible impress on the history of the development of Indian music, particularly Hindustānī music.

ĀMĪR KHUSRAU (KHASRU) (1253-1325 A.D.)

He was an Indian, and composed poems in Persian. With the real name Ābul Ḥāsān Khusrau Dihlabi, he was born, in 1253

'Tānsen kahata yug yug jiyo jiyo'. The rise and continuity of the *Senī Gharāṇā* through centuries are an eloquent testimony of the recognition he achieved and the respect he commanded.

According to the *Ākbar-nāmāh* of Ābul Fazl, Tānsen died in 1589.

MĀNSIṂHA TOMAR
(Accession 1486 A.D. Death 1519 A.D.)

Ruler of Gawalior, Mānsiṃha was a musicologist and musician rolled into one. In his attempt to develop north Indian vocal music, he assembled some talented maestros in his court, including Sultan Hussain, Sekh Bahāuddin, Bakhsu, Māhmud, etc. He composed many *Dhrupada* songs, and invented a novel *rāga* called *Mānihā Kalyāṇ.* His outstanding contribution to musicology is the Hiṇdī work, entitled *Mānakutūhala,* laying down the number of *Rāgas* and explaining them in an attractive style. In order to propagate this type of song he convened a marathon Music Conference attended by the veterans and connoisseurs. Considering their views, he created, out of *Dhruva Prabandha-saṃgīta, Dhruva-saṃgita* by which the artistes set much store even to-day. The king's most active and helpful associate was his consort, Mṛganayanī, who was herself a lover of music and versed in the musical lore. Their joint efforts led to the foundation of an institute of music in the fort-city of Gwalior.

It was at this time that Sultan Husain of Gujarat tried to transform Indian *Rāga-saṃgīta* into Irānian *Saṃgita.* Sultān Sekh Bahāuddin attempted to break up Śāstric *Saṃgīta* in order to give rise to various *Dhūns* of lighter vein. The king made exemplary efforts to save *Saṃgīta* of both the Śāstric and *Rāga* types.

The king's *Mānakutūhala* was translated by the learned Phakīrullāh under the title *Rāgadarpaṇa.* It contains Mān Siṇha's views leading to the creation of *Dhrupada.*

In 1519 Mān died, but the atmosphere of music that he

created survived for a long time. Voices were stilled in the royal courts, but myriad throats pulsated with the *Dhrupada* songs which the king tried to propagate.

GOPĀLA NĀYAKA

(13th. century)

Very little is known about this eminent musician and composer. He was the royal preceptor of the king of Vijaynagar in South India. His charisma in vocal music earned him the sobriquet *Nāyaka.* According to some, however, it was his family cognomen. Having lived there for a long time, he adorned the court of Rāmacandra, ruler of Devagiri, as his court-singer. Mālik Kāfur, General of Ālāuddin Khilji, led an expedition to Devagiri in 1307 A.D., and having defeated Rāmacandra took him to Ālāuddin along with Gopāla. Thenceforward, Gopāla settled in Delhi. We have it, on the authority of Veṅkatamakhin, that he was unrivalled in *Prabandhagīta* and *Deśītāla.* He is stated to have been an adept in *Prabandha* of the *Āli* class, consisting of 32 *Rāgas.* Gopāla flourished in an age of *Sālagạ-sūḍa.* He was versed in the mixed mode.

That was the secret of his great fame. Kallinātha, the most renowned commentator of the *Saṃgītaratnākara,* has reeorded a deep meed of praise for Gopāla's genius. Having composed *Prabandha-gītas* in Hindustānī language, in imitation of Sanskrit *Prabandha* songs, he set them to sonorous tunes which enraptured the music-lovers of his time. These songs still command respect. Before composing such songs, he used to sing Sanskrit songs. His songs, written in elegant and graceful language, and sung with impeecable melody, earned the admiration of the learned and the connoisseur alike. His *Dhrupada* songs are still sung with sincere devotion.

BAIJU BĀURĀ

(C.15th. cent. A.D)

A renowned singer and composer, perhaps he is the same

Baiju who is included among the twelve *Nāyakas* (music maestros) named by Hakim Karam Imām in his work, *Mādnūl Musikī* (1853 A.D.). According to some, more vocalists than one were known by the name Baiju. The famous Baiju, whose real name was, perhaps, Baijnāth, was a man of indifferent temperment having little material pursuit. Hence, he was given the epithet Bāurā (mad). He has left many songs of his own composition, some having heen composed in four *Tüks* and others, in *Bṛj Bhāṣā*, are of the *Cautāl* and *Dhāmār* types. According to some musicologists, it was Baiju who innovated the name *Dhrupad* from the older term *Dhruvā*.

VIII
MAṄGALAGĪTA

Gītamaṅgala or *Maṅgalagīta* bas been in vogue in India since remote antiquity. The *Mahābhārata* (Droṇa, 5.41) refers to *Gītamaṅgala* sung by bards and panegyrists. The word *Maṅgalagīta* occurs also in Drona 69.11. In the *Nāṭyaśāstra*, there is mention of *maṅgala-stuti-gāna*, with benediction, at the commencement of dance, song, instrumental music and a dramatic performace. It is stated that, when such a song began to be sung, Maheśvara (Śiva) awoke. There are references to *maṅgalagītas* having been sung to rouse kings from their sleep. For example, we may refer to Bhāravi's *Kirātārjunīya, (stutigīti-maṅgala*, I.38).

In the *Saṃgīta-ratnākara* (Prabandhādhyāya-d 303b-304a), Śārṅgadeva holds that a *maṅgala-prabandha* should be sung in *Boṭṭarāga* in *Vilambita laya* (delayed rhythm or tempo). Such a song should be composed in auspicious words like *Śaṃkha, Cakra*, etc. As an alternative, he suggests that it should be composed in *maṅgala-chandas*. In his commentary, Kallinātha says that *maṅgala-chandas* means that every foot should consist of five *cakāra-gāṇas*. In the stanzas 297(b)-298(a) in composed in prose, verse or in a mixture of both, and which is to be sung in the *Bhāṣā-rāga* called Kaiśikī and in *tāla Niḥsāru* and at the end of whose *padas* or, at the end of the half, *Svara* is used.

KĀLIDĀSA (C.5th cent. A.D. Earlier than 634 A.D.)

ABHIJÑĀNA-ŚĀKUNTALA

The term *Rāga* occurs in Act I (Sūtradhāra's speech after V.4.; King's speech after verse 5; Act V (King's speech after verse 1)

In the first context above, the commentator Rāghavabhaṭṭa (16th cent.) takes *Rāga* to denote *gītadhātu, i.e., the wording of a song. In I.5, the following words occur: gītarāgeṇa................ etc.*

Here sāraṅga is taken by some to be the name of a *rāga.* Vide Ranade in *Jour. of Music Academy,* Madras, XI,1940, pp.90-94; XII, 1941,pp. 80-84

Others, however, do not agree with the above view. According to them, *sāraṅga* means nothing but an antelope. Vide O.C. Ganguly, *Jour. of Music Academy, Saṃgīter Tihās* in (Bengali), II, latter part, p.481, footnote.

SELECT BIBLIOGRAPHY

MUSIC
(VOCAL AND INSTRUMENTAL)

TEXTS AND TRANSLATIONS

(Names of authors are arranged in the English alphabetical order)

AHOBALA or AHOBILA : *Saṃgīta*, ed. T.G.Sastri, Travancore, 1925, ed. K. Vedāntā-Vāgīśa, Calcutta, 1936; with Bengali trs., Calcutta,1959; published at Hathras, U.P.1941.

ĀRṢEYA BRĀHMAṆA of *Sāmaveda,. ed. A.C.* Burnell, Mangalore, 1876; Intro., pp.XXViii, XLi-XLViii.

AŚOKAMALLA: *Nṛtyādhyāya*, ed. P.Shah,

GOS., 1963; with Hindī gloss by V.Gairola.

BHARATA: *Nāṭyaśāstra*, ed. M.Ghosh, Calcutta, I, 1967; II, 1961; R. Nagar, with comm. *Abhinavabhāratī* of Abhinanavagupta, Delhi, 1981;

Ed. M.R. Kavi, GOS, Vol I, 1956 (2nd. ed.); Vol II.

1934; Vol III, 1954.

Kāvyamālā ed., 1894.

Trs. into English, by M.Ghosh, Calcutta, 1951.

Trs. into Eng. by a Board of Scholars (Indian Books Centre, Delhi).

Trs. into Bengali by S.C.Bandyopadhyay, I, Calcutta, 1980. II, Calcutta, 1982. III, Calcutta, 1982.

There is a *Nāṭyaśāstra-saṃgraha* by U.Govindācārya, ed. A.K.M. Row Sahib, K.V. Sastri, G.Nagaraja, Vol.I, 1953; Vol. II, 1961.

Gītālaṃkāra, ed. and trs. into French by A. Danielou and N.R. Bhatt, Pondicherry, 1959.

BHATKHANDE, V.N.: *Abhinava-rāga-mañjarī*. 1921.

CIKKABHŪPĀLA, M : *Abhinava-bharata-sāra-saṃgraha*, ed. R.Satyanarayan, Mysore, 1960.

DĀMODARA : *Saṃgīta-darpaṇa*, Hathras, U.P., 1950.

DATTILA: *Dattilam*, ed. S.Sastri Trivandrum, 1930.

An ed. published in Leiden, 1970.

Bengali trs. by P.K.Ghosh.

Eng.trs. in *A Study of Dattilam* by M.Loth.

GHANAŚYĀMADĀSA : *Saṃgīta-sāra-saṃgraha*, ed. Prajñānā-nanda, Calcutta, 1956.

GOVINDĀCĀRYA, U : *Nāṭyaśāstra-saṃgraha*, ed. A.K.M. Row Sahib, L.V. Sastri and G.Nagaraja, Vol.I.,1953. Vol.II, 1961.

HṚDAYANĀRĀYAṆA: *Hṛdayaprakāśa*, ed. with Bengali trs. and notes by P.K.Ghosh, Calcutta.

JAGADEKAMALLA : Same as Kavicakravarti (q.v.).

Jaiminīyam Sāmagānam, ed. B.Bhattacharya.

JĀYASENĀPATI : *Nṛtyaratnāvalī*, ed. V.Raghavan.

KĀŚĪNĀTHA APĀTULASĪ : *Saṃgīta-sudhākara*, 1917.

KAVICAKRAVARTĪ : *Saṃgīta-cūḍāmani*, ed. B.J.Sandeshara, Baroda, 1958.

KUMBHA OR KUMBHAKARṆA : *Saṃgītarāja*, ed. P.Sarma, I, Varanasi, 1963. *Nṛtyaratnakośa* (part of the *Saṃgītasāra*) ed. R.C.Parikh and P.Shah, Vol.I.1957.

MATAṄGA: *Bṛhaddeśī*, ed. K.S.Sastri, Trivandrum, 1928.

Mṛdaṅga-lakṣaṇa—anonymous work in Purāṇic style.

NANDIKEŚVARA : *Abhinaya-darpaṇa*, ed, with Eng.trs. and notes, by M.Ghosh, Calcutta, 1975 (3rd ed.);

trs. into Eng., Cambridge, Mass., 1917.

See *Mirror of Gestures* with Intro., Eng. trs. and illustrations, by A.K. Coomaraswamy and G.K.Duggirala, 1970;

Bharatārṇava, Ed, K.B. Sastri, Tanjore, 1957; with Hindi exposition by V.Gairola.

NĀNYABHŪMIPĀLA : *Bharata-bhāṣya*.

NĀRADA : *Saṃgīta-makaranda*, ed. Telang, Baroda, 1920. Ed. and trs, into Bengali by P.K.Ghosh, Calcutta, 1988.

Nāradīya Śikṣā, ed. (with Sobhākara's comm.), Varanasi, 1893; ed. S.Samasrami, Calcutta, 1890;ed. with intro.,

Eng. trs. and notes, S.C. Banerji, Calcutta, 1983, ed. P.Jha (with editor's Skt. comm.), Tarakesvar (Hughli); Vis. 2037, Bengali trs. by R.Mitra, Calcutta.

Also published in Tanjore.

Pañcamasāra-saṃhita or *Pañcama-saṃhitā* Published in S.C. Banerji's ed. of *Nāradīya Śikṣā* referred to above. Trs. into Hindī by L.Tiwari.

NARAHARI CHAKARAVARTĪ: Same. as Ghanaśyāmadāsa (q.v.).

Nṛttasaṃgraha (Anonymous), ed. P.Shah; ed. P.Ghosh, 1956.

PĀṆINĪYA ŚIKṢĀ

PĀRŚVADEVA: *Saṃgīta-samayasāra*, Ed. T.G.Sastri, Trivandrum, 1925.

PUṆḌARĪKA VIṬṬHALA: *Rāgamāla*, being published in

Bengali Journal *Sāṅgītika*, Calcutta, from issue No. 2, April 1989 with Bengali trs. and notes by Pradip Ghosh.

PURĀṆAS - *Vāyu*, Chs, 86, 87

Mārkaṇḍeya, i. 34-35; XXiii

Saṃgītasudhā., ed. P.S.S. Ayar & S. Sastri, Madras, 1940.

RĀMĀMĀTYA : *Svara-mela-kalānidhi*, ed. M.S.R. Iyer, Annamalainagar, 1932; pub. from Hathras, U.P. with Hindī comm.

SĀRADĀTANAYA : *Bhāvaprakāśa*, ed. K.S.R.S. Siromani, GOS, 1930.

ŚĀRṄGADEVA : *Saṃgīta-=ratnākara*, I (CH.1), Adyar, Madras, 1943 (with comm. of Kallinātha and Simhabhūpāla) II (Chs. 2-4),

Do, 1959

III (Chs.5-6), Do, 1951

IV (ch.7) Do, 1953.

Ed.H.Apte, Vol.I, 1896, Vol. II, 1897 (Ānandāśrama Skt. Series).

Ed. M.S. Iyer with Eng. trs., Tranvancore.

Eng. trs. of ch.I. Adyar, Madras, Ch.VII (Eng. trs, in *Brahmavidyā*, Adyar Library Bulletin, Vol. XXiii, 1959).

Chs.I, II-IV Eng. trs. by R.K. Shringy, Varanasi, 1978, 1989. Bengali trs. by *Sures Chandra Bandyopādhyāy, Calcutta.* 1379 B.S. Ed. with Hindī comm., Hathras, UP

ŚAURĪNDRAMOHANA ṬHĀKUR: Saṃgīta-sāra Samgraha, Calcutta.

SOMANĀTHA: *Rāgavibodha.* ed. S.Sastri, Madras, 1945; ed. K.B. Deval.

SOMEŚVARA: *Abhilaṣitārtha-cintāmaṇi* or *Mānasollāsa*, III, ed.

G.Shrigondekar, Baroda, 1961.

Music and Dance sections, cr.ed. by V.Raghavan.

ŚRĪNIVĀSA: *Rāga-tattva-vibodha.*

ŚUBHAṂKARA: *Saṃgīta-dāmodara,* ed. G.Sastri and G.G. Mukhopādhyāya, Calcutta, 1960.

SUDHĀKALASA: *Saṃgītopaniṣad-sāroddhāra,* ed. U.P.Shah, Baroda, 1961.

TULAJĀJI : *Saṃgīta-sārāmṛta,* ed. S.S.Sastri, Madras, 1942.

VIṢṆUSARMAN: Nom-de-plume of V.Bhātkhande (q.v.).

WORKS IN ENGLISH

Agrawal, V.K. : *Tradition and Trends in Indian Music.*

Ambrose, K. : *Geschichte der Musik,* Vol. I,pp 41-80

Classical Dances and costumes of India. 1950.

Ananda-padmanabhan, C.S. : *Veena,* New Delhi, 1982.

Augustus. W.N. : *Music of India.*

Ayangar, C.R.S. : *Indian Dance.*

Bagchi, P.C. : *India and China.*

Bandyopādhyāy, S : *The Music of India.*

: *Indian Music through the Ages 2,400 B.C, to the present Era.* Delhi. 1985.

: *The Origin of Rāga.* 1978.

Banerji. S.C. : *Fundamentals of Ancient Indian Music and Dance,* Ahmedabad, 1976.

Banerji, P. : *Erotics in Indian Dance*

: *Basic Concepts of Indian Dance.*

: *Apsaras in Indian Dance,* New Delhi, 1982.

: *Dance of India* with Foreward by Uday Shankar, 5th. ed. Allahabad, 1956.

: *The Folk-Dance of India,* 2nd.ed., Allhabad, 1959.

: *Art of Indian Dancing,* New Delhi, 1985.

Bartholomew, W.T. : *Acoustics of Music,* New York, 1948.

Bhaduri, M. & Chatterji, S. : *The Art of Hindu Dance,* Calcutta, 1945.

Bhandarkar : *Study of Ancient Music,* Bombay.

Bhatkhande.V.N. : *A Short Historical Survey of the Music of Upper India.*

Bhattacharya, A : *A Treatise on Ancient Hindu Music, Calcutta,* 1978.

Bhattacharya : *Ethno-musicology and India.*

Boatwright, H. : *Indian Classical Music and the Western Listener.*

Bose.M. : *Melodic Types of Hindusthān,* Bombay, 1960.

Bowers. F. : *The Dance of India.*

Caitanyadeb, B. : *Music of India, a scientific study,* 1981.

: *Musical Instruments of India*

(history and development)

Clements, E : *Introduction to the study of Indian Music*, London, 1967.

: *Indian Music* , London, 1917.

Coomaraswamy, A.K. : *The Dance of Shiva*, 1982.

Cousins. M.E. : *Music of the Orient and Occident*

Cultural Heritage of India (R.K..Mission, Calcutta), Vol.III (Article on The Cultural Aspect of Indian Music and Dancing).

Denielou, A. : *Northern Indian Music*, Vols.I, II, London, 1949, 1954.

: *Intro, to the Study of Musical scales* 1979.

: *The Rāgas of Northern Indian Music*, 1980.

Day, C.R. : *The Music and Musical Instruments of Southern India and the Deccan*, 1974.

Deba, B.C. : *The Music of India* , New Delhi, 1981.

Deval, K.B. : *The Hindu Musical Scále and the Twenty-two Śrutis, Poona*. 1910.

: *Theory of Inidan Music as Expounded by Somanātha*, 1926.

Devi, R. : *Dance of India* with an Appendix on *Indian Music* , Vārānasi, 1984.

Earnest, C. : *Intro. to study of Indian*

Music, Allahabad, 1966.

Encyclopaedia of Indian Music with special reference to Rāgas, 3 vols. bound in one.

Engle, C. : *The Music of the Most Ancient Nations*, 1865.

Ethel, R. : *The Story of Indian Music*, London, 1928.

Felber, E. : *The Indian Music of the Vedic and the Classical periods*, Vienna, 1912..

Foxstrangways, A.K. : *The Music of Hindustān*, Oxford, 1965, Reprint 1975.

: *The Hindu S~ale*, Leipzig, 1967-68.

Framjee, F. : *Text-book of Inaıan Music, theory and* practice, ed. Hathras. UP, 1986.

French, P.T. : *Catalogue of Indian Musical Instruments*.

Gangadhar : *Theory and Practice of Hindu Music*, Madras.

Ganguli, O.C. : *Rāgas and Rāgiṇīs*, Baroda, 1948.

Gautam. M.R. : *The Musical Hertiage of India, New Delhi, 1980.*

Ghosh.N. : *Fundamentals of Rāga and Tāla with a new system of notation*, Bombay, 1968.

Goswami.C. : *The Story of Indian Music*, Bombay, 1957.

Goutam, M.R. : *Musical Heritage of India*, New

Delhi, 1983.

Guru Gopinath : *The Classical dance pose of India.*

Hampiholi, N.K. : *The Theory of Indian Rāgas* with one hudred and eleven new Rāgas, Dharwar, 1953.

Hindu Music and the Gāyan Samāj, Bombay, 1887.

Jairazbhoy, N.A. : *The Rāgas of North Indian Music*, Oxford.

Jones and Williard : *Music of India*, 1962.

Jones. W. : *On the Musical modes of the Hindus.*

Kapil Vātsyāyan : *Classical Indian Dance in Literature and the Arts.*

Kaufmann, W. : *The Rāgas of South India*, Bloomington, 1976.

Kavi, M.R. : *Bharatakośa*, Delhi, 1983.

Keskar. B.V. : *Indian Music, Problems and Prospects*, Bombay, 1967.

Khare, G.S. : *Some Thoughts on Hindu music*, Poona.

Khokar, M. : *Traditions of Indian Classical Dance*, 2nd. ed., New Delhi, 1984.

Krishnarao : *First Steps in Hindu Music*, London.

Krishnaswamy, S. : *Musical Instruments of India*, New Delhi, 1967.

: *Psychology of Music*, Mysore.

Kunst, J. : *Hindu-Javanese Musical Instruments*, 2nd. ed. (Trs. from Dutch), The Hague, 1968.

Kuppuswami and Hariharan : *Indian Dance and Music Literature*—a select bibliography.

Lakshmanapillai, T. : *Travancore Music.*

Lath, M : *A Study of Dattilam.*

Mani (Mrs.) : *Indian Music*, Madras.

Marcel-Dubois, C. : *Les instruments de Musique de L'Inde Antique*, Paris, 1941.

Marcotty, T. : *The Way of Music*, 1980.

Menon, R.K. : *Indian Classical Dance*, 1980.

Menon, R.R. : *The Sound of Indian Music.*

Misra, S.S. : *Mānasollāsa of Someśvara, a cultural study*, Banaras.

Mudaliar, C. : *Oriental Musiç in Staff Notation, 1892.*

Naidu, C.T. : *Hindu Music.* Madras.

Nijenhuis, Te : *Musicological Literature*, Fasc.1 of Vol.VI of *History of Indian Literature* by J.Gonda, Wiesbaden, 1977.

Peterson, J.D. : *On the Grāmas or Musical Scales of the Hindus.*

Pillai, T.L. : *Travancore Music and Musicians.*

Pingle, B : *History of Indian Music*, Calcutta, 3rd. ed. 1962.

Popley, H.A. : *The Music of India, Calcutta,* 1950

Prajnānānanda, S. : *Historical Development of Indian Music*, 2nd. ed., Calcutta, 1973.

Premlatha, V. : Music through the ages.

Rāghavan, V. : *Encyclopaedia of Technical Terms in Music, Dance and Drama* (to be published).

Rām, V.B. : *Glimpses of Indian Music.*

Rāmgopāl : *Indian Dancing.*

Ranade, G.H. : *Hindustāni Music and the Outline of its Physics and Aesthetics.* Poona, 1951.

Ranade, A.D. : Keywords and concepts : *Hindustani Classical Music* New Delhi, 1990.

Rao, T.V.S. : *Studies of Indian Music.*

Ravindranath, P.K. : *Bhāvam, Rāgam, Tālam, Nāṭyam* a handbook of Indian Dance, Bombay, 1980.

Rosenthal, E. : *The Story of Indian Music and its Instruments*, London, 1928 (Reprint, 1971).

Sahukar, M. : *Indian Classical Music.*

Sambamoorthy, P. : *History of Indian Music*, Madras, 1981.

Sanyal, A.N. : *Rāgas and Rāgiṇīs.*

Schmidt : *Essays on Hindu Musical Scale and Twenty-two Śrutis.*

Seetha, S. : *Tanjore as a seat of Music* (during 17th., 18th. and 19th, centuries), Madras, 1981.

Shahindra : *Indian Music*, London.

Simon, R. : *The Musical Compositions of Somanātha, Leipzig*, 1904,

Sinha, P. : *An Approach to the study of Indian Music*, Calcutta, 1970.

Singarachari : Kṛishnamachariar refers to his works, pub. from Śaśilekhā office, Madras.

(*Vide Hist. of Class.Skt. Lit.* 1974, p. 883).

Srinīvasan, R : *Indian Classical Dance.*

Subbarao, B : *Rāganidhi*, Vol. I, Poona, 1956.

Swarup, B. : *Theory of Indian Music*, Agra, 1933.

Tagore, S.N. : *Six Principal Rāgas of the Hindus*, Calcutta , 1877.

Tagore, S.M. : *Indian Music from Various Authors*, Vols.I, II, 3rd.ed., 1882.

: *Short Notices of Hindu Musical Instruments.*

: *Seven Principal Musical Notes of the Hindus with their Presiding Deities*, Calcutta, 1892.

: *Hindu Music from various authors*, Calcutta 1965.

: *The Musical Scales of the Hindus*, Calcutta, 1884.

: *Universal History of Music*, Calcutta, 1896.

: *History of Music.*

: *Six Principal Rāgas.*

: *Music and Musical Instruments*

of South India, Calcutta.

Telang, M.R. : *Twenty-two Śrutis of Indian Music*, Bombay.

Tarlekar, G.H. : *Musical Instruments in Indian Sculpture*, Pune, 1972.

Thirumalavyanaidu : *Studies in the Nāṭyaśāstra.*

: *Hindu Music*, Madras.

Vātsyāyana : *See Kapil Vātsyāyana.*

Vedānta, P. : *A New Intro. to Indian Classical Music.*

Veer, R.A. : *Music of India*—history and development, 2 vols.

Venkatacalam : *Dance of India.*

Verma, K.M. : *Nāṭya, Nṛtta* and *Nṛtya*, 1957.

Vishnudas, S. : *Hindu Music and Rhythm.* Paris, 1930.

White, E. : *Approaching Indian Music.*

Williard, N.A. : *A Treatise on the Music of Hindustan*, Calcutta, 1834.

Wood, A. : *The Physics of Music*, 1945.

BENGALI

Bandyopādhyāy, Sures Chandra : *Bhārater Jñān Vijñān*, I, Calcutta, 1366 B.S. (Chapter on Musicology).

: *Saṃgīta-ratnākara*, Bengali trs.

Bandyopādhyāy, Gopeswar : *Saṃgīta-candrikā.*

Bandyopādhyāya, K. : *Gītasūtrasāra*, 1934.

Bandyopādhyāya,

Rāmaprasanna Bandyopadhyay	:	*Saṃgitamañjarī.*
Banik, P.	:	*Mṛdaṅga-darpaṇa.*
Chakrabarti, Mrigaṅka	:	*Tālatattver Kramavikāś,* Calcutta, 1986.
Chaudhuri, Pramatha and Debi Chaudhurāni, Indira	:	*Hindu Saṃgīta.*
Datta, Devavrata Goswami, K.	:	*Saṃgītasāra,* 2nd, ed., 1879.
Gupta, Murari	:	*Saṃgīta-prakāśikā.*
Mitra, Rājyeswar	:	*Ārya Bhārater Saṃgītcintā,* Calcutta.
	:	*Saṃgītasamīksā,* Calcutta, 1975.
Mukhopādhyāy, Harinārāyan	:	Saṃgīte parivartan, 1931.
Mukhopādhyāy, Dhurjatiprasād	:	*Sur or Saṃgati.*
Prajnānānanda	:	*Saṃgīta O Saṃskṛti,* I, Calcutta, 1953.
	:	Do, II, Calcutta, 1956.
	:	*Rāga O Rūpa, Darjeeling.*
	:	*Bhāratīya Saṃgīta Itihās* I, Calcutta, 1961, (2m) II, Ist half, Calcutta, 1978(3rd ed.); II, 2nd half ,1979 (3rd. ed.).
Ray, Rabindralāl	:	*Rāganirṇaya.*
Ray Chaudhuri, B.K.	:	*Bhāratīya Saṃgītakoṣa,* Calcutta, 1372 B.S.
Sanyal, Amiya	:	*Prācina Bhārater Saṃgītacintā.*

Sen, Rādhāmohan : *Saṃgīta-taraṅga*, Calcutta.

Sen, Ksitimohan : *Vedottara Saṃgīta*, Calcutta, 1984

Thakur, S.M. : *Yantrakoṣa*. 1875.

HINDĪ

Misra, Rāmsebak : *Tālaprakāśa*.

Paranjape, S.S. : *Bhāratīya Saṃgītkā Itihās*, (from Vedic times to Gupta Age)

Sarmā, B.S. : *Tālaprakāśa*, Hatharas (U.P.), 1978.

: *Bhāratīya Saṃgīt kā Itihās*.

MĀRĀṬHĪ

Bhatkhande, V.N. : *Hindustāni Saṃgīta-paddhati*, I, 1910;

II, III, 1914.

IV, 1932.

DANCE

(Some texts, mentioned under Vocal and Instrumental music, partly deal with dance too. Hence, those texts are mentioned here also).

TEXTS AND TRANSLATIONS

Aśokamalla : *Nṛtyādhyāya*, ed. P.Shah, G.O.S., 1963.

Bharata : *Nāṭyaśāstra*—See under Music.

Cultural Heritage of India : (R.K. Mission, Calcutta) III, (C.R.S. Aiyangar, The Cultural aspects of Indian Music and dancing.).

Dhanañjay : *Daśarūpaka*,. ed. and trs. G.C.O. Haas, 1912.

Ghanaśyāmadāsa : *Saṃgīta-sāra-saṃgraha*. See under *Music*.

Ghosh P.ed. : *Nṛttasaṃgraha*, 1956.

Govindācārya, U. : *Nāṭyaśāstra-saṃgraha*, ed. A. K. M. Rowsahib, Sastri and Nāgrāja, Vol. I. 1953; Vol. II, 1961.

(Mahārāṇā) Kumbha : *Nṛtya-ratnakośa*, ed. R.C. Parikh and P. Shah, Vol. I, 1957.

Nandikeśvara ; *Abhinaya-darpaṇa*, ed. M.M. Ghosh, 1957.

Nārada : *Saṃgīta-makaranda*, ed. M.R. Telang, G.O.S. 1920.

: *Nṛttasaṃgraha*. ed. P.Ghosh, 1956.

Narahari Chakrabarti—Same as Ghanaśyāmadāsa (q.v.).

Pārśvadeva : *Saṃgīta-samayasāra*, ed. T.G. Sastri, TSS, 1925.

Rāmacandra and Guṇacandra : *Nāṭyadarpaṇa*, ed. G.E. Shrigondekar and L.B. Gandhi, G.O.S., 1929.

Sāgaranandin : *Nāṭaka-lakṣaṇa-ratnakośa*, ed., M.Dillon, Vol.I,1937.

Sāradūtanaya : *Bhāvaprakāśa*, ed. K.S.R.S. Siromani, G.O.S., 1930.

Śārṅgadeva : *Saṃgīta-ratnākara*.See under Music.

Someśvara : *Mānasollāsa* or *Abhilaṣitārtha-cintāmaṇi*, ed. G.K. Shrigondekar, G.O.S. Vol. I, 1958; Vol.II, 1961.

Subhaṃkara : *Saṃgīta-dāmodara*, ed. G. Sāstri and G.G.Mukherji, Calcutta, 1960.

Sudhākalasa : *Saṃgītopaniṣat-sāroddhāra*, ed. U.P. Shah, G.O.S. 1961.

STUDIES

ENGLISH

Ambrose, K. : *Classical dance and costumes of India*. 1959.

Ayangar, G.R.S. : *Indian Dance.*

Banerji, P. : *Erotics in Indian Dance.*

: *Art of Indian Dancing*, New Delhi. 1989.

: *Apsaras in Indian Dance*, New Delhi, 1982.

: *Dance of India*, with Foreward by Udayshankar, 5th.ed. Allahabad, 1956.

: *The Folk-dance of India*, 2nd, ed., Allahabad, 1959.

Banerje.S.C. : *Fundamentals of Ancient Indian Music and Dance*, Ahmedabad, 1976.

Bhāduri, M.& Chatterji, S. : *The Art of Hindu Dance*, Calcutta, 1945.

Bhavani, E. : *The Dance of India*, Foreward by Kamalādevi Chttopādhyāy, Bombay, 1965.

Bose M. : *Classical Indian Dancing*, Calcutta, 1970.

Bowers,F. : *The Dance in India.*

Coomāraswāmy, A.K. : *The Dance of Shiva*, 1982.

Devi R. : *Dance of India* with an appendix on Indian music, Vārānasi, 1984.

Guru Gopinath : *The classical dance-poses of India.*

Kapil Vātsyāyan : *Classical Indian Dance in Literature and the Arts.*

Khokar, M. : *Traditions of Indian classical dance*, 2nd ed., New Delhi, 1984.

Kuppuswāmi and Harihharan : *Indian Dance and Music literature—a select bibliography.*

Menon, B.K. : *Indian Classical Dances.* 1967.

Naidu S. and Pantulu, V. : *Tāṇḍavalakṣaṇa* or *Fundamentals of Ancient Hindu dancing*, 1980.

Rāgini Devi : *Dance of India.*

Rām Gopāl : *Indian Dancing.*

Ravindranath, P.K. : *Bhāvam, Rāgam, Tālam, Nāṭyam* Bombay, 1980.

Srinivasan, R. : *Indian classical dance.*

Tarlekar, G.H. : *Studies in the Nāṭyaśāstra.*

Vātsyāyana, K.	:	*Classical Indian Dance in Literature and the Arts*, Delhi, 1977.
Venkatacalam	:	*Dane of India.*
Verma, K.M.	:	*Nāṭya, Nṛtta and Nṛtya* 1957.

BENGALI

Adhikāri, Subhadrā	:	*Bhāratīya Nṛtyakalā*, Calcutta.
Bandyopādhyāya, Sures Chandra	:	*Saṃgīta-ratnākara* (Bengali trs. with an outline of Sanskrit literature on music and dance, glossary and bibliography), Calcutta, 1379 B.S,
	:	*Nāṭyaśāstra* (Bengali trs. with introduction, summaries of chapters, etc), Vols, I—III, Calcutta, 1980, 1982,1982. Vol, IV in Press.
Chattopādhyāya, Gāyatri	:	*Bhārater Nṛtyakalā*, Calcutta, 1985, (3rd ed.).
Debi, Pratimā	:	*Nṛtya.*
Pal, Snigdhā	:	*Nāṭya-nṛtta*, Calcutta.
Roy Chaudhuri, Manjulikā	:	*Nṛtye Bhārat*, Calcutta.

JOURNALS, YEAR-BOOKS, REPORTS, COMMEMORATION VOLUMES., ETC.

(Besides the Journals, noted below, the Reports of All India Musical Conferences may also be consulted.).

ENGLISH

Annals of Bhandarkar Oriental Res.Institute, Poona, XV, 1934 (O.C. Ganguli- Non Aryan Contribution to Aryan music).

All-India Oriental Conference, 1924 (Paper read by M.E. Cousins—*Eastern and Western Music*; by M.Ponnu Sami, Swaras; by K.N. Sitārām, *Place of Chidambaram in Evolution of Dance in India*; by K.V. Srinivasa. Ayanagar- *Abhinaya*; by M.R. Kavi *Nānyadeva on Music*.

Bhārati 1925 , 94 (K. Bhairavamurti- *Music*).

Hindusthan Standard, Pūja Annual, 1950 (Prajnānānanda- The forgotten *Indian Culture*, IV. 1939 chapter of Indian music) P.C. Dharma, Musical Culture in the Rāmāyaṇa)

Indian Music Journal, Vols. I,II, 1912-13 (Article by H.P. K.Rao)

Indian Review, Madras, XVI, 1054 (Kannolmal, *Indian Music*).

JASB. IX. VII (A.Wesharp -*Psychology of Indian Music*).

I.No.2 (V.V.N. Chary—The early writers on music)

II.No.22 (DO).

Journal of Music Academy Madras. III (C.Halugar-Some names in early Saṃgīta literature)

IV (C. Halugur—Some names in early saṃgīta literature).

E.Felber—The Indian Music of the Vedic and the Classical Period)

1930 (C.Halugur-Intro. to the study of Bhāratīya Saṃgīta-śā-

XIV (O.C.Ganguli—Dhruvā, a type of old Indian stage songs).

XIX (C. Halugur—The Indian Origin of the violin)

XXIII, 1952. (V.S.Agrawala—Some early reference to Musical Rāgas and Instruments) XXIV (C.Halugur-Why is Mṛdaṅga so called)

XXXIII (C.Halugur -some early references to musical *rāgas* and musical instruments).

The following articles are stated to have been published in this journal, but no references are given. Vide Svāmī Prajnānānanda, *Bhāratīya Saṃgīter Itihās*, (in Bengali), Vol, III Appendix, Calcutta, 1994 B.S.

V. Rāghavan	:	Music in Palkuriki Somanātha's works.
	:	Music in the Bṛhaddhamra-Purāṇa
	:	Music in some Jain works.
	:	Music in the Haṃsavilāsa
	:	The Pārijāta-haraṇa Nāṭaka of Nārāyana Tīrtha.
	:	Naṭī's song in the Abhijñāna-Śakuntala
Swāmi Prajnānānanda	:	The Charyā and Vajra-Gītis
	:	Some Rāgas and Tālas in Rājā Mān Sing Tomar's Time.
G.H. Ranade	:	The Naṭī's song in the Prelude to the Abhinjñāna-śakuntala of Kālidāsa.
O.C. Gangooly	:	The Naṭī's song.
	:	Naṭī's song in the Abhijñāna Śakuntala.

Journal of Royal Asiatic Soceity of Great Britain and Ireland,

1936 (M.S. R.Aiyar—The question of *Grāmas*)

1935 (A.H.Fox-Strangways - The *Gāndhāra-grāma*).

Journal of University of Bombay, XVIII, 1949 (C.R. Sankaran and B,Chaitaya Deva-Postulational methods and Indian Musicology).

Krishnaswāmy Iyengar Com.Vol. (Sambamoorty—A History of Indian Opera).

Poona Oreintalist, IV, July, 1927 (L.S. Bhatta—The mode of singing of Sāmagāna).

Reports of All-India Musical Conference.

Sāngītika—a quarterly musicological journal published from Calcutta.

Sanskrit Research, 1916 (K.B.Deval—Theory of Indian Music as expounded by Somanātha).

The Four Arts Annual, 1935(K.M.Sen Sāstri—Music in the Vedic age)

The Hindusthān,, 1940 (O.C. Gānguli—The Meaning of Music).

USIC Centre News, Almora, 1942 (V.S.Agrawala—Dance terminology from Kālidāsa : 1943 Vol. V(O.C. Ganguli—A new document of Indian Dancing).

Uttaramandrā, I, 1940 (P.C. Bagchi—The diffusion of Indian Music in ancient times).

Year book of Oriental Art and Culture, London, 1925 (A.K.Coomarawamy—Dīpaka-rāga).

Besides the above, the following journals, containing articles in English on various matters relating to music are published.

Journal of Musicological Society, Baroda.

A useful book is the *Encyclopaedia of Indian Music with speical reference to the Rāgas* , Delhi, 1986 Indian Books Centre

Journal of Musicological Society, Baroda.

A useful book is the *Encyclopaedia of Indian Music with speical reference to the Rāgas* , Delhi, 1986 Indian Books Centre (2nd. ed.).

INDEX

[Asterisk indicates foonote. Technical term alphabetically listed in Chapter IX are not mentioned here]

A.D. to one Saifuddin, a protégé of Sultan Iltutmish. His mother was an Indain. Even as a young man, he showed talent in literature and music. Included among the twelve *Nāyakas*, mentioned in Hakim Muhammed Karam Imām's work, *Mādnūl Musiki*, Ḳhusrau was Poet Laureate and Chief Courtier under Dehli Sultns Kāykobād, Jālāluddin, Ālāuddin Khilji and Giyāsuddin Tughlak. He came under the influence of his spiritual preceptor, Nijāmuddin Āuliyā. Besides several noteworthy works in Persian, he composed many *Gāthās* and *Caturdaśapadīs*.

A music maestro, he proved his talent in his rivalry with Nāyaka Gopāla, the great musician in the court of Ālāuddin Khilji.

Among his exploits are the introduction of the musical modes Kāwl, Tarāṇā, etc, and the combination of Indain songs with Persian songs. He has been immortalised in the domain of music by his introduction of the type of songs known as *Kheyāl*.

He breathed his last in 1325 A.D.

TĀNSEN (d. 1589 A.D.)

Born sometim between 1520 and 1530 A.D. Tānsen was a musical Titan in the medieval age. His original name was Rāmatanu and his Brahmin father was named Makarand Pānde belonging to village Bihaṭa close to Gwalior. The family finally settled in Gwalior. Quite early in age, he became attracted to music. Among his *Saṃgita gurus* was the eminent Haridāsa Svāmin of Vṛindāvana. When Tānsen was established as a reputed vocalist, he was installed as the court-musician of the ruler of Bāndhavgaḍ in 1555 A.D. But, in deference to the wish of Akbar, he had to join the court of Akbar at Agra in 1562.

Besides being a singer of a very high order, he was a composer too. He composed songs sung in *Rāga Kānāḍā (Cautāl)* which, having been sung in the royal *Darbār* of Rāmacandra, came to be known as *Darbāri Kānāḍā*. In the *Sthāyī* parts of songs, he wrote *'Rājā rām guṇanidhān'*. In the *Ābhoga* portions, there was the line